AF375465

Real Estate Investing For Beginners (2 in 1): Build Your Property Empire& Passive Income With Rental Properties (& Managing Them)+ Negotiation, Tax Strategies& Air BnB

By Unlimited Potential Publications

Rental Property Investing: Build Wealth & Passive Income With Properties, Flipping Houses, Air BnB & How To Manage Your Rentals + 10 Negotiation Tips (Real Estate For Beginners)

By Unlimited Potential Publications

Table of Contents

Introduction

What you are reading right now might be the roadmap to a more prosperous future. And if you're reading this, congratulations on taking the first step and getting your copy of this eBook. You bought this because you have an interest in real estate and think you might have what it takes to become an investor.

Let's get one thing out of the way first and foremost: it's not as easy as you think. In fact, this isn't something that's going to make you thousands, hundreds of thousands, or even millions of dollars tomorrow. It's going to take plenty of work to achieve success.

Still with us? Good. By doing so, you've pre-emptively accepted the fact that it won't be easy.

But you know you have the patience and the willingness to work hard to ensure that you will find success in real estate investing. That's why you've continued on. Because most of the people who picked this book up might have already stopped reading after the second paragraph.

One thing you'll want to realize is when building your real estate empire, it won't take just you to pull it off. It takes the right kind of people at your side to help you out in any way they can. They are experts in their own right.

They are bankers, legal experts, accountants, real estate professionals, and everyone in between. They are right in your downtown area or just a state away. No matter where they are, you may find someone who will help you achieve levels of success in real estate.

Do you want to make more money than possible?

Let's talk about you for a moment. You're someone who is probably sick of the boring, mundane lifestyle. You get up, work your 9-to-5, come home, eat dinner, relax, and sleep. Then you repeat the process over again for five days a week.

Sure, the paycheck may bring steady and slightly predictable income. Yet, it may not seem like enough to pay the bills or go on vacation. You feel like trading your time for money is just the nature of life.

But guess what? We live in an age where people are making their own money and working their own hours. They are doing it in so many ways.

People will scoff and say, 'well that's not a real job'. Let's face it, doing business isn't something for everyone. And not everyone is cut out for it.

However, don't let someone else's limited beliefs discourage you. You can make as much money as you like without slaving away at a 9-to-5. But you still do need to put in the work for it.

What better way to jumpstart your income like investing in rental properties? Yes, becoming a landlord may just be the one thing you can do to generate the income that you want so you can be able to do what you want with it.

Why real estate?

You're probably thinking about making money. You want to start some kind of business so you can make your own income and become your own boss. It's possible to do just that.

And it can be done with real estate. The reason why real estate is so popular in terms of making money is simple. People are looking for a place to live or operate their business.

And most people would rather rent a place to live as opposed to purchasing it. Eventually, your tenants may become homeowners themselves. But for now, they have the financial means to rent a place from you.

Rental properties are pretty much everywhere. It's a matter of finding one that will yield a good return on your investment. You will learn how to find the right property later on in this book.

Who are we?

This is a book based on the knowledge and information gathered by those who have invested in rental properties and have made a good amount of money doing it. They know the ins and outs. They know what to do in order to acquire properties.

Other than that, they will share with you the strategies and tactics you can do to find a piece of property that is perfect for renting out. We'll also show you ways to secure financing as well. And we'll show you how to build your real estate network from the ground up.

The Benefits of Rental Properties

While building your rental property empire, you'll be putting in quite a bit of work. However, the rewards at the end are pretty sweet. What exactly are the benefits?

Here's what you'll enjoy:

- **More passive income:** You'll be earning more money. If you work hard and follow the proper steps, you may even acquire enough properties to make even more money as you go. Imagine making the same amount of money you make a year, but you make it in a month's time.

- **You'll understand deeply about real estate:** Whether you know little to nothing about it, you'll have a basic understanding of it by the time you have finished reading this book. Plus, you'll be able to gain more knowledge from it when you reach out to other real estate professionals.

- **You'll know the process about tenancy:** You'll learn how tenants apply for a rental space, move in, sign the lease agreements, and move out. Of course, let's not forget all the in-between things that go along with it.

- **You'll learn the ins and outs of business:** Having rental properties will be like a business. You'll understand how to operate it as such using ways to acquire properties, marketing your vacancies, fulfilling the demand for rental properties, calculating your cash flow, and more. Believe us, it's more exciting than you think.

Where to go from here?

At this point, you know of the benefits. You won't be able to enjoy them unless you follow everything you learn in this book. This isn't something that you read about and use the material to converse with your friends.

Almost everything you'll read about in this book has actionable steps that you can take to assure yourself great success in real estate. It won't work unless you put it into action. It's as simple as that.

From here, you now have two choices: one, do you just decide that rental properties aren't going to be right for you? Or two, be willing to put in the work, be proactive, and make the necessary moves to ensure you acquire your first property and make money?

Remember, this is an opportunity for you to say goodbye to the mediocre 9-to-5 lifestyle and say hello to financial freedom. At the end of the day, the choice is yours. If you are ready to accept the challenge, let's turn the page to begin Chapter 1.

Chapter 1: First Time Doing A Real Estate Business? Then Start Learning Now

Starting a real estate business isn't easy. It requires time, work, commitment, and dedication. If you're reading this after the introduction, you may have known that and have accepted the challenge.

With that said, stick with us. Because we'll be showing you the ins and outs about starting a real estate business. You'll learn about what you need to know and the kind of people you want to connect yourself with as you start out.

Let's get one thing out of the way: running a real estate business as a one-person band is almost next to impossible. You'll need a good amount of people helping you out along the way. That's why it's important to build a good solid network (which we will elaborate on more later on in the chapter).

And as always, it's good to look before you leap. Especially when starting a new business. We'll explain why later.

In the meantime, let's get started:

Starting A Real Estate Business and What You Should Know About It

Before diving into the idea of starting a real estate business, you need to know what it's all about. You have to know what you are getting into and what the whole thing entails. Everyone that gets into the real estate business has a certain set of goals that they want to achieve.

Perhaps they are looking for an extra stream of income. Or maybe they are looking to get into a new industry after spending time doing business in another. Each person is different, and their goals are unique.

There is a certainty that you will make money if you run the business properly. How you go about using that money will be up to you. You can set aside money for yourself and set another amount for re-investing in other properties.

One thing to know is that of those who have declared over a million dollars or more on their taxes, about 71 percent of them had been involved in the real estate business in some way. So, there may be some sweet tax benefits that you can take advantage of along the way.

With that said, let's cover a few basic things that you need to know about starting a real estate business:

Is a real estate business profitable?

The short answer: yes. However, there is a caveat. You can make it profitable so long as you are able to be smart with your assets.

Let's explain this in a brief example: let's say that you want to make money in real estate by increasing the value of the property.

Flipping or Rehabbing

One good way to do it is to find a house that might need a little TLC (or a fixer-upper if you will). This is known as 'flipping' or 'rehabbing'. And it's one of the fastest ways to make bank when it comes to real estate.

In fact, you can actually do this repeatedly using a method known as BRRRR. If you don't know what that means, no worries. The next chapter will have a section explaining it in further detail. At this point, the property value has no place to go but up.

But there's another caveat: you have to put in the money to improve the property's overall quality. This means that there needs to be repairs and maintenance that need to be done to the property you have purchased.

This means setting off money to the side that will go towards any initial repairs (including unexpected ones when something else is discovered). Granted, you don't have to do all the repair work and the like yourself. You can hire professional contractors to get the job done for you.

After all is said and done, the fixer upper is looking better than ever. From there, you can rent the place out to tenants or have it appraised prior to selling it outright. So, the value of the property will be way better than before you acquired it.

Profits Through Income

Another way to make your real estate business a lot more profitable is by acquiring properties and renting them out to tenants. These properties can either be residential or commercial. Since you are most likely new to the game, you should be better off acquiring residential properties.

However, you could acquire a commercial property assuming you have the cash. Just remember, while the rent for commercial properties will be even higher, the expenses will be higher as well (compared to residential properties). But to make it easier, go with residential properties for now.

You can collect rent by renting out apartment units or even single-family homes (among other property types). Keep in mind that aside from the income portion, you'll also need to factor in expenses as well. These include insurance, property management fees, any loan payments, and so on.

Now that you have a good understanding on how to acquire profits, it's time to discuss what is also known as the other 'moving parts'. These are some things that you'll want to keep in mind while you are starting a real estate business.

It's important to implement some of these steps and not skip through them. Not only because it will allow you maximum results. But missing pieces of the business puzzle will make things a bit more disorganized.

Plus, running the business will be frustrating enough. So, let's lay out some things before moving further:

Know your business goals

When it comes to success, it takes planning. Succeeding in business by way of some 'shot in the dark' strategy will be impossible from the get-go. So, you'll want to plan and prioritize what needs to be done when it comes to your business goals.

What are your personal goals? What about your professional and financial goals? How do they all tie together?

These goals should influence you to start and build a real estate business from the ground up. Also, consider looking ahead. Where do you plan to be in five, ten, or even twenty years?

How will you get to where you want to be in those time frames? That's when you need to strategize, evaluate, and even make some changes if needed. The goals you set will keep you focused while allowing you to take action on them.

One kind of goal framework to adopt is the SMART framework. This stands for Specific, Measurable, Attainable, Relevant, and Time-Bound. You want to use this framework for both short-term and long-term goals.

Do your research

This is a big one here. Research is important especially when you are starting a real estate business. Particularly when you want to scope out the first ever property you want to acquire.

Your research has to be in-depth and detailed. When doing this research, you have to gather some pertinent information. This includes the median home values, rental prices, amenities in the neighborhood, and more. Simply put, it all comes down to your financial goals and the kind of real estate you want to acquire.

So, if you are looking for single-home fixer uppers, find an area where you might be able to find one. Or if you are looking into commercial real estate, then your local downtown area will always be a good place to start. Either way, doing research and putting in the time to find the right kind of property will be important.

In fact, we would go so far to say that you should NEVER skip this step. Because a lack of research and preparation will lead to one bad deal after another. You want a positive return on investment, not a negative one.

Keep your finances in order

Your finances must be in good shape. Especially when there's a good chance you may need to borrow money from banks or lenders. This means making sure that your credit score is in good standing.

Yes, there are ways to acquire financing. And you can get involved in real estate without putting down a single penny. However, it's better to be prepared for all possible options than never.

You want to take a look at your existing accounts and current investments. If you have any debts that need to be paid off, focus on doing so before even making the first major move in your real estate business. Being able to straighten out your financial affairs might put you in a better position to get approved (or even pre-approved) for a loan.

Sharpen your business strategy

After getting your finances in order and doing plenty of research, it's time to lay out the business strategy itself. This includes writing out a business plan that includes all the tools and resources you plan on leveraging from the start.

Your business plan should include your mission statement, marketing strategy, and what the initial income and expenses will be among others.

Form a Real Estate LLC

An LLC is a business structure that is set up so your business costs don't interfere with your personal finances. This is a great way to keep your finances separate so your real estate properties don't involve any personal reliability. Depending on your state, there will be different fees and regulations that will be tied into establishing an LLC.

However, the concept will usually be the same. This includes the following:

- Confirming the state's regulations

- Choosing a unique business name

- Filing an Article of Organization with your state

- Creation of an operating agreement

- Publishing an intent to file (if required)

- Application of a tax ID number via the IRS.

Plan your marketing strategy

You can market your real estate business using various channels. But it's important to know what your unique value proposition is. What makes you stand out amongst the other competitors in your industry?

Also, you may want to consider the idea of putting together a mission statement and the core values of your business (which should be included in your business plan). You'll want to come in with a battle plan on how you want to reach out to your potential customers.

Here are some marketing approaches to consider when marketing:

- **Direct mail:** This marketing method is tried and true. And it still reigns supreme in the Digital Age. Direct mail has become more of a 'road less traveled' method because many people are using digital marketing.

- **Email campaigns:** If you have an email list of potential leads, this method would be perfect. You can send emails to potential buyers or sellers of property that you are interested in acquiring. List building is important, and it will take time to put one together. But other than that, it's one of the best (if not most cost-effective) ways to market your business.

- **Social media:** Because it's the Digital Age, every business owner and their mother will be using social media to market something. So, it will become hyper competitive at best. However, you can spread out your marketing on various social media channels like Facebook, Instagram, Twitter, or even LinkedIn. It all depends on who your initial buyers are and where they frequent on social media.

- **Networking:** If there is one reliable marketing channel that will assure you success in real estate, it's networking. Where do you begin? See if there is a real estate event in your area. If there is one, attend it. Meet real estate professionals that know their stuff. They will also be more than happy to help you get started with your own real estate business.

Five Benefits for Starting A Real Estate Business

What are the five benefits for starting your own real estate business? Here's what they are:

- **Tax benefits galore:** Those who are in real estate will take advantage of so many tax benefits when it comes time to file. You get to keep more of your money compared to someone who has grossed the same amount of money working a regular job. Crazy, right? The government tends to reward real estate investors better than those who work a 9 to 5 (which makes quitting it a lot more appealing once you get money rolling in).

- **Cash flow:** Of course, you can get a good amount of cash flow coming in. The cash flow is the money you get once all of your income and expenses have been factored in. This is extra money that you can keep to yourself or reinvest it in other properties. It's your call either way. The more properties you own, the greater your cash flow.

- **Appreciation of value:** The property you own can also appreciate in value. This can happen by paying off any loan you may have that's tied to the property. Despite the fact that the economy can go in one direction or the other (including the housing market), the property value will appreciate over time regardless.

- **Control of the property:** You own it, you control it. There's no better way to say it. The property is tied to you, not some other Company CEO, Wall Street banker, and so on. So, do what you want with it (so long as it's within the legal parameters).

- **Security in retirement/finances:** If there is one thing that you might be aiming for, it is financial security. Your real estate portfolio might be part of your entire retirement plan. The more financially secure you are for the future, the better. And what better opportunity to acquire more security by putting together a real estate business?

There Are Many Ways to Invest Your Money in Real Estate

As mentioned before, there are two major ways to invest money in real estate. You can make money with the 'flip' or 'rehab' approach. The other way is by rental income.

But did you know that there are other ways to invest your money in real estate? Let's take a look at some of the other ways to go about putting your money in real estate and seeing a good return on investment:

- **Mortgage notes:** This is a great way to ensure that you have some passive income. You can buy a mortgage note and receive monthly payments that also include the interest and the principle. In a sense, it's like receiving income as if you are renting out a property. The good thing about mortgage notes is that you can invest in real estate without having to jump through so many hoops like real estate licensing, taxes, or abiding by local regulations and the like.

- **Real Estate Investment Trusts (or REITs):** Like mortgage notes, REITs allow you to invest in real estate without even buying or managing a property. REITs are publicly traded and can also be available in non-tradable forms. However, the SEC highly discourages non-traded REITs because of the high fees, illiquidity, and the potential that they could become worthless over time. Publicly traded REITs are liquid and can provide you with a dividend.

- **Real Estate ETFs and Mutual Funds:** You can purchase exchange-traded funds or ETFs and mutual funds that may be based on specific sectors. One of those sectors of course is in real estate. There are mutual funds that specialize in real estate development or even property management firms. Like REITs, these are highly liquid, and the costs are usually low.

- **Using the 1031 Exchange:** The 1031 Exchange involves like-kind properties. The number 1031 is based on the tax code allowing you to sell a real estate property and using the funds to purchase another property with value that is equal or greater. Sometimes, you may take advantage of the exchange and find a property that is more profitable than your previous one.

- **Refinancing:** You can refinance your mortgage if you so choose to do so. One awesome benefit you can get out of it is you can easily obtain a loan with lower interest. Another benefit? Lower mortgage payments.

The People You'll Meet Once You Get Started

You will be getting in touch with people that will help you through the process of building your real estate business. We will go over who you'll meet and why they're important in Chapter 4. These are people who are knowledgeable in more ways than one when it comes to investing and maintaining your real estate properties.

Get Your Head Straight Before You Jump In

Yes, there is real money involved. And yes, you can stand to get a substantial amount to the point where you are financially secure for the rest of your life. However, you need to do one thing before you jump into the real estate business.

Here are some tips that you absolutely need to take to heart before getting into it all:

Keep your emotions in check

There is nothing more thrilling than getting money in the bank (even if it's five or six figures a month) from real estate. However, you can get caught up in what may be an 'expected outcome' and fail miserably to the point where you might give it up. However, it's important to get into the business with a level head.

So, it's better for you to know the numbers and determine if it's the right investment or not rather than just say 'yes' without thinking twice. It's better to use your gut rather than your emotions.

Accept the fact that you need to put in the time

Building a real estate business from the ground up takes time. And by this, we don't mean putting in an hour here or an hour there. And it also doesn't mean going into research mode constantly (meaning you read all this info and never apply it). As far as time is concerned, this will be a long-term thing.

How long exactly? About a year or even 18 months tops. So, you need to accept the fact that you've got to be in it for the long haul in order to succeed.

Never stop trying and don't give up

Failure only happens when you give up. Yes, there will be setbacks. There will be shortcomings.

But it's all part of the process. Just because one property seller or a loan lender says 'no', it's not the end of the world. There's an opportunity waiting to be taken every day of the week. And there are those so oblivious to it that they don't know it's staring at them in the face.

So, take that opportunity when you see it. But make sure you do your due diligence, so you know it's the right one to take.

Focus on one thing at a time

It's true that you can overload yourself. Whether it's focusing on too many tasks or real estate opportunities, it's better to stand back, take a deep breath and focus on one thing. Many of us were not made to be juggling so many things at once.

When you focus on one thing at a time, your focus will be invested heavily on that one thing. You can pay attention to other things at some point. But focus on the priority tasks and the like first before all else.

Final Thoughts

If this is your first foray into real estate, the sooner you start learning the ins and outs, the better. Starting a real estate business is no easy task. And it won't just take one person to get the job done.

There are many ways to make money through real estate. But your most common ways of doing so is by flipping properties or renting them out and earning monthly income. Putting together a business plan with a solid list of goals and keeping your finances in order is key.

Also, the benefits will be even more awesome once you're in the thick of it. Just remember, you need to keep your emotions in check and accept the fact that building a real estate business from scratch will take time, effort, and yes even money.

But don't let the tasks intimidate you. This will separate you from those who want to try something just to make a quick buck, but give up after finding out how complicated things are. You're in it for the long haul and you want to attain success no matter what.

If you are in it to win it, then there's no turning back now. At this point, you can accept the challenge and move on to the next chapter. Or you can just say 'you know what, this ain't for me' and move on to something else.

In the event it is the latter, stop reading this now. Otherwise, accept the challenge, keep reading, and let's talk about choosing a rental property and why getting cold feet is the last thing you ever want to deal with. Let's move forward and get moving.

Chapter 2: You're Choosing Rental Property Investing? Don't Get Cold Feet!

Now that you have decided to move forward in building your real estate business, there might be little room for turning back now. So, if you are dealing with 'cold feet', you can either press on and find out that it's not so bad to build a business that gives you absolute freedom.

Or, you can focus on something different. Other than that, let's move forward. Because we have a lot to talk about on the subject of rental property investing.

Investing in rental properties is by far one of the best ways to generate profit from a real estate business. All you need are properties like a single-family home, a multi-family home, or even an apartment complex to rent out to tenants. Granted, like any other business that you approach, the task itself isn't easy.

But if you are an absolute beginner, we highly recommend rental properties. Not only will it be easier for you in terms of managing the finances, but you'll also be able to crunch a few numbers while looking at properties to acquire. This 'number crunching' will help you determine whether or not the property will be a good return on your investment.

But we'll talk about the numbers later on. This chapter will focus on rental properties and why it will likely work to your advantage. You'll want to make sure that you are up for the challenge.

Speaking of challenges, we'll talk about those and the difficulties that come with investing in rental properties. They will be brief since we'll touch more on them as we go farther in the book. But once you get a good idea of what you're dealing with, you'll be more than prepared.

Lastly, you know that there is a lot of money to be made. We'll touch on that briefly as well. Finally, we'll talk about how investing in rental properties works (including the moving parts that go along with it).

Let's dive right in and get started:

Getting Real Deep with Rental Property Investing

As a beginner, there's a good chance (about 80 percent or more) that you'll wind up looking at rental properties. In fact, they will more than likely be the starting point for many real estate property investors like yourself. The reason is simple: you are getting recurring monthly income through tenants via rent payments.

However, you have to understand that with the rewards come the risks. We'll be taking a look at some tips that will help you find your first ever rental property. These tips were made to not be ignored, so pay close attention.

Here's what they are:

Are you cut out to be a landlord?

This is a simple 'yes' or 'no' question. But before answering it either way, think deep about it for a moment. Are you someone who is a 'handy' person?

Are you up for fixing broken pipes at three in the morning? Or are you willing to hire a property management company to get the job done knowing that it can cost more?

If you answered 'yes' to either of these questions, then there's a good chance that you are cut out to be a landlord. It's up to you whether or not you want to deal with the repairs yourself or outsource them to a contractor or property management company (so long as you have the cash set off to the side). You may be cut out for being a landlord if you have the capability of putting together a team of reliable people who can handle such things with your property like repairs, appraisals, and so on.

Be sure to pay down any personal debt

Do some investors carry debt? Yes. But that doesn't mean you have to.

We're talking about personal debts here. Student loans, medical bills, or even your kid's college education (assuming you are older and have kids in school). The sooner you pay it off, the better.

Lock in a down payment

If you are looking to secure a rental property, then it's important to find one where you have enough to lock in a down payment. Keep in mind that some properties will have a larger down payment requirement compared to properties that are considered owner-occupied. How much of a down payment do you need?

Try 20%. The reason why is because there won't be mortgage insurance on rental properties. For example, if the rental property is roughly $200,000 to buy out right then you'll need at least $40,000 for the down payment.

You can secure this money usually through a bank loan. You can easily be pre-approved so long as you have no serious debts (we weren't joking about personal debts and why you need to pay them off).

Location, location, location

This is the one word you'll keep hearing until the day you're done with real estate (or when you die). Either way, the big 'L' word that pertains to rental properties is location. You want to pay attention to what might be the best location possible in terms of a good return on investment.

Your property should be in an area where it's on the up and up rather than declining. When you are looking for a rental property, there are some factors that need to come into play. For example, what are the amenities in the neighborhood?

Furthermore, how low are the property taxes? What's the average commute time for most residents? The deeper you dig, the more data you'll gather on the area and whether or not it would be a good place to find a rental property.

The location of the rental property will have an effect on the overall value itself. There is no need for you to choose a property located on a rough end of town because it's cheap and you want to save money. Remember, all the amenities and positives you can find because of the location will often mean a larger pool of potential tenants.

Buy or finance: what is better?

If you have enough cash to purchase a property outright, then it's obvious that 'buy' is the clear choice. If you don't have enough cash to purchase a property outright, then financing would be your next best option. However, in terms of the latter, you'll want to take a look at your options.

Also, it will depend on your business goals. For example, if you are looking to make money by the flip/rehab way, then you'll want to consider a hard money loan for financing purposes. We'll explain the best way to go about doing this in a later chapter.

For everything else, there's always the personal loans. You put down 20% for the down payment, and then you have other expenses like the mortgage, operating expenses, and so on. Consider your ROI when figuring out which option is better for you.

If you choose the financing route, this next tip may apply to you:

Stay clear of high interest rates

Did you know that interest rates for rental properties are higher than traditional mortgages? Now that you do, it's important to find a mortgage that has lower monthly payments. That way, it won't have to eat a lot into your monthly profits.

The goal for a positive ROI should be around 10 percent. Keep this in mind when you are crunching numbers while searching for the right property. Another thing to keep in mind is the maintenance costs, which should be at least one percent annually of the property's value.

When calculating to find the right margin, also take into account the other expenses like property taxes, HOA fees (if applicable), insurance, property management, repairs, and so on.

Things happen at any time, day, or night. For this reason, it's good to plug in the figures that will be enough to cover any kind of unexpected costs. How much should you set off to the side each month? Consider at least 20 to 30 percent of your rental income.

Prepare Yourself: Are You Up for The Challenge?

Whether it's one rental property or five of them, there will be challenges. And each property might have its own challenges. One may need urgent repairs while another is dealing with a pest problem.

So, it goes to show you that not all properties will always have the same challenges. But there are challenges that can start before, during, or after you have tenants occupying the property. We will be diving deep into these challenges later on in the book.

But the most common ones will be covered right now. They include:

- **Repairs and maintenance:** These might be needed at any time whether a tenant occupies the property or not. The cause for these never takes a day off, nor does it care if the property is occupied or not. Be prepared for any needed repairs, small or large.

- **Unreliable tenants:** There are two kinds of tenants: those who pay on time and those who don't. This is where a screening process for tenants is handy. You can do this by yourself or via a property management firm.

- **Financial challenges:** These will exist no matter how far along of the journey you're on. You might get rejected for a loan, have tenants skipping out on rent, or sinking in a lot of money into repairs. They come in different shapes and sizes. So you best be aware of them.

Why Rental Property Investing Is for You?

There are plenty of reasons why rental properties are perfect for beginners like you. And we'll take a look at the reasons why shortly. Rental properties do have their advantages and disadvantages. But they are a lot easier to manage and maintain.

Aside from that, here are a few other reasons:

You're in control

Simply put, you own the property, and you can do what you please. It's not tied down by anyone else, nor will you be restrained from making such decisions by banks or other entities. This means you're in control of how much you can charge for rent (within reason), how to use the property, and so on.

Appreciation of property

The property that you acquire will appreciate over time. And you can use what is known as leverage. This is explained as using a small amount of money for a down payment or the like, while borrowing the rest in multiples ranging from four to twenty times more of the purchasing price.

An example of how leverage works is this: Let's say you use $20,000 of your own money and borrow $80,000. This means you can buy property that is $100,000. Your property may appreciate by a percentage over the next 10 or so years. The appreciation will be on the entire asset, not your own money.

More money for you

Isn't it nice to have a little extra money in your pocket? Well, the good news is that it is possible when you have rental properties of your own. But remember, it all comes down to the income and expenses.

Take the monthly income with the expenses and there is your cash flow. If you are in the positive, that's good. If you're in the negative, you may want to consider making adjustments to the expenses that you are spending on. While we're on the subject of expenses, set aside 5 percent a piece on monthly maintenance and vacancy costs.

Tax write-offs

Rental property owners will get plenty of tax deductions. What qualifies as tax write-offs? Let's take a look at the following:

- Interest paid on the mortgage

- Insurance policy

- Travel expenses (if you own properties outside of where you reside)

- Property taxes

- Maintenance repairs

It goes to show you that it pays to have rental property. Whether it's just the one or multiple, things will tip the scale in your favor if you are smart with your finances and rely on those who can handle things like the day-to-day property management and other things that one person obviously cannot do.

You're Going to Make A Lot of Money with This Business

It's possible that you will make a lot of money with a real estate business. Especially if your portfolio consists of just rental properties. However, don't expect to get rich overnight with just one rental property.

But there are plenty of benefits that you will get out of this. The positive cash flow, the tax benefits, and so on. Obviously, this will go without the usual downsides like unreliable tenants, unexpected repairs, and the like.

We'll be talking about the whole money-making aspect of running a real estate business later in the book. But consider this section a brief synopsis of one of the biggest benefits that you can get out of it. Plus, we don't want to divulge any further details or spoil it for you.

An Overview of How Rental Property Investing Works

To give you a good idea of how the entire process works, this list will be an overview of how rental properties work. Pay attention to this as this can serve as one of your roadmaps to success. We'll also use a similar approach when the time comes to talk about the BRRRR approach.

In the meantime, here's how the process typically works:

1. Purchase the property

You find the property that you are interested in after doing some analysis. This includes the kind of ROI you'll get in total after factoring in the income and expenses. You'll also need to find out if the property is in a good location and is valuable enough to be a good investment.

2. Do any necessary repairs or renovations

Nine times out of ten, you're going to need to do a thorough inspection of the property itself. If you find anything that needs to be fixed, take care of it as soon as possible. Furthermore, you'll need to determine if there is a need for any renovations.

From there, get as much done as you can in terms of these repairs or renovations. You can do them yourself or hire a contractor to do it for you.

3. Rent out the property

Afterwards, you can rent out the property to tenants. It's important to market your vacancies wherever there is high traffic. You can advertise by social media or use old school approaches like direct mail or flyers.

When you are accepting applications, field through them to determine who would make a great tenant. We highly recommend background checks and doing reference checks as well. It would be a lot easier if you hired a property management firm to do this for you.

4. Hold on to it and collect income

You might have long-term plans as far as holding on to the property is concerned. You can generate income so long as you own the property yourself. You also have the option to refinance the property so you can easily obtain another loan and acquire subsequent properties.

Once again, we'll discuss that later on when we discuss the BRRRR strategy.

5. Keep the financials in check

Throughout the month, you want to regularly check the financials to see that you are still maintaining a positive cash flow. Vacancies can be filled or unfilled from month to month or depending on the length of the lease. If the income and expenses are the same, keep moving forward.

But it's better to double check your finances to see if there is anything amiss. You'll never know what will happen between one day and the next.

Final Thoughts

Rental properties are a no brainer, even for the newbie real estate investor. Yes, there are some pros and cons to it. But you'll be able to handle them properly with patience, due diligence, and the ability to delegate any responsibilities if needed.

Rental properties are a great way to jumpstart your bank account once you're in the real estate business. And your entire portfolio will probably consist mostly of them. You can have apartment buildings, single-family homes, and even a few commercial properties.

It is important to do your due diligence first and foremost to ensure that the property you're interested in is worth it. One piece of property may yield a negative ROI because of the conditions of the surrounding area. Or the property may be in disrepair.

Your property value may even get dragged down even if it looks better than the surrounding buildings. That's why choosing a location is important. And you also want to take a look at what's close by in terms of amenities, the commute time, and so on.

Don't let the tasks and responsibilities of owning a rental property intimidate you. So long as you play it smart and stick with it for the long haul, success will be assured.

Chapter 3: Make Sure That Your Finances Are Straight, This Is No Get Rich Quick Scheme

Repeat the following: 'I will get my finances in order before moving any further.' Again. One more time.

We cannot stress this enough. Before you even make the first major step in starting your real estate investment business, you have to make sure your finances are in strong shape. That means taking a look at your personal debts and paying them down to a point where they can be manageable (or paid off altogether).

Also, a reminder that your real estate business is no 'get rich quick scheme'. Don't expect a million dollars to magically appear in your bank account the day after you acquire your first rental property. In the words of that famous commercial, 'that's not how any of this works'.

Even after your finances are in good enough shape, you still have to deal with the financing aspects of the real estate business. Applying for loans, dealing with rejections, and so on. After that, there's still the balancing act of finding the right cash flow after factoring in the income and expenses.

This chapter will answer all your burning questions about the financials when you're starting out. Questions like, 'How much is this going to cost me?' or 'do I need a reserve fund?'...and similar questions like that.

By the time you finish up this chapter, you will have at least a basic understanding of the financial aspect of the real estate business (specifically things you'll need to know about loans and the like). We'll also be talking more about the numbers and how to crunch them together so you can get a good deal out of every agreement you jump into.

Let's sharpen those pencils, dust off those calculators (you'll need them later), and get right to it:

How Much Will It Cost You?

This is the million-dollar question that every aspiring real estate investor asks. Granted, the answer probably isn't a million dollars. Before we move any further, let's make a quick adjustment of the mindset.

If you are planning to make money in real estate, don't consider spending money on things as something that's going to 'cost' you. Think of it as an investment for something better. So instead of asking 'how much will it cost me', ask yourself 'how much will I invest'.

Get the idea? You're investing in your future long before investing in your first property. As for the question of how much you'll need to invest, the answer is 'it depends'.

It will depend on the expenses that you are willing to spend. Some of them are completely optional. And there are those expenses that are so necessary that you'd be crazy to not spend money on them. What are some of the costs that are considered necessary?

Let's take a look at the following costs that you should consider with rental properties:

- **Down Payment of loan and interest:** Unless you intend to purchase the property outright, the next best thing would be to consider a down payment on the loan plus interest. As mentioned earlier, the down payment will usually be 20 percent of the purchase price. On top of that, you'll also want to put down an extra percent for the interest itself. If you really want to play it safe, consider 25 percent as the down payment.

- **Property taxes:** Of course, property taxes are a necessary evil. And it will vary depending on the property that you purchase. It will also depend on where you live. And one more thing, this is one expense that could increase or decrease without warning. If you want to stay ahead of the curve, you may want to pay attention to what your local and state governments are doing (even if you hate politics).

- **Maintenance:** This is one of those required expenses that you'd be insane to forego. Indeed, things happen anytime, no matter what they are. One good rule of thumb is to set aside a total of 10 to 12 months' worth of rent to cover these costs. If you want to talk percentages, budget anywhere between 10 to 15 percent of the annual rent. For example, if you have 20 units renting out at $1000 per month ($20,000), you'll earn $240,000 annually in rent. Therefore, the annual reserves should have $24,000 to $36,000.

- **Insurance:** The insurance policy you get will depend on factors like where you live and the kind of property it can cover. When considering insurance policies, consider some of the environmental problems that occur on a regular basis. If you live close to major bodies of water, get a policy that covers floods. If you live in an area that's prone to wildfires, you better get a policy that covers fire damage. Also, discuss rates with insurance representatives and find the best policy that works in your favor.

- **Association (HOA) Fees:** If your property has an HOA formed, then there will be additional fees. As such, make sure that they are included in your budget. If you want to avoid them, find a property that is not under the jurisdiction of an HOA.

- **Utilities:** This is somewhat optional. You can defer the utility payments to the tenant, or you can include it within the rental agreement of what it will cover. If you intend to cover utilities in your rental agreement, you'll need to get estimates from the utility companies to get an idea of how much gas, electricity, water, etc. is used per month.

- **Looking for tenants:** Yes, finding tenants to fulfill your vacancies will eventually be an investment. For this reason, it would be a good idea to provide a non-refundable application fee to offset any costs. $25 would be a good place to start and some even command higher application fees. This is typical of property management companies that own several apartment buildings.

- **Vacancies:** In the world of real estate, you'll always be dealing with people coming in and people going out. So, vacancies will be common. However, there is no telling how long a vacancy will stay vacant. You might want to set aside one to two percent of the property value every year. Do not assume that your vacancies will be fulfilled every month of the year. You can allow two months of vacancies at most.

Now that we've covered the costs that you need to consider, what is a specific number that you need to know? How much of a minimum amount do you need to get started? The answer is 20 percent of the property value.

So, if the property value is $100,000, then it will need to be $20,000 upfront. Oh, and keep in mind that there are closing costs that will be around five percent of the purchase price. But remember, you'll need additional money for cash reserves just in case things happen BEFORE you even get around to renting out the property.

Will You Be Needing A Reserve Fund?

As hinted in the last part of the previous section, the answer is yes. A reserve fund is something you'll build up using money that you set off to the side. This will be useful in the event of unexpected instances such as sudden repairs, unannounced vacancies, and so on.

A reserve fund will also be your saving grace if there are big problems that have suddenly appeared. We're talking things that go beyond the costs of your monthly rental income. If you have a reserve fund that will cover enough of the costs, then you'll want to be in good shape.

It's good to know that you will be prepared for the worst no matter how many properties you own. It should be large enough to cover any of the common, but unexpected issues that happen with rental properties and other real estate. Better to be prepared than never at all.

How much money you'll need to set aside in the reserves will depend on several factors. These include but are not limited to:

- The property's location
- Age of the property
- Property type
- Number of united
- The last time the property was updated
- Your level of risk aversion

Do you want the specific numbers? Well, you'll get them. Because we have a few specific numbers that we want to throw out.

Here are some of our recommendations:

- **$5000 per property:** This is a good starting point for most rental properties. You can grow the number until it reaches $10k to $15k max. To start, you want to use a base and add on a portion of the rental income to ensure more growth. If you want another specific number, you may want to set aside 10 percent of your rental income per month for reserves.

- **If you are less risk averse:** Consider starting off with 3 months' rent in total for your reserves. This should cover at least the required expenses like the mortgage, taxes, interest on the loan, and insurance.

- **If you are more risk averse:** Starting off with 6 months' worth of rent will be enough for those who are risk averse. It will cover the expenses we've mentioned in the previous example and also any additional expenses.

Now that you know some more of the specific numbers, you'll want to refer back to this section if you ever get stuck or run into a financial snag. Sometimes, you might just start off with the less risk averse option just to be on the safe side rather than have more of it as originally intended.

Knowing the best practices of building a reserve fund will help you out immensely in the long run. Because you will run into problems that will require you to use the reserve fund. Over time, you will probably have plenty of it to keep you covered for years.

Imagine having a colossal disaster on your hands and not stressing out about it. Why? Because you know you have the money to take care of it.

If you are going forward without a cash reserve, it's the equivalent to riding a motorbike at night without any headlights. Oh, and it's completely dark too without the moonlight or anything else. In other words, don't go any further without building up a cash reserve.

How Much Do You Know About Real Estate Financing?

You might know the basics of real estate financing. Or you may not know any of it. Either way, this book will help you understand the terminology that you need to know and understand so you don't get confused or 'fly blind' as you go about starting your real estate business.

In this and the next sections, we'll be going deep into real estate financing, so you'll know things like loan-to-value, loan-to-cost, and so on. But what's so important about financing?

The importance of financing is that it covers the conventional and non-conventional ways of acquiring a rental property. Financing is your best option if purchasing the property outright cannot be done due to being low in funds. Yes, there are ways to finance a rental property including loans.

Keep in mind that there are loans that you can put to good use such as conventional bank loans, hard money loans, and so on. There is also bank and creative financing as well. What's the difference between the two?

Let's take a look at them:

- **Bank financing:** In plain English, you're basically getting a loan from a bank. This is one of the common ways to go about your financing for properties. You apply for a loan, it gets looked over, and you're either approved or rejected. Loan requirements will differ from bank to bank, so that's why you'll need to explore your options rather than be dead set on one financial institution in particular.

- **Creative financing:** The words 'creative financing' is the non-conventional way for financing. This includes approaches like a master lease agreement, seller financing, and personal loans to name a few. These financing options will vary in terms of the credit requirements, flexibility of the loan term, and even the processing speed.

The important thing to remember is that you'll want to invest in a property that will give you a positive cash flow. Otherwise, you'll be in a much deeper financial hole. And it may be hard to pay back the loans if you have a property that is generating a negative return on investment.

Get A Good Understanding of Loan-To-Value and Loan-To-Cost

What is the difference between a loan-to-value and a loan-to-cost? We'll delve into that further in this section. We'll weigh the pros and cons of each, so you'll know what to expect.

Also being discussed is the loan-to-after repair value or ARV. In the meantime, let's dive right in and discuss it all:

Loan-to-Value explained

The loan-to-value ratio or LTV is what is used when you're determining the amount that is necessary for a down payment. This will also determine whether or not a lender will extend a line of credit to a borrower. If the LTV ratio is at or below 80 percent, borrowers can apply for the lowest interest rates possible when financing for a property.

In order to understand the LTV ratio, this means understanding the formula that makes it up. Here's what you need to do:

- To get the LTV ratio, you have to divide the mortgage amount over the appraised property value. Therefore, the formula looks like this: **LTV = MA/APV**

For example, let's say the property that you want to acquire has an appraisal value of $200,000. The down payment is $40,000. So now, you'll need to borrow $160,000.

160,000/200,000 = .8 (80%)

Therefore, 160,000/200,000 comes out to .8 or 80 percent. So, you're right at the ideal LTV ratio. Again, if the ratio is at 80 or below, you'll be in good shape in terms of paying off the loan with low interest rates.

Let's try another example. Let's say the rental property is the same price, but the down payment is double ($80,000). Since you put down $80k, then all you need is $120,000 to borrow.

Now, let's crunch the numbers:

120,000/200,000 = .6 (or 60%)

As you probably notice, the higher the down payment, the lower the ratio will be. However, if you are a low-income borrower, obviously the LTV will be higher. There are lenders that have mortgage programs for these types of borrowers including Fannie Mae and Freddie Mac (among others).

How the LTV is used

The LTV will be used by lenders to offer mortgage and home equity borrowers the lowest interest rates possible. If the LTV is higher than 80 percent, it will not exclude any borrowers from being approved. The only difference is that they may pay more in interest compared to someone who has a lower LTV.

If your LTV ends up being above 80 percent, you should strongly consider private mortgage insurance. Keep in mind that this may add up to anywhere between 0.5 to 1 percent annually on the total loan amount. These PMI payments will be required until you manage to reduce the LTV to 80 percent or less.

Also, the LTV ratio will work in your favor in terms of your loan application. The lower it is, the better. But that isn't a guarantee.

Pros of an LTV

- The lower, the better in terms of interest rates and easy loan approval

- Reduces over time with PMI payments

- A high LTV will not mean rejection of a loan application

- It does not include any additional mortgages like a second mortgage or a home equity loan

Loan-To-Cost Ratio

Now, we'll discuss the Loan-To-Cost ratio (LTC). Without wasting time, let's break down the formula of the LTC ratio:

LTC = Loan Amount/Construction Cost

A higher LTC will mean that the project will be much more of a risk for lenders. Lenders will only finance projects that have an LTC of up to 80 percent (there's that magic number again). Like the LTV, the lower it is from 80, the better.

The LTC will usually come in handy if the rental property is more of a commercial real estate project. So, what does the LTC ratio tell you? This is determined to calculate the percentage of the loan amount that the lender will be willing to provide when you want financing.

Let's take a look at the LTC formula at work:

Suppose you have a commercial real estate project with construction costs ranging out to $250,000. Let's say the lender provides you a loan for $200,000. So:

200,000/250,000 = 80 percent (or .8)

In this instance, $200,000 seems like a risk to borrow since the LTC is right at the limit. Therefore, the less money the lender gives you, the lower the LTC will be. However, if the construction costs are higher, that's when the LTC gets reduced.

What's the difference between the Loan-to-Cost and the Loan-to-Value ratio?

Both the LTC and LTV ratios are similar to one another. But there are slight differences. The LTV is a comparison of the total loan given for a project that goes against the value of the finished project (after repairs and renovations).

The LTC is based on the future value of the project once it is completed. One common way to determine the value is by doubling the hard costs. In our example above, the hard costs were $250,000.

Let's say the total loan was $350,000. So:

350000/500000 = .7 (or 70 percent)

So, the LTV ratio of the project is 70 percent. Not bad at all.

- The size of the loan will be based on the total cost of the project as opposed to the appraised value. Actual costs will give the lenders more accurate data

- LTC provides the borrower with funding based on the expectation of what they're spending on construction costs and the like

- The cost for construction and renovation for each project is usually difficult to determine at the outset

- Loan amounts based on the LTC could be smaller than loans that use an ARV. This can be due to the property's estimated value once repairs have been completed.

Loan-after-repair value (or ARV) explained

The ARV or the after-repair value is defined as the value of the property after it has been repaired or rehabbed. Obviously, the value will differ when compared to the condition before repairs. Here's the formula that you want to use to determine the ARV:

Purchase Price + Value from Renovations = ARV

One rule that you need to abide by is the '70% rule'. The bid price for property must not exceed 70 percent of the ARV minus the estimated repair costs. The reason why this is the rule of thumb is because it will allow real estate investors to make an ROI of 30 percent.

So the formula is like this:

(ARVx70) - Estimated Repairs = Maximum Purchase Target

So, let's plug in some numbers:

Suppose the value of the property after repairs is $500,000. And the cost of repairs will be roughly $75,000. Let's calculate the maximum price:

$500,000 X 70 percent - $75,000 = $275,000

Therefore, the maximum purchase target is $275,000. Do not pay any more of the maximum purchase target than you need to, or you'll end up bleeding cash.

Real Estate Financing Options that You Should Know

There are plenty of financing options that are available for real estate. Earlier, we mentioned two of them: bank financing and creative financing. There are other financing options that we'll be taking a look at as well.

Without further ado, let's dive right in:

Creative Financing

Starting with the non-conventional way of financing, we'll dig deeper into creative financing. This is intended for a real estate investor to purchase a property under a certain situation. Specifically, if the investor in question has bad credit or a credit history that can easily disqualify them from a standard loan, creative financing is the best possible route.

If your credit history is shot, then this might be the clear option going forward. What kind of creative financing techniques are available to you? Let's take a look at a list:

- Private loans
- Lease options
- Credit partners
- Loans from IRA owners
- Equity partnerships
- Purchases that are subject to the mortgage

What makes this option even more appealing is that it's flexible, fast, and can work in any market condition. So, if the market is good or bad, creative financing will still work to your advantage. On top of that, there is no limit to how many loans you can have (so long as you pay them off in a timely manner).

As well as that, creative financial methods are not as risky. So, you won't need to put anything up for collateral unlike bank loans. This may seem like the easiest route to take if you want to waste little or no time with bank applications.

If you have straightened out your finances and paid off debts, you can try and give this kind of financing a shot. But when it comes to your own finances, just because it's for those with bad credit and the like, doesn't mean you shouldn't pay off debts.

Conventional Bank Loans

This is the common road that real estate investors take whenever they are in good financial standing. Meaning their credit is in good shape and they have shown that they are reliable in paying back the loan.

As mentioned before, conventional bank loans require a 20 percent down payment of the property you are purchasing.

Your personal credit history and credit score will determine whether or not you get approved for the loan or not. However, financial institutions will differ in terms of the qualifications that you'll need to meet for a loan. The more stable your credit and payment history is, the better your chances are of getting approved.

Hard money or 'fix-and-flip' loans

Hard money or 'fix-and-flip' loans are short term loans that carry high interest rates. So, you'll need to put it to good use and fast. The best way to do it is by using the money to purchase a property, repair or rehab it, and then sell it or rent it out.

Then, you can refinance the property and pay off the loan in time. We'll dig a lot deeper into this when we talk about the BRRRR method. Hard money loans will be easy to acquire despite the fact that your credit and income get checked anyways.

The interest rate for these loans can go as high as 18 percent and can depend on the lender. If you have a list of hard loan lenders on hand, be sure to consider the interest rate as one of the driving forces behind your final decision.

How Leverage Works in Real Estate

Leverage is using money that you borrow to purchase property. The way this works is that you purchase the property rather than cover the purchase price outright. And it's one of the reasons why it's one of the best ways to finance your real estate projects.

The intent behind leverage for real estate is you'll want to be able to increase your returns with money that you are borrowing without putting in a lot of your own money into it. It will allow you to purchase a property that costs more than the amount that's available or have it distributed across multiple properties in your portfolio.

You can use leverage if you don't have enough cash to purchase your target property outright. Or you can do it in order to maximize your returns while putting less of your own cash into the property itself.

Either way, leverage can work to your advantage if you are smart with it. However, there are risks that you need to avoid. Let's take a look at what they are:

The truth is that you want to keep your expenses low. High payments for a loan will equal high leverage. And that will eat into your finances or risk putting you in an even greater financial quandary if things go south.

If you are unable to make the payments, you'll find yourself in a much deeper hole. So be sure to pay your monthly payments on time and make sure they are low and reasonable.

Depending on high levels of appreciation

Yes, property will appreciate over time. But don't count on it and shoot yourself in the foot. If you do so, you may overpay on properties.

One thing that you need to do is plan out your investments that are leveraged and sort them out by three different scenarios: best, worst, and most likely.

Allowing good financing to lead to a bad purchase

Plenty of investors have overpaid for properties. Why? Because they think that high-leverage financing was the best thing to do.

However, it's quite the opposite. Even with a little cash outlay, not every property would be considered a good purchase. You'll want to take a look at the property and consider the current and expected market trends, respectively.

You'll want to make sure whether or not the property is overpriced or if there is any room for appreciation. If the room for appreciation is little to none, then you want to consider finding another property. Otherwise, you're in deep trouble.

Forgetting about cash flow

At the end of the day, it's all about the cash flow. And if you overpay or use leverage improperly, that cash flow won't flow as freely as you think. If your investments take a nosedive, you'll be losing money instead of gaining it.

Brush Up Your Math, You'll Be Needing It

Sure, math probably wasn't your favorite subject in school. But what you might not realize is that it holds the most value in so many ways. Especially when you'll be doing some real estate investing.

You don't have to be a math genius to crunch some numbers and determine whether or not you're getting in on a good investment or not. Everything you'll use math wise is simple enough as it is. We'll be taking a look at a few math formulas that you'll need to ensure that you can properly crunch the numbers while searching for your first and subsequent properties.

We'll make these as simple as possible because we're not huge fans of complicated math formulas. But rest assured, these formulas you need to know about won't stress you out in the slightest.

Let's begin with the first one:

1. Price to Rent Ratio

The price to rent ratio will be the average property price divided by the average rental income. Therefore, the formula looks like this:

Average Property Price/Average Annual Rental Income = Price to Rent Ratio

The goal here is to find a property that is financially sound in terms of investing in it. You'll want to find a low price to rent ratio (typically anywhere between 1 to 15). If the ratio is anywhere north of 15, then you may want to consider affordable properties that will help keep it low.

2. The Net Operating Income (NOI)

This is basically another name for the word 'cash flow'. The net operating income is the amount of income that you get using the following formula:

Monthly gross income - monthly expenses = NOI

Chances are the income will be from rent paid by your tenants. And you also might have additional income from the property itself including pet fees, income from laundry, vending machines, or any other amenities that charge a fee. There are different kinds of non-rent income that you can consider to ensure that your NOI is in the positive.

3. Cash-on-Cash return (COC)

The Cash-on-Cash return or COC is roughly the same as the ROI calculation (which we will get to in a bit). The COC is calculated as follows:

Annual pre-tax cash flow / total cash invested = COC

The number you get from this is an indication of what you might expect on your investment. However, it should not always be a reliable figure as it may differ from the actual ROI itself. The reason being is because you are using cash flow figures that do not include taxes.

It also does not include mortgage amortization. This COC model should be used if you are focusing on a yearly ROI.

4. Capitalization Rate (Cap Rate)

The Cap Rate is the ratio between the net operating income and the sale price. Therefore, the formula is this:

NOI/Sale Price = Cap Rate

For example, let's say your net operating income is $20,000 a month. But we'll be gunning for a cap rate using the annual monthly income. Divide that by the sale price (let's say $500,000) and you get the cap rate.

So, for example, this is what you do:

$20,000 x 12 = $240,000

$240,000 / $500,000 = .48 (or 48%)

So the cap rate is 48 percent. With this cap rate, you'll expect at least a 48 percent return on investment. Not too shabby. However, if the cap rate goes up, then the price/earnings valuation multiple will decrease.

The cap rate is a great tool to determine whether or not the property you want to invest in will yield a good ROI.

5. Cash flow

The cash flow is definitely something you want to include in your figures for obvious reasons. To calculate the cash flow, you take the net operating income and minus by the debt service (not the expenses). Bet you didn't expect that, did you? But it's true. So here's the formula:

NOI - Debt Service = Cash flow

What exactly is the debt service? You are subtracting the NOI with the amount you repay if you have a loan.

6. Return on Investment (ROI)

The return on investment is your cash flow divided by the cash you invested in the property. So, let's say the cash flow you have after subtracting the NOI from the debt service is $12,000 per month. But you are shooting for an annual figure. Therefore, $12,000 times 12 is $144,000. Let's calculate the rest with the amount you've invested in the property (we'll say $300,000):

$144,000/$300,000 = .48 (48 percent)

So for example, if you already invested $300,000 into the property and take in $144,000 in NOI every year, that's a 48 percent investment. Again, not a bad number to have.

Note: Use online calculators if needed

To help you save time and perhaps money, you should consider using online calculators to help you get accurate numbers for cash flow, ROI, cap rate, and so on. Check out the following calculators from these sites:

https://www.calculator.net/real-estate-calculator.html

https://www.fortunebuilders.com/real-estate-calculator/

Final Thoughts

Your finances must be in good shape even before you start considering the type of financing you need for your real estate properties. Even after you've acquired your first property and have tenants moving in, it's important to make sure that your finances are in order.

You absolutely need to consider having a cash reserve handy in the event that you run into any unexpected expenses along the way. The same goes once you have things up and running. It doesn't matter if you own one or five properties, having cash reserves handy is the smart thing to do.

Also, keep the equations listed above in mind. Especially when you are looking for a property that will generate monthly income. Get to know some of the equations like the Loan-To-Value ratio (LTV) or the Loan to Cost (LTC).

Don't forget, you'll also need to consider the loan-after-repair ratio should you be dealing with properties that need a little fixing up after being acquired. Also, leverage is your friend when it comes to investing in properties (only when done right). Lastly, don't forget to factor in things like cash flow, return on investment, the cap rate, and so on. Crunching numbers is all part of the game.

Even if you hate math, it will serve as your useful ally whenever you have the goal of making money in real estate. It will even be your best friend that will help you get out of a potentially bad investment (while saving you money in the process). Take your time with these calculations and be sure to focus on one of them at a time.

Lastly, keep the minimum and maximum numbers in mind (like the LTV and LTC). The lower the maximum number (i.e. -- 80 percent) the better. However, if you are looking at ROI, the higher the number, the better.

Chapter 4: Hiring and Working with the Important People of Your Real Estate Team

As we have said before, real estate investing is dang near impossible to do as a one-person band. That's where your real estate team comes in handy. In this chapter, we're going to show you how to hire the people that will be perfect for your team.

It's obvious that you need more than a pair of hands, eyes, and ears to help you find the best property to invest in. You may think that it's hard to do. However, you may not have to start too far off to find people who you can trust and are willing to help you grow as a real estate investor.

We'll talk about how to find people such as a property manager, an attorney that can handle all your legal affairs, who to go through for insurance and so on. These are people who will likely stick with you in the long term. The key here is to choose your people wisely.

In business, you may think that you've hired the right people. However, when tensions mount and tempers flare, then it gets to the point where you have two people not speaking to each other for an indefinite amount of time. So, who do you hire?

Let's answer that question and then some right now:

Start Looking Within Your Family

Before you say anything, there is nothing wrong with a family operated business. And let's not talk about stuff like nepotism or the like. That's totally off the topic.

But if you are looking for people that will help your business grow, you don't have to look any further than your own family. However, considering such an option requires you to look over a few things. For example, is it legal to hire family members?

The answer: it depends. But you'll want to check out any federal, state, or even local laws that will allow or prohibit family members being hired by you as an employer. This is one of the many reasons why you'll want an attorney as part of your team overall.

They will be knowledgeable of the laws in question. They will point out which laws allow family members to work together (or the laws saying otherwise). Another legal thing to look at is child labor laws.

You cannot simply have minors under a certain age working for your company. That's when you need to review the federal, state, and local laws pertaining to this. If you have a child that is of the minimum labor law age, then you may consider a small role for them (like groundskeeping).

Also, take a look at the IRS tax policies regarding family members as your employees. For example, you can withhold income tax if you employ a parent or spouse. However, you cannot withhold FUTA taxes from their income itself (with the exception if your child is 21 years old or older).

The Pros and Cons of Hiring Family

When hiring family members, you'll want to know about the pros and cons in general. What will be the positives of having family on your real estate team? What will be the liabilities?

Let's take a look at them right now:

Pros:

- **They have strengths and weaknesses:** You might have a family member that can capitalize on a few strengths that they may have. And they also might have some weaknesses that you know about. You can help them capitalize on the former by assigning them a role that they know they'll be competent at. Do you have a member of the family that can work the books with ease? Hire them as a bookkeeper. Do they have a good eye for property acquisition? Hire them as one of your scots.

- **You know who to include on the team:** You are well aware of the skill sets that your family members have. There are members of your family that will have a skill or two that will benefit your business. However, there are others in your family that possess irrelevant skills that will not help your business out at all.

Cons:

- **Some family members do not have the skills:** The truth is, you have family members that won't be a good fit for your business. And that's what you need to understand right off the bat. That's because they won't know what they're doing or will even be qualified for such a job.

- **Your other employees may not appreciate it:** The word 'nepotism' might get flown around a lot. Some employees may resent you for the fact that you have family on staff. And thus, they blame their lack of opportunities solely on that. Regardless, treat all employees the same way whether they are family or not.

- **Unproductive family members:** Lack of productivity really brings down a business. And for that reason, they'll fall behind on various tasks. As such, you may have a family member that may be hired for something but doesn't put in the amount of work that they're supposed to. At this point, it's either have them work as much as the rest of the employees or cut them loose.

The truth is you can start with family as your employees. However, you'll want to make sure you are hiring the right family members. Pay close attention to what they're strengths are and determine whether or not they will be beneficial for your business.

Accountability Partner is Not Only for Fitness Purposes

If you are looking for someone who will help you propel your real estate business, it's an accountability partner. This is someone who will help you keep yourself accountable whenever you need to meet a certain set of goals (be it short-term or long-term). Accountability partners are not just for fitness purposes anymore.

You can have an accountability partner who will help you in the long haul get from zero to six figures over time. Do not confuse them for mentors. These are people who know you can get from point A to point B, but want to make sure that you get there.

What to Look for in an Accountability Partner?

So, what exactly do you need to look for in a reliable accountability partner? Let's take a look at a few characteristics that will make one stand out over the others that may have potential:

Genuinity: Having a genuine friend as your accountability partner is a plus. Why is that? Because they can respect you not just as an individual, but also as a business person. They know of your hopes, dreams, and aspirations. And they will do their best to help you get there.

Availability: You and your accountability partner must realize that you both have to be respectful of each other's time. You don't want someone who will be busy all the time. And you definitely don't want anyone that will never make time for you. If you need someone to talk to, make sure that you have an accountability partner that will always have time to chat with you if you run into any problems or concerns.

Clarity, honesty, and tact: You want someone who is not afraid to be honest with you. At the same time, you want someone who will give you a straight answer rather than beat around the bush. This is what separates some of the best accountability partners from those who may be considered 'wishy-washy'. Straight, clear, and to the point is what you'll want from an accountability partner.

Similar industry, different perspective: Keep this mantra in mind when looking for an accountability partner. They need to be in a similar industry, so they have a clue about what they are doing. At the same time, you want them to be looking at your goals and aspirations from another angle. This way, they can help you incorporate various strategies including where to invest and whether or not the area itself is viable for a good ROI.

Having an accountability partner is a must whenever you want to build a business. There are three reasons why you would want one on your side each and every time. Let's take a look at them:

- **Your partner will keep you on track:** The one true thing that an accountability partner does is keep you on track. That's it. They help you stay on track with your goals and complete the tasks that need to be done day after day.

- **They are willing to be a gauge for success:** Your accountability partner wants you to succeed. They also want to let you know how close you are getting to succeeding. You can also measure each other's success and compare.

- **They help you become smarter:** They will help you become more knowledgeable in real estate. They will relay 'need to know' information. And they will keep you in the know of things when it comes to real estate news and so on. But they want you to be aware of it so you can make any necessary changes, if needed.

Agents, Brokers, and Realtors

We'll be talking about agents, brokers, and realtors and the roles they play. We'll also talk about the differences in responsibilities and how they earn money. Take a closer look at each one:

Agents: Real estate agents are people who are licensed to assist in buying, selling, or renting properties. One of their chief responsibilities is bringing the buyer and seller together to ensure that a deal is done. In addition, their responsibilities include carrying offers and counteroffers and making sure that both clients are aware of any requirements that need to be met before the deal is approved. Real estate agents get paid by commission fees. While they may not get the entire commission, it's usually split up as follows: Listing agent, buyer's agent, the listing agent's broker, and the buyer's agent's broker. For example, if the commission is 8 percent, all four parties will get 2 percent a piece.

Brokers: Real estate brokers do pretty much the same tasks as real estate investors. Brokers will work with buyers in terms of looking for property based on the criteria set by their own clients. There are also seller brokers that are responsible for determining market values of the property that their client wants to sell.

At the same time, they use listings and show properties to buyers including those that are being sold by their client. There are three types of brokers: associate brokers, managing brokers, and principal or designated brokers.

Brokers typically get paid by taking a share of the commissions earned by the real estate agents that work for them. Brokers can make their own deals and therefore do not need to split their own commissions.

Realtors: Realtors are professionals in the industry and are members of the National Association of Realtors or NAR. One of the main things that gets confusing is that realtors and real estate agents are considered the same. However, there are some differences. To become a realtor, they must have a real estate license that is valid and active. And they must be active in the business itself. They must also have no sanctions based on unprofessional conduct and also have no pending or recent bankruptcies. Realtors get paid based on commission and will usually have it split between other agents.

Finding A Real Estate Professional

Now, it's time to find a real estate professional that you can trust. The question is: who will you want to be a part of your team? Do you want a real estate agent or a broker? Or do you want a realtor who may have a deep network of real estate professionals that you can leverage if and when needed?

The first question is where to find them. Let's take a look at some of our recommended methods in finding a good real estate professional:

- **Ask your friends or family**

- **Do online research (i.e.: [Your City] + Real Estate Agents)**

- **Attend open houses in your local area**
- **Drive around the neighborhood (and see who's selling houses along with the realtor they are going through)**

Characteristics to look for while finding a real estate professional

When you are looking for a real estate professional, the ultimate goal is to find someone you can trust. This means that you'll have to find one that has these characteristics that we'll list below. With that said, here's what you need to look for:

- **Someone who is a problem solver:** When it comes to creating solutions, a real estate professional does just that. They know how to make a property more marketable for buyers or investors.

- **They are self-motivated:** Like you, they are self-motivated entrepreneurs that are hungry for success. It takes drive, determination, and smart decision making for both of you in order to get where you need to be.

- **Honest and have integrity:** Obviously a huge factor here. If they have honesty and integrity, you'll be better off giving them your trust. However, don't dive in just yet. You want to be sure you are working with the right person. And you want to make sure whether or not they are going to screw you out of a good deal.

- **They have an interest in houses and architecture:** Most of those who are in real estate have some sort of interest in houses and architecture. So, they're not just in it for the paycheck. With knowledge about the houses and the kind of architecture and design, they are reflected as more professional and an expert on all things houses in the eyes of the buyer or seller.

- **An engaging personality:** They are someone that is willing to have a conservation with someone. They are patient, always willing to ask or answer questions, and connect with people who are interested in purchasing a property or selling one.

- **Attention to detail:** Real estate agents need to pay close attention to detail. If they are able to, they will have a long and successful real estate career. And they can be one of your most trusted members of your real estate team.

- **They understand the housing market:** Whether it's the broad market or the local market, the real estate professional you want to partner up with is someone who understands it. This will help them give you a good idea on when it's the right time to purchase a piece of property and what part of the local area to steer clear from.

- **A robust network:** There is no doubt that a real estate professional will have a network of people. Not only will it have other real estate professionals, but everyone else from property managers, lenders, attorneys, and so on. They will gladly refer you to people within their network if there is a need that you want fulfilled.

Working with One

Once you've found a real estate professional, you'll want to know how to work with them. At the same time, you always want to make sure that you are working with the right person. You want someone that you can trust and will never screw you over.

When speaking with a real estate professional that you are interested in working with, it's important that you ask questions. Gauge their knowledge of the real estate business and the housing market. Do they sound like they know what they are talking about or do they sound like an idiot?

Also, are there any pre-existing connections between you and the real estate professional? If they are related to your family in any way, don't choose them. And simply don't choose them because you grew up down the street from them either.

It all comes down to someone who is experienced in the field and also has a professional reputation. So yes, it's better to be picky about which real estate professional you want to work with before you hit the ground running.

What about 'double agents'?

Double agents are just something you hear about in spy movies. There are such things as dual agents in real estate. In rare cases, they do work.

But nine times out of ten, you want to steer clear from them. Not only are they not good to work with, but in eight states (Alaska, Colorado, Florida, Kansas, Maryland, Oklahoma, Texas, and Vermont), being a dual agent is against the law. Who is a dual agent you ask?

A dual agent is someone who is a real estate agent that represents both the buyer and the seller in a transaction. However, this will create all kinds of problems as it can create some conflicts of interest. If anything, avoiding 'dual agents' will be key when you want to invest in real estate.

Instead, you want to go with an exclusive agent. They need to be exclusive to buyers or sellers. If you want to buy properties, a buyer's agent will obviously be your go-to person. When it comes time to sell the property, a seller's agent should be somewhere in your network.

When to get rid of a real estate professional?

Hopefully, the real estate professional that you choose is someone that you can trust and will always be honest and transparent with you. However, if they are causing you problems, it's better to let them go rather than keep them around.

However, you want to think this decision through before doing anything else. It's better to repair a relationship first to see if both you and the real estate professional are on the same page. They may have a style or performance that you may not agree with.

Or they may have failed to meet certain expectations. Iron out the wrinkles before doing anything else. If all else fails, that's when you notify the professional that you want to terminate the working contract between the two of you.

To help avoid problems, you want to do your due diligence on the real estate agents that you are interested in working with. Keep a close eye on what they're saying and take notes. It will come down to who you want to work with based on experience, competence, and credibility.

Hiring A Property Manager versus Self-Management

The next most valuable person on your team is a property manager. This is someone who will help handle tenant issues on your behalf. Plus, they are also responsible for determining which tenants can rent your properties and who cannot based on the policies and conditions that you set forth.

Of course, you have the option of managing the property yourself. This means you handle all the tenant applications and decisions. Plus, you have other responsibilities such as getting in contact with the right people in the event you need repairs or some other issues taken care of.

What option will work best for you in the long run? That would depend on how much work you are willing to handle. Let's take a look at some differences between property management versus self-management:

Property management

Pros

- A property manager does the heavy lifting, so you don't have to. It makes your work as a property investor a lot easier. Plus, it's less stressful

- They are well aware of the market and will usually handle the nooks and crannies of property management

- They can handle problem tenants, so you don't have to. Especially when it comes to missed payments, damage to the property, and so on.

- Often useful when you own numerous properties. So long as they manage them well, your properties will be in good shape.

Cons

- With property management, it comes as an additional expense. It might be a necessary evil if you choose not to manage the property yourself.

- You might end up with a property manager who may be incompetent and not know what they're doing. So, it's best to screen for property managers should you go that route.

- Some property managers may not meet your expectations. They may be subpar in performance and manage the properties in a way that you did not ask for them to do.

Self-Management

Pros

- You can save property management fees

- You can manage it better than anyone else, if you believe you can

- You have even greater control over the tenants that occupy your properties

- You'll have top priority over the property (especially if it's the only one you own)

- Self-management is no easy task. This includes chasing down late payments, possible late-night calls about urgent repairs, and performing inspections that happen from time to time

- You might not have up-to-date information that may be needed for tax and legal purposes

- Your real estate resources may be limited compared to those who opt to have someone else manage the property

After looking over this list of pros and cons, it's up to you to determine which will be better for you in the long run. If you don't want to juggle a lot of responsibilities, chances are the property management option will be more suited for you. However, if you have just a couple of properties within the same area, you may try your hand at self-management.

If you plan on owning multiple properties over the course of your lifetime, property management will always be the smart decision going forward. You cannot be everywhere all at once. Plus, you may have property that is hundreds of miles away from where you are.

Being Insured Can Lessen the Burden

Making sure that your rental properties are insured will be one of your priority tasks as a real estate investor. Disaster can strike anytime and anyplace. On top of that, the damage may be greater than you would expect.

What does insurance cover anyways? When looking for an insurance policy, it's important to find something that will cover the following:

- Floods
- Fires
- Natural disasters
- Damages beyond the control of tenants or owners

The more your insurance policy covers, the better. The reason why insurance is worth looking at (and worth purchasing) is because it will soften the blow in terms of any incidental expenses. Without insurance, the repairs and maintenance will take a considerable bite out of your cash flow.

In order to get a property insured, the first thing you want to do is shop around. Which property insurance policy will serve you best in the long run? And if you plan on owning multiple properties, can you cover them under the same policy?

Let's take a look at some additional tips that will help you find the right insurance policy:

Know the kind of coverage that you're getting

Insurance policies don't just cover things like the disasters that can cause damages. But you'll need to have your bases covered. You'll want things like liability coverage and even loss of rent coverage (especially if the property becomes uninhabitable for a lengthy period of time).

Know the different types of rental insurance policies

There are three kinds of rental insurance policies: DP-1, DP-2, and DP-3. DP is short for 'dwelling property'.

So, what's the difference between the three? Let's take a closer look:

DP-1: If you are looking for the cheapest form of insurance, DP-1 will be what you'll need. You will get basic coverage. This policy will cover named perils of disasters. If the disaster or peril is not mentioned in the policy, the insurance company will not reimburse you for the damages. Reimbursements will be on an actual cash value basis. The insurer will pay you for any damage except for wear and tear (or depreciation).

DP-2: This will give you slightly better coverage compared to DP-1. Like DP-1, named perils that fall under the DP-2 policy will be covered as such. Again, unnamed perils and disasters will not be reimbursed. One major difference is that a DP-2 insurance plan can cover burglary damages while DP-1 may not do so. Insurers will reimburse you for damage based on the current market prices and can do so without taking depreciation into account.

DP-3: The most expensive coverage. This will give you the broadest coverage of the three. This will protect you against all perils except those that are excluded in the policy. This will be provided on the basis of a replacement cost.

Explain to your tenants about renter's insurance

Let's talk about rental insurance for a moment. This is separate from your insurance policy. Your policy is not responsible for any damages to the tenant's possessions. That is why it's important to encourage them to get renter's insurance just in case things happen.

This will lessen their burden after the fact since the insurer will reimburse them for any property that is damaged. You hold your tenants in high regard. So be sure that they are covered in ways that you cannot provide for them.

How About Those Involved in Fixing?

The final piece of the puzzle in building your team are those who are contractors, handymen, and repair specialists. As mentioned before, damage can occur at any time. And you want some go-to people on your contact list.

When looking for someone who will do the repair and maintenance work, you'll want to find someone who is competent, can do most repairs and maintenance, and also has a good response time.

Do you need a handyman or a contractor?

There will be times when you will need to ask if a handyman is needed on the property or if you need a contractor. The answer to this question is that it depends. If the repair or maintenance project is small, a handyman will be the go-to person.

One thing to keep in mind is that there may be laws that may allow the kind of work a handyman can do. For example, in California, a handyman is only allowed to do work that totals out to about $500 plus labor and parts. If a handyman does $500+ worth of projects, they must hold a license for a specific area that they focus on.

For example, if a handyman specializes in plumbing and bathroom remodeling, they must have a license as a plumbing contractor. However, a handyman will be useful for small projects.

If the repair, maintenance, or renovation project is large, that's when a contractor will come in handy. Especially if it's a contractor that is focused on a certain area such as plumbing, kitchen remodeling, and so on.

Hiring a handyman or contractor

If you are considering the idea of hiring a handyman or a contractor, you'll want to take a moment to interview any candidates that you're interested in adding to your team. Ask them about their track record, their areas that they specialize in, and references.

Always make sure that you check with references to see if things check out. You will be around this person on your properties and work closely with them. So, find someone you can trust and have a positive record.

After adding your handyman and contractors, be sure to have a written agreement drawn up so it details the project, the cost, and the frequency of payments. Also, you may want to keep on the lookout for handymen or contractors that ask for a full payment upfront prior to the project.

While hiring a handyman or a contractor may be an extra expense, it might be better if you choose not to manage the property yourself.

Final Thoughts

Having a team at your side will be important. You'll have the right kind of people who will deal with any issues you may have. At the same time, you have people who specialize in one area of real estate.

Obviously, you'll want to work with a real estate professional who is exclusive to one part of the process, not a dual agent. A property manager might also be a valuable asset if you don't want to perform any self-management tasks. Let's not forget that you'll need someone to take care of the insurance policy just in case things happen.

Finally, when things do happen, you want to have a handyman and contractors in your network. That way, when something needs repairing or maintenance, you can give them a call at any time. These are people who you can trust and will stick with you in the long haul.

Be sure to screen for these people thoroughly so you don't run into any issues. When you do, a big plus is always asking for references. That way, you'll know who you're dealing with and you can make the decision to add them to your team or find someone else.

Chapter 5: Everything You Need to Know in Finding Houses

One of the best things about a real estate investing business is finding a property that will be great for your portfolio. However, finding the right one can be difficult and it will take time.

This chapter will be focused on what you need to know about finding your first property. You will learn how to use due diligence to your advantage. The farther you go into it, the more you'll know about the property and be able to determine if it's a good find based on the numbers.

Furthermore, we'll be discussing the what, how, where, and who aspects of purchasing a house. Also, don't skip this chapter if you want to overcome your fears of diving into one bad deal after another. Speaking of which, we'll show you how to avoid scams.

We'll also talk about foreclosures and how they might be a good addition to your portfolio. Next, we'll discuss what house hacking is and how it might work to your advantage in real estate. Lastly, you'll learn about why now would be a good time to start creating your real estate network from the ground up.

If you're ready to know more about houses and how you can find one as your first property, let's get going:

What You Should Know About Due Diligence

With any kind of investing, due diligence is what you usually need to do. You want to make sure that you are looking at the assets in question before you take the great leap with money. This includes stocks, bonds, and yes...even real estate.

Due diligence is defined as an investigation or a review to confirm that the investment you're looking to make is legitimate. You want to double check and make sure that the data is accurate before making an investment. At least 99 percent of the time, doing your due diligence will get you out of a potentially bad deal or a scam deal.

With due diligence, you want to go as deep as you can to get the right information. So, what is the information that you need for real estate transactions? Let's explain what you need to find.

When it comes to due diligence, it all comes down to the metrics and the types of information you need to have on hand. Each bit of information is different depending on what you're investing in. Due diligence metrics in stocks are way different than those in real estate.

Because of this, we're going to show you metrics on what you need to know when you look at one property. You need to know these numbers (and possibly crunch some of them) in order to determine whether or not it will be a good investment on your end. Let's take a look at the stages of due diligence that need to be performed before an offer is ever made:

The Neighborhood and Area

Population: The population of the area of interest will be key. Because a higher populated area could mean more valuable property. If you are in a major city, there may be suburbs that are closer to the downtown area. A lower populated area could also mean cheaper property values as well.

Job growth: If you want a good indicator of how good the housing market is for an area, take a look at the job growth. Is the local economy doing well? Or is it faltering due to layoffs and job loss? If the job growth is negative, you might be second-guessing the idea of investing in a property in such an area.

Percentage of occupied rental properties: How many households are occupied by renters? If there are more people renting than buying houses outright, then that could serve as a good opportunity to find a single-family home that you can use for rental purposes.

Vacancy rates: How many rental properties are vacant during a calendar year? To calculate this, take a look at the number of days the property has been occupied and divide by 365. For example, if a property has been occupied for 120 days [120/365 = .33] then the vacancy rate is 33 percent. This means for a third of the year, the property has been vacant.

Median rents: How much are people paying for rent monthly? What's the average? This will give you a good idea of how much you want to set the rental rate for your property.

Crime rate: You want your tenants to feel safe in the area that they are living in. If they are in a high-crime area, then odds are you'll be on the losing end of the deal. Make sure that the crime statistics in your area of interest are accurate.

Neighborhood and school rankings: Your tenants may have children that want to go to a good school (and maybe close to where they live). How is the neighborhood overall? Are there amenities nearby? Is it commuter friendly? These will factor into the actual rankings for both neighborhood and schools.

Gross rental income: What's the current gross rental income? Will it match up with your intended cash flow target? If necessary, will it mean increasing the rent?

Additional income info: What other income is there? Are there fees that the tenants pay? Do they charge late fees for missed rent? Are there any application fees? These are what you need to look for.

Expenses: What are the expenses that the current property owner is paying? Utilities? Property management? How much are they setting aside for repairs and maintenance every month?

Property taxes and insurance: How much are they paying in property taxes every month (or year)? Are they currently covered under an insurance policy? Can that policy be transferred from one holder to another? Or do you need to get your own?

Cash reserves: Does the current property owner have cash reserves? If so, how much?

Future improvements: What are some future improvements in the works? How long will they take before completion? What's being added to the property?

Due diligence after an offer is made

If you think the due diligence is finished after an offer is completed, think again. You still need to do more of it when there's an offer on the table. Here are some things that you need to do as part of the post-offer due diligence:

Physical inspections

You want to see if the property is in good shape. That's when you want to inspect the entire property from top to bottom. This includes checking to see if the HVAC and plumbing system is in working order.

But it doesn't stop there. You'll also want to take a look at the roof and the structural integrity of the property. Also, see if there has been an inspection for any lead-based paint before 1978. Safety is very important for those who will be occupying your properties (including those with young children).

Depending on where you live, you may need to do an inspection for radon gas or defective drywall (especially if the property was built during the previous decade). If the property is near an area where flooding occurs, you'll want to see if there is any verification of a flood zone. If the property is in danger of being flooded, then you want to consider flood insurance.

Financial Due Diligence

Next, we go back to the financial side of things. This means taking a look at statements that document profits and losses that are for the current year and date back to the last two years. Also, you want to take a look at the tax returns, income, and expenses of the previous owner (information given to the IRS).

Next, you'll want to take a look at the current rent roll. How many tenants are there and how much are they paying in rent. Then you need to take a look at the lease terms for each tenant. Some leases are different because of the different expiration dates.

You'll also want to pay attention to the other terms of the lease such as the deposit amount or any unique agreements made between the tenant and the previous owner. These unique agreements include but are not limited to discounted rent in exchange for something a tenant can do like landscaping.

You'll also want to look for any additional fees that the previous owner has charged tenants. These include pet fees and deposits. You'll need to compare the pro forma information from your pre-offer due diligence and compare it to the numbers that you have on hand now since they will differ from one another.

Don't forget, you'll also need to take a look at any existing contracts made between the former property owner and any other businesses such as contractors, property management companies, and so on. Also, you'll want to be aware of any repairs and capital improvements that were made prior to the acquisition (along with any invoices or proof of payment on file).

Check for any loan or legal issues

If your property is under an HOA, you'll want to take a look at any covenants and restrictions ensuring that the property can be rented. You may also want to check for any pending litigation between the previous owner and any former tenants. You also want to make sure that the property appraisal matches the purchase price on the contract.

The last thing you want to do is get yourself in a legal battle for something that you didn't do. Sometimes, a former property owner may pass off their problems onto someone else. This is one of the biggest reasons why doing your due diligence is important.

The What, the How, and the Where of Finding Houses

In this section, we'll be talking about the 'What, How, and Where' of finding houses. We'll be taking a look at what kind of properties are available for an investor, how you can look for them, and where to look.

This entire section will be chock-full of valuable information that is only designed to be applied. Don't read through this and just keep it there for useless information. This will not work unless you take action.

Knowing what kind of property that's available is half the work. But knowing how to look and where is the other part. Now, let's start off with the 'what' portion of looking for a house:

What kind?

There are different types of houses that you can own and rent out. We'll be taking a look at what kind of houses you can buy and rent out. Each type is different, but they will provide you with a good amount of income from one or multiple tenants.

Let's take a look at the different types of houses that will make a great rental property for your portfolio:

Single-family homes

Single-family homes are regular individual houses designed for a single family to occupy. They may apply to some different property classes like luxury homes or even vacation homes. Single family homes consist of a number of bathrooms and bedrooms.

For example, a house with two bedrooms and two bathrooms would be a single-family home. Even a luxury home with 12 bedrooms and eight bathrooms would fall under the category of a single-family home as well. For single-family homes, the lot size and square footage will vary from one property to the next.

You get more space and also the ability to expand if needed. Plus, it offers more privacy for tenants compared to other property types.

However, there are some disadvantages. Some single-family homes may be under an HOA, which means there may be certain rules and restrictions. If the home is in an HOA neighborhood, unfortunately they may not be rented out if the HOA agreement explicitly says so.

Multi-family homes

Multi-family homes can be a property that includes several units. These units can be rented out separately and you can charge the same amount of rent or slightly more (depending on the measurement of the unit). One thing to be aware of is multi-family homes should not be confused for an apartment complex or the like.

However, there are apartment buildings that can be considered multi-family homes. For this reason, you can still rent out to multiple tenants if you so choose. These multi-family homes can be perfect for generating a good amount of monthly income.

Multi-family housing would be great for getting rental income since you'll be renting out multiple units. At the same time, lenders will be favorable towards those who own multi-family homes (especially if you live in one of the units). You can get financing as if it were a primary home so long as you reside on the property itself.

However, if you want to look at appreciation, multi-family properties don't appreciate as fast as single-family homes. The fees for financing these properties will be even higher. And acquiring a loan for the purpose of purchasing a multi-family home may be even more challenging compared to other properties.

Townhomes

Townhomes are similar to single-family homes. These are also known as row houses because they have a distinguishable characteristic of being two stories high and at least one wall that is connected to a neighboring property. These townhomes are usually modern, so they can be very attractive for both buyers and even potential tenants.

The great thing about these townhomes is that they may be closer to a more populated area. They will be close by to various amenities and may boast some pretty cool views. If you want a house that is underrated in terms of investment opportunity, a townhome just might be right up your alley.

One of the best things about owning a townhome is that some of the expenses that you normally deal with like maintenance and repair will be reduced. Especially if the townhome development is part of an HOA. Yes, you still will need to incorporate repairs and maintenance in your expenses, but they will be much lower than usual.

However, potential tenants may not be too happy with the shared wall. If privacy is one of their 'make or break' demands, then they will not find a townhome as something they want to live in. If a potential tenant cannot handle a lot of noise, then a townhome won't be for them either. Lastly, townhomes may be expensive to buy depending on the area that you live in.

Distressed Properties

Distressed properties are houses that are considered fixer-uppers. You can purchase the property for a below market price and then put in the needed repairs and maintenance. Once completed, you can sell the house outright for a higher profit or rent it out and refinance it.

Referring to the BRRRR method as we pointed out in chapter two, you can purchase the property, repair or rehab it, rent it out, and then refinance it so you can pay off any loans or the like. The only place for the valuation of the property to go with distressed properties is up.

One of the downsides with distressed properties is that you might run into some issues that may come as a surprise. This means you may be spending a little more than your expected budget. Also, you'll need to get the repairs and maintenance done in a shorter period of time (especially if you need to pay off a hard money loan).

Foreclosures are a great property to snag up for a good price. Later on in this chapter, we'll discuss what they are, how important it is to understand them and how you can acquire one. You'll also learn about the advantages and disadvantages of them as well.

Retail Properties

Are there properties that will allow you to run a retail business on the lower level while having a habitable living space up top? The answer is yes. And what's great about this is that you can own a retail business while racking up additional income for a rental property.

Or if you don't own the retail business, you can get income from both the business owner and the tenant separately (unless the business owner lives on the same property like an upstairs apartment). Either way, retail properties are a good opportunity to generate income.

However, there are some expenses that you need to keep separate. If there are issues with the retail business, you may be paying higher expenses as if you were tending to a commercial property. But if there are issues with the residential side of the property, then the expenses will be charged like it would with an apartment building or a single-family home.

How to Look for Rental Properties

Now that you are aware of the type of properties that are available, it's time to figure out how to look for them. In today's digital world, it's easy to find them online. However, you might want to mix it up a bit and perhaps use some offline methods as well.

In this section, we'll show you where exactly you can find these properties using the specific methods below:

Online tools

Even today, more people are relying on the Internet and even mobile apps. There are dozens of rental listing websites that you can start with. These include Craigslist, NextHome, GottaRent, RentSeeker, Apartments.com, and more.

When using online tools, you can take advantage of the filtering features. This way, you can whittle down the properties that you are looking for based on a certain criteria. If you are looking for single-family homes, you can check out realtor websites or MLS listings via brokers like Coldwell Banker, ReMax, and so on.

Bulletin boards

Online isn't the only place to find properties that you can buy and rent out. You can check out bulletin boards that are in your local area. These can include high traffic areas like banks, supermarkets, shopping malls, and other local businesses where there are community bulletin boards.

If you are planning on purchasing apartment complexes that provide student housing, consider looking at bulletin boards on college or university campuses.

Classified ads

Just because the Internet is dominating everything, doesn't mean that classified ads have gone the way of the dinosaur. Your local newspapers will be a good place to start. Also, if you have large regional newspapers that have a statewide or regional coverage area, take a look at those too. Sometimes, you may have to go outside of your local area to find the property that fits your criteria.

Rental guides

Typically, these guides are free. You can find them on street corners or store entrances if they are available.

Signs

You know those signs that say 'vacancy' or 'no vacancy'? Yep. You'll be hunting around your area of interest for these signs.

You can find these and other signs like 'for rent' in neighborhoods as well. If you are interested in acquiring any houses or apartments, you can call the owner and ask questions. When will there be vacancies? What is the asking price for the property?

Dig into as much information as you can so you can make an offer at some point in the future should the property of interest be suited for you.

Where to Look?

Location, location, location. One word said three times over. And you'll be hearing that an awful lot when you build your real estate portfolio.

You won't get tired of it because it's one of the mantras you'll remember while looking for one property after another (assuming you want to invest in more of them). The first thing you need to do is choose an area of interest of a potential market.

Nine times out of ten, most real estate investors will start in their local area. That's because they want to be close by to the property should anything happen. However, that's not always the case.

You can acquire properties from a long distance. Whether it's a hundred miles away or even two states over, there is a property that could fit your personal criteria. All you need to do is hire a property manager to take care of the day-to-day operations and you can collect income and have a nice steady cash flow.

As far as where to look, you'll want to take the following into consideration:

Cost of housing

You'll want to be in an area where the cost of housing is affordable. This will help determine the potential ROI for investors. At the same time, it will also determine whether or not the property will be useful in terms of being a rental property or otherwise.

One thing to pay attention to is the national average. As of this writing, the national average of purchasing a home is over $272,000.

Demand and opportunity

If you're an investor, you'll want to find a property in an area where the demand for rental units is high. The higher the demand, the better the opportunity. In order to determine the demand, you'll need to take into account some of the following things: population growth, unemployment rate, rental-rate growth, job opportunities, etc. Also, you'll want to take into account another national average.

In this case, take a look at the unemployment rate nationwide. This will change from month to month as the jobs reports and the unemployment figures are released every first Friday. For example, the jobs report for the month of March will be released on the first Friday of April.

As a real estate investor, you want to mark these days on your calendar especially when you are constantly searching for rental properties.

What type of neighborhood is the property in?

The types of neighborhoods are usually a thing of personal preference. However, you'll want to consider neighborhoods that are occupied by a specific group of people. These can be families, students, or even young professionals.

No strategy is a 'golden strategy' for all. But you'll want to find a neighborhood that dominates the market for that area. For example, if college rentals are dominating the local housing market, then that's a good opportunity to invest in a student housing complex.

Keep in mind that there may also be downsides to this as well. In the example of student housing, there may be parties that rage on late into the night and may lead to damages because of some rowdy, drunk, revelers. And that may mean more money to set off to the side because of repairs.

Insurance costs

The insurance costs will differ from one area to the next. In other words, not all locations will be insurable equally. Also, you'll want to take a look at areas that are susceptible to certain disasters. For example, you might find that the insurance policies may be higher for areas that are prone to wildfires.

Insurance policies do not come cheap. Especially when the policies are designed to give you extra coverage because you're in an area where disasters can occur regularly (fire, floods, etc.).

Walkability

One thing to pay attention to is the walkability of a neighborhood. How easy is it to walk from various stores, public transportation stops, parks, and so on? If it's easily accessible, this can be a huge selling point for investors when looking to fulfill tenant space.

However, the farther the tenant may need to walk, the less walkable it might be. Some won't mind walking a mile to the nearest store. But others will. So, consider any place less than a mile from the property to be walking or biking friendly.

Nearby amenities

What's close by? Is it a recreational center? A golf course?

Is there anything for the kids? Are there any grocery stores nearby? These are the things that you want to pay attention to.

Again, you want to make sure that it's a 'skip and a hop' away as opposed to a long drive. Because it's more convenient for someone to head out, get in, get out, and head back home in the quickest time possible.

Public transportation options

Are there any public transportation options in the area? If so, how far are they from the property? What types of transport are available?

If they are near public transportation, that's a huge plus. On top of that, it will command a higher price just for the convenience.

Avoiding Scams

Scams are all over the place. And you can be sure that in the real estate niche, there is bound to be a scam or two out there that may prey on newbie investors like yourself. That's why you'll want to learn about some of the most common real estate scams that have long sucked in many newbies and left them out to dry.

But knowing us, we've managed to track down some of the most common scams, so you know what they are and how to avoid them. These are some of the most common scams related to real estate:

Escrow Wire Fraud

This happens when you receive a phone call, email, or text from someone claiming to be from an escrow company. They give you instructions on where to wire escrow funds. These fraudsters even try to make it look real by setting up a website, email address, and phone number.

To protect yourself from this kind of fraud, you'll want to refer back to the original documents that were given to you by your lender. Call the phone numbers and see if the escrow wiring instructions you have received were real. Also, do not click on any links (via email or text) or send money online without verification from an authorized person that is associated with your lender.

Loan flipping

This involves predatory lenders that claim to refinance mortgages. These scammers are known for charging high fees and often target seniors with memory problems. If you have not requested the help of lenders but they are seeking you out, then you may want to avoid them.

To prevent getting caught up in this kind of scam, work with known banks and lenders. Also, question the fees and penalties that are presented if needed.

Foreclosure relief

This is the kind of scam that targets those who may be falling behind in their mortgages. Because of public records, the scammers can access this and know who is behind and who isn't. From there, they will call the person up and claim to offer foreclosure relief.

Those who want to avoid this scam must speak with a loan service provider while working to modify your current loan. A scammer who discourages you from talking with your lender is a huge sign that you may be dealing with a scammer.

Rental scams

These rental scams pop up in places like Facebook or Craigslist. The way this is done is that scammers will use photos from a previous listing or from a different property. This is a scam that is known to target younger persons from age 18 to 29.

One way to be wary of this scam is to be suspicious of anyone who asks for upfront cash before you see the property in person. No landlord or property manager would charge anyone a ridiculous amount of money just for a showing.

'We Buy Houses'

There is a scam out there where a firm claims to buy houses while giving you money for it. However, while there are some that may exist and use legitimate means, there are scammers that claim to be 'investors'. They give out all kinds of information that you don't need.

Plus, they ask you to pay an application or evaluation fee. Let's not forget, they also ask for your bank account information. Whatever you do, do not give them anything.

On top of that, do not sign any papers or even the deed to your house without the consultation of your attorney or the escrow company.

Understanding Foreclosures

Foreclosures happen when the bank evicts a resident after they have missed multiple mortgage payments. It starts with the notice of default, followed by the foreclosure filing, the notice of the sale, and the eviction.

You can get a foreclosure property at a lower price. On top of that, you can close the deal a lot faster. And it will also be a good investment property that you can turn into a rental.

However, one of the greatest disadvantages is that you may never see the home or inspect it before purchase. This means that repairs may be needed once everything is all said and done. Lastly, you also may need a ton of cash to buy it.

How About House Hacking

House hacking is something that can be done if you are planning on acquiring multi-family properties. For this to happen, you want to reside in one of the units and consider it your primary residence. From there, you can have renters of the other units pay the mortgage and other expenses.

As you can see, the concept is pretty much the same as everything else. You use the rental income and take a portion of it to pay any expenses including the mortgage itself. You can also do this using other strategies to pull it off.

You can even rent the property room by room or even rent out an RV on the driveway of the property. If that isn't a crazy way to do real estate, then we don't know what is.

Start Creating Your Real Estate Network

Later on in this book, we'll be discussing the creation of your real estate network. Already, you may have a bare bones structure already built in. And from there, you can simply build the network from the ground up.

This network should include your fellow real estate investors. Sure, while some of them may be your competition, they also share similar goals as you do. And you can all learn from each other in terms of how to become better landlords and investors.

Creating a real estate network will take time and effort. And it will also take due diligence as well. That's because you want people in your network that you can trust. And these are people who will help connect you with other people whenever you need a problem solved (and you shall return the favor whenever someone needs something from you).

Final Thoughts

Finding houses doesn't always have to be difficult. But as long as you know what kind of rental property you are looking for, you'll be in good shape. It's important to know how to look for properties, where to find them, and who to buy them from.

Also, be sure to keep your eyes open for any scams that may exist. The last thing you want is to lose your hard-earned money and never see it again because of a scam or a deal gone wrong.

Remember, purchasing foreclosures may be a good way to acquire properties. However, you may need a little extra cash because of the repairs that may be needed in the long-run. If you are considering the idea of acquiring a multi-family property, consider house hacking as a great way to generate more income.

Chapter 6: Taking Full Control of The Deals

As a real estate investor, you'll be doing quite a bit of wheeling and dealing. Especially when you're going to build a solid portfolio. In this chapter, we'll be talking about the importance of real estate valuation and appraisals.

You'll understand how important they are and how each property is appraised. You'll learn about the different approaches of valuation and appraisal. You'll even learn how to evaluate deals so you can be sure whether or not it will be profitable on your end.

Before any deal is made, you want to make sure that the property is in good shape. That's when we'll talk about property inspections. This is where you'll approach inspections and how they work from a buyer's point of view.

This will show you exactly how to go about setting up a budget, so you know how much you'll need to spend on repairs and renovations. Every good offer should go without a hitch. So, we'll show you how to go through the process of making an offer and what to avoid while doing so.

Negotiation will also play an important role in getting the best deal. In this chapter, you'll learn 10 different negotiation strategies that you can incorporate while you are looking to get the best deal possible. This will include counteroffers and give you an overview of the closing process.

If you are planning on making a deal that will be below the market value, we'll talk about what you need to look for. And lastly, we'll discuss the closing process, so you know what to expect when the paperwork is prepared, signed, and ready for processing.

This is one of the many all-important chapters that you DO NOT want to skip in this book. Especially when you want every deal to be a good one. Let's get started:

Real Estate Valuation and Appraisal

Property valuation is a process that determines the economic value of a real estate investment. Here, this will determine what is considered a fair market value of the price itself. Likewise, the seller may be willing to sell his or her property to an informed buyer at a price that may seem to be reasonable for both parties.

Both parties will have relevant information. No one will be forced to buy or sell the property. The property value itself and the selling price are not always equal to each other.

At times, a seller can sell the property right off the bat even if the price is below the fair market value. They may be doing this out of desperation or distress. This may not always happen, but it's good to know nonetheless.

An appraisal is done to determine the value of the property itself. There are three methods of going about doing this. Regardless, the appraisal process will include data that will need to be used such as national, regional, city, and neighborhood averages.

Once the data is gathered, the appraisal process uses the following approaches:

Approach #1: Sales comparison

This is an approach often used in the appraisal of single-family homes. This is better known as the market data approach. This will estimate the value of the property and compare it to the value of properties that have similar characteristics.

These properties are known as comparables. To provide an accurate comparison, the following must be taken into account:

- The comparing properties must be similar to one another

- Has been sold in an open and competitive market within the last year

- Sold under usual market conditions.

These three comparables will be used in the appraisal process. Other comparables include size, location, and other relevant features. Also, you'll want to take into account the other qualities such as the age and condition, the date of the sale (and any economic changes between the date of the sale and the current day), location, and physical features.

Approach #2: Cost Approach

This approach is used to estimate the value of any properties that have been improved over a period of time. With this method, this will use separate estimates such as the building and the land that the property is built on. Also, this approach will take depreciation into consideration.

Other things that will be taken into consideration is the cost of the repairs and renovations if needed. The current costs will also play a role in this approach. Also, the value of the land as if it were vacant must also be taken into account as well.

Approach #3: Income capitalization

This is better known as the income approach. This is a method that is based on two things: the rate of return the investor wants and the net income that is produced by the property of interest. These will be used to estimate the overall value of the property itself (such as apartment complexes and the like). The income capitalization approach is simple and straightforward. And it will determine the potential income and expenses that will go along with this property.

As a newbie to real estate investing, you'll find this to be a very easy approach. You'll be able to determine how much income you can generate from rental rates and the expenses that will be taken out to ensure that you have a positive cash flow every month.

Evaluating Deals

In this section, we're going to show you how to evaluate every deal so you can determine whether or not it will be profitable on your end. This may require some data and even crunching the numbers. Again, we want you to get the best deal possible each and every time.

You do not want to fly blindly into a deal only to realize that it was a bad deal, and it is too late to turn back. We'll be talking about the kind of information you need to gather, as well as the tools you need to use to gather said info. You'll also learn about the property details and what you'll be getting out of the deal itself.

How can you evaluate a deal? We'll show you how to do it step by step, followed by a few rules that you need to follow while doing so. Let's take a look at what you need to do, first and foremost:

Gather the property details

The property details include the name of the property, the street address (including the city, state, and zip code), and the square footage. You should also include information for the date that the information was prepared followed by the name of the person preparing the details.

Calculate the purchase details

You'll want to take a look at the market value, the assessed value and then the purchase price percentage of market value. Other information that needs to be included are the purchase price, the equity at purchase, the down payment, and the mortgage amount. Last but not least, you'll want to include pertinent costs including the closing, renovation, and out of pocket costs.

Rental information

Take into account the number of rental units that are available in the area of interest. Also, take into account the going rate for rent. The figures you want to put together is the rental rate and the renovation costs (both monthly and annually).
This includes two percent rent of the purchase price and renovation costs. Also, take into account the vacancy rate and also the gross operating income. Another thing you need to do is get the average rent per unit.

For example, let's say you have five units: two of them are $650 per month, one is $850 per month, and the last two are $700 per month. Let's add them up:

- 650 * 2 = $1300
- 850 * 1 = $ 850
- 700 * 2 = $1400

In total, that's $3560. Now divide that by five and you get $712 as a rental average. For the annual average, simply multiply by 12 (which gives you $8544). This is a good opportunity to play around with some rental rates to see what is considered reasonable enough not just for your cash flow, but to ensure that you are getting a good ROI out of the deal.

Estimated Financials

These estimated financials include the estimated operating expenses, net operating income, annual debt service, and the estimated cash flow (including cash flow per unit). If you want to quickly evaluate each deal, use at least 50 percent as the operating expenses for any property. As an option, you can utilize calculated financials and use specific figures rather than estimated numbers.

For example, you can opt for $500 or $502.01. Likewise, you use $550 or $553. Round it to the nearest $5 dollars if need be. To make it easier, stick with the estimated financials since you may not have an idea of an exact number.

Other analysis

If you want more numbers to analyze, you can also include one-time prices such as the purchase price per unit, renovated price per unit, the gross rent multiplier, and more. This is also a good time to calculate the cap rate as well.

When should you purchase the property?

This is where the numbers will give you a good indication. There are some requirements that you need to follow. These may include the following:

- The monthly rent or GSI must exceed two percent of the renovated price.

- The cash flow per unit is $100 or more

- The debt coverage ratio is greater than 1.2

If the property meets the criteria, then that should be a green light to purchase the property. However, if some of the figures do not meet the criteria, recalculate until it does. Or you can move on and find another property that will pass the test.

As part of your evaluation, you want to analyze the property's overall cash flow. What does this entail? Let's take a closer look:

Mortgage payment: Depending on the lender, you'll factor in things like the property tax and the insurance payments. Typically, these can be paid altogether. However, if you don't pay them along with the mortgage then you'll want to account for these items separately.

Utilities: This will usually vary. You can cover utilities such as water, cable, and trash while the tenant will be responsible for the lights. If you acquire a multi-unit property, determine what the tenant will pay out of pocket for utilities while choosing which utilities will be covered under their lease agreement.

Property management fees: This will be included should you opt for a property manager to take care of the day-to-day operations. The standard figure for such a fee is 10 percent of the total collected rent. If you collect $1500 in total rent, then the property management fee is $150.

HOA fees: If the property is under an HOA, then you'll want to include this fee in your expenses. This may apply if you are renting out townhomes or single-family homes depending on the neighborhood the property is on.

Vacancy: Setting aside an amount in the event of vacancies will be a slippery slope. For a specific figure, consider setting off a percentage of cash as if you are dealing with five to ten percent of your units being vacant.

Maintenance: Things happen. Almost to the point where they need to be repaired or replaced outright. Set aside at least 10 percent every month as a cash reserve for maintenance and repairs. If the property is an older home, you might want to consider setting aside a little more money per month.

Rental income: Self-explanatory. The rental income will be the rent per unit. If you have multiple units, the rental rate per unit may vary.

Remember, the cash flow is the net operating income minus the expenses. For example, if the total net operating income is $1500 per month and the expenses are roughly $650, then the cash flow should be $850. And that's just for one property.

5 Rules to Keep in Mind While Evaluating A Property

1. When you buy, you make money

To explain this, when you buy an investment property, you are aware that the purchase is about the money you'll get from rent. It's about what you'll get for an ROI. It doesn't matter if the kitchen flooring is linoleum or hardwood.

When you buy, you know of the factors that go into whether or not the property is worth purchasing. Keep in mind that if you choose to find a property on an MLS listing, don't expect the return on investment to be massive. That's because the MLS will allow you to pay 10 to 20 percent less than the listed price.

2. Use the 55 percent rule for NOI

If you want to calculate the NOI, this is where your number crunching skills will come in handy. The 55 percent rule will be exercised as follows: Take the gross rent for the year and multiply it by 55 percent (or .55).

Let's take a look at the following example: let's say the gross annual rent is $45000 (assuming you have five units at $750 per month for rent). Now multiply that by 55 percent like so:

$45000 * .55 = $24750.

Therefore, your annual NOI will be $24750. The remaining 45 percent will go towards other expenses such as insurance, vacancies, maintenance, utilities, repairs, and so on.

3. Use the cap rate for property comparisons

Part of the analysis is pitting one property against the other in a battle to see which one would fare better. Keep in mind that at the end of the day, the numbers never lie. In case you have forgotten the formula for the cap rate, it's the net operating income divided by the purchase price.

So for example, we use the $24750 in the previous example and the purchase price is $300,000. Let's calculate it:

$24,750/$300,000 = 8 percent

Ideally, you want the cap rate to be anywhere between 6 to 8 percent. Since the cap rate in this example is 8 percent, that's a good property.

However, let's say that you're looking at a building with 10 units. The gross rent per month is $3,000 (or $36,000 a year). The purchasing price is $450,000.

Here's the calculation:

$36,000/$450,000 = 8 percent

Once again, we have a property with an eight percent cap rate. If needed, you'll want to whittle it down to the exact decimal. Sometimes, the smallest number might be the best option even by a razor thin margin.

Let's say for instance you settle with the property that's $450,000 because it's dead on the money for a cap rate. Keep in mind that the down payment will usually be 20 percent of the purchasing price. In this example, the down payment for this property is $90,000.

If the net operating income per month is $3,000, you'll want the financing cost to be less than that amount. So, you'll want to up the ante a bit. Instead of putting down a 20 percent down payment, opt for 30 percent?

Therefore, put down $135,000 instead of the usual 20 percent. This way, you can get a positive cash flow while giving yourself a head start on the mortgage payment (and you pay it off quicker).

Transaction costs are not the best thing to deal with. Especially when you are making real estate deals. For this reason, you'll want to minimize them as much as possible.

It's not common for real estate investors to spend 15 percent in total. That's five percent for purchasing the property and ten percent when you sell it. For a $450,000 property, that's $67,500 of your money spent the whole way.
The costs may even consume any appreciation value of the property. Even if you put down a good amount of money for your property and sell it quickly, the transaction costs will take up at least half of what you get.

Property Inspection

If you want to inspect a property, then you want to do this from the buyer's point of view. Home inspections are pretty much the requirement before a sale event takes place (in most situations). Even if the property in question is a fixer-upper, an inspection must be done to ensure how much money you are willing to put in on repairs and renovations alone.

Getting right to it, a home inspection will entail a thorough inspection of both the inside and outside of the property. A home inspector will be looking at the following:

- HVAC and plumbing
- Any appliances that are inside the house (i.e. -- Refrigerator, dishwasher, etc.)
- Electrical system
- Structural integrity including the foundation, walls, roof, etc.
- Outside of the property including the fence, lawn, home exterior, etc.

A property inspection will range between $300 to $600 depending on the size of the property and the rates the home inspector charges. The length of time for an inspection will also depend on the size of the property. Smaller sized properties will take one to two hours max while larger homes will take an upwards of six hours.

When choosing a home inspector, it's important to take a look at things like reviews. How many of them are positive and authentic? What are people saying about them?

Also, you may tap into your existing network of real estate professionals and be referred to one or two of them. That might even be the route you go with subsequent properties as well. As long as you have a real estate professional that you can trust, there's a good chance that you'll take them at their word.

Don't be afraid to ask questions as you and the inspector go through the home. That's because you'll want to assess the damage and get a good figure of how much it will be to repair it. Be sure to note any potential costs that the inspector gives you (if any).

What happens if a home inspection goes bad?

There's always the chance that a bad home inspection can occur. But keep in mind that 'bad' doesn't necessarily mean dire straits. If one does occur on the property, bailing out may not be the smartest decision.

Even a bad home inspection can be important to buyers. That's because it could give them some more options on what to do with the property (including the kind of financing they need to acquire it). In the event of a home inspection, the seller can be responsible for any repairs or pay you the amount needed for them to be done.

Either way, it's a win-win for you because it lessens the amount of money you spend on repairs overall. You get a credit at closing, but you will still need to pay the remainder of the repairs if and when needed.

Estimating repairs

During the home inspection, you'll want to get a good idea of how much money you'll need in order to get the repairs completed. Once again, it's always a good idea to walk through the inspection when it's being done on site with the inspector.

Have the inspector give you ballpark estimates, so you have a preliminary budget. Keep in mind that the figures may not always be accurate. You could get the repairs done under or over budget.

In the case of going over budget, this may be due to any discoveries you may find after an inspection. Things can happen in the time between the post-inspection and the sale. So, you want to keep your bases covered if needed.

Take into consideration what needs to be repaired and renovated. While the house value will be increased, the costs will be quite hefty depending on the amount of work that needs to be put in.

Avoid the Mistakes in Making an Offer

When it comes time to make an offer, you want it to go off without a hitch. This means making sure there are as few mistakes as possible. One false move and it can derail the entire transaction.

Before we unveil the top seven mistakes that you need to avoid, let's take a look at the offer making process itself:

Get a comparative market analysis (or a CMA)

A CMA will always be used during the offer process. This will help determine the true value of the property in question. Of course, this includes the characteristics such as the square footage, number of bedrooms and bathrooms, and other pertinent information.

Also, you'll want to take a look at which properties are currently on the market, which ones are in escrow, and which ones have a closed escrow. You'll want to go back as far as the last six months. These properties must be located within a minimum of a ½ mile to a max of 1 mile radius.

Pay attention to things like the sold price instead of the list price. Also, pay attention to the adjusted average sales price. You can also compare it to other properties and determine whether or not the units and lots are the same size, if the number of bedrooms and bathrooms are the same as the property you're looking at, if they are close to each other, and so on.

Look at the market trends

What kind of market is the area in? Is it a buyer's market or a seller's market? You'll know just by taking a look at the neighborhood.

If you hear stories about buyers making multiple offers before one gets accepted, that's when you'll know that it's a sellers' market. If you hear of stories about a buyer getting a great deal on a home that's been on the market for a lengthy period of time, then the market is a buyer's market.

Basically, it takes word of mouth and asking around to determine the kind of market the local area is. However, you'll want to take certain factors such as the list price to sales price ratio, any seasonal issues that may arise, and the average number of days that homes in the area are on the market into consideration.

Know the facts about the property and the seller

Not only will you need to know things about the property like how long it's been on the market, but it's good to know what the seller's motivation and priorities are. Why are they selling it?

What price do they want? Keep in mind that the seller may sell the house for a reasonable offer (even if it isn't the price they originally wanted to settle with). A seller may need money for something, or they might be making mortgage payments on another home and don't want to pay an additional one.

Also, the competition is something you want to keep any eye on. Because you might not be the only person interested in the property.

Make your best offer on your first offer

You want to make the best offer possible at the outset. Keep in mind that the seller may counteroffer to ensure that you pay more. You may even offer a price higher than the seller expects. If you offer something that's $10,000 above the asking price compared to someone making one $5,000 above, then you might snag the property without the seller giving a counteroffer to the other.

Stay within the price of which you are pre-approved for. That way, you can make monthly payments at the new price (albeit a higher one at that). Also, don't make an offer that is above what the property could be appraised for.

7 Mistakes to Avoid

Now that you have a rough idea of how the offer process works, here are the mistakes that you need to avoid while making one:

1. Rejected for pre-approval of mortgage

If you cannot get pre-approved for a mortgage, that might put you at a disadvantage. Sellers will nine times out of ten favor those who are pre-approved for financing. That's because the pre-approval lets them know that they will have the money once the deal is done.

2. Bidding the pre-approved amount in its entirety

If the bank hands you a loan that's $450,000, resist the urge to make an offer that is the same amount. This could hurt you in the long-run should you go about doing this. Also, it will obliterate any breathing room that you'll have for negotiating.

The less you spend, the better off you'll be.

3. Not doing your research

This includes researching the market and the seller of the property. The more intel you have, the better prepared you'll be to make an offer. This research should go beyond the comparables and the price that it's listed for on the market.

As for the seller, if you have their names, do some research on them. Their social media profiles should give you a clue on the kind of people you are working with. If anything, don't be creepy or stalkerish.

Keep any intel you may have on them to yourself. But use it to help put together what may be the perfect offer that they cannot not refuse.

4. Lowball offers

Don't lowball the seller. If the property is worth $350,000, don't offer $250,000. If you do so, the seller will basically freeze you out and you blew it. Simple as that.

5. Too many contingencies

Having too many contingencies is the equivalent to jumping through too many hoops. And the more hoops that need to be jumped, the less likely the closing will be a success. Keep those contingencies to a minimum to ensure that the deal goes without a hitch.

What are contingencies? We're talking about things like home inspection, the ability to acquire financing, and so on. Don't make it more complex than it has to be.

6. Using the same agent as the seller

Three words: conflict of interest. The short answer to this problem: hire a buyer's agent. Remember the part where you should not work with dual agents?

This is reason number one why you should never ever deal with dual agents at all.

7. Allowing your emotions to get in the way

You might be in awe of the home's features. But don't let that get you to the point where you can buy it and have your budget busted after the fact. Get a buyer's agent who will not only keep their own emotions in check, but will make sure to keep yours in check as well.

Even if the home looks good inside and out and you love it to death, you may not always be on the winning end of the deal.

Negotiating Your Way into The Best Deal That You Can Get

We'll be taking a look at ten negotiation strategies that can work to your advantage to ensure that you get the best deal possible. This is an important section that you want to make sure that you have in your arsenal with every deal you find yourself in. Some sellers will be reasonable while others may take a little work to finally budge.

With that said, let's take a look at the following strategies:

1. Know the seller's personality type

There are four different 'color coded' personality types for sellers: red, blue, green, and brown. Once you get a good idea of their personality type, it will give you an idea of how to approach them. Let's break down each personality type in detail:

- **Red:** These are people who may have their emotions on their sleeves. They are transparent and have nothing to hide. They usually field offers from people they know first before anyone else. They'll try to get to know you better (to the point where you and the seller address each other on a first name basis). Feel free to share common interests and passions.

- **Blue:** Sellers with this personality will usually have no clue about what they want. They are emotionally open and tend to share stories that are of heartbreak. They are loyal to the decision they make and put other people first before themselves. However, they can be jumpy and scare off easily. Take your time with them and lead them to an offer that they are comfortable with. Nine times out of ten, they're looking for someone who will define what they need for themselves.

- **Green:** This is someone who is all business. Unlike a red, they are not in the business of making friends. They care more about the numbers than personal lives. They want to keep their cards close and receive an offer as soon as possible. When dealing with this personality, ask what their end goals are as far as selling the property is concerned. Also, have them make a reasonable offer by asking them.

- **Brown:** Like the green, they are not looking to make friends with the buyer. However, they are more direct with their end goals and have little time for dilly-dallying. So, keep the relationship professional and be prompt. Also, give them a straight answer as to whether or not you can help them achieve the goals they set forth.

2. Be aware that the negotiation will be an uphill battle

Yes, there is money at stake. And there may also be emotional attachments to the property. Also, you want to be aware that the seller will have expectations that may be based on the market.

3. Focus on the win-win, not 'winner take all'

Negotiations and offers should not be about who wins and who loses. The goal here is to ensure that both sides come out with a win. The seller gets a good amount of money out of the deal and you have a property that you can rent out and generate income with.

This will allow the both of you to focus on the solutions rather than the issues. Don't make the process a war between you and the seller. You have your best interests at heart and so do they.

Meet in the middle and the both of you will find something that will be worth striking a deal.

4. Use an escalation clause

An escalation clause is something that you can use to ensure that you better position yourself to get the property when there are multiple offers. This includes making an offer above the market price, but not exceeding a specific price in particular. The highest written offer will be sent along with the acceptance to the respective agents involved with the buyer and seller.

5. Use the market value instead of the asking price

Depending on the market, you may want to use the market value as your starting offer as opposed to the asking price that the seller has set forth. So typically, you'll want to shoot for a price that is slightly lower than what the seller will likely accept.

Do not confuse this with lowballing them (which is offering them a price much lower than the asking price). They may accept the deal or come back with a counteroffer (while not scaring off what appears to be a strong buyer).

6. Be aware of the following tactics

One of the tactics to watch out for is nibbling. Nibbling may be something that a seller may not like. That's because the buyer will want to purchase the property while asking for something a little extra. However, the seller will mostly not accept because it will eat away at the profits (hence the term nibbling).

Another thing that buyers tend to do is known as the 'hot potato'. The buyer may not have enough money for some reason or may not qualify for purchasing it at such a price. The buyer will present a problem and will try to pass it onto the seller and make it their problem.

As a seller, you may want to stay sharp and not give the buyer any room. As a buyer, you'd be smart not to do these tactics.

7. Learn the basics of persuasion

There are six basic building blocks of persuasion: reciprocity, scarcity, authority, consistency, liking, and consensus. You'll want to persuade people to act in a certain way. You can add on something extra and that could put the seller in the position to do you a favor just for being good to them.

8. Embrace the 'no'

Needless to say, the word 'no' is going to be thrown around a lot. Whether it's you saying it or the seller, this is a good word that the both of you will be accustomed with. A 'no' can move the deal forward and that's when the negotiations will begin.

9. Learn what the seller needs from the deal

It's important that the needs of both parties should be met. That's why you need to know what they are before reaching a fair deal. Don't be afraid to ask these questions towards the seller or even the agent representing them. Get a backstory on the property including the number of kids they've raised or whether or not the property was an investment property (kind of like what you're looking for).

10. Meet the seller in person, if needed

Face to face meetings with the seller are important. Because you'll be able to tell whether or not they are authentic and serious about selling the property or if they are just giving you the runaround. Meeting them will give you a good idea to get to know them better and know the personality type of the seller.

Also, in-person meetings will help you stand out. It will put you in a more favorable position since other buyers may not be so keen to meet with the seller themselves.

Counteroffers

A counteroffer is a conditional acceptance. It's the seller stating, 'I accept the offer on the condition that you agree to this and that'. You will face three options: either you accept the counteroffer, submit a counteroffer of your own, or walk away.

If you want to negotiate these counteroffers, it would be best to have your agent help you out. Your agent will get a good idea of what the seller wants and assist you in putting together a counteroffer of your own should you present one.

Also, you'll want to learn something known as 'quid pro quo' or 'something for something'. You can get something from a seller under the condition that you give something that they want. In a common situation, the seller will want to close the deal at a higher sales price.

They should give you something in return as part of the deal (hence something for something).

Purchasing Below Market Value

Is it possible to purchase a property at a below market value price? The short answer: yes. However, there are a few types of properties that will allow you to purchase at such low prices.

Two of the most common properties are foreclosures and fixer-uppers. One of the biggest caveats of acquiring either of these properties is the need for extra cash. That's because there's a good chance that a lion's share of it will be going towards repairs and renovations.

The goal is obviously increasing the value of the property and selling it at a much higher price when the time comes. Or you can command a higher rental rate once everything is fixed up. Either way, purchasing BMV properties might be an easier route for you to take if you are new to real estate.

Closing and Settling the Paperwork

Finally, it's closing time. Your offer has been accepted and it's time to make it official. You'll be reviewing a purchase agreement, which is a real estate contract that was arranged between you and the property seller.

Keep in mind that the purchase agreement should not be confused with the offer. The offer is a proposal with conditions that is used to buy the property. It is drafted by the agent of both the seller and the buyer.

The buyer will pay the agreed upon amount and the seller will transfer the deed of the property over to them. In the terms of the agreement, this includes the price, closing target date, offer expiration date, the money deposit amount (in earnest), and details regarding who will pay for the title insurance, inspections, and so on.

Also included are adjustments regarding property taxes, utilities, and other fees. Typically, it will be the responsibility of the buyer from this point forward to handle all the repairs and maintenance (although the seller may have done some repairs beforehand).

Final Thoughts

Making sure that the deal is done before any repairs are being made is important. Yes, the seller may do some repairs ahead of time. However, it may be up to you to finish where they start.

After acquiring the property, it is all up to you to take good care of it. And, you'll want to consider adding value to the property in more than a few ways. Be sure to brainstorm a few ideas on how to make the property more valuable and appealing before setting a budget.

Remember, if any repairs or renovations need to be made, you'll want to make sure that your modifications will be all up to go so the place is habitable for a tenant.

Chapter 7: Planning and Preparing Before the Fix

This chapter will cover the repair and maintenance of a rental property. Now that you have a property in your possession, the next thing you need to do is get it fixed up. For most properties that are in need of repairs, the valuation has no place to go but up.

However, there is one caveat. You have to put in the work to ensure the place is in better condition than it was when you bought it. We'll be discussing the condition of the rental property in addition to how you can add value to the property.

You'll have a battle plan to work with before you even get the repairs started. Of course, this will be a major project that will take a good amount of money to complete. That's why we'll be discussing how you can make a budget and why it's important to have one.

We'll also show you how to stick with it the best you can. We'll even weigh the pros and cons of fixing it yourself versus hiring professionals to do it for you. At the end of this chapter, you'll already have a decision made on who will get the job done.

We'll talk about how to set up a schedule based on the tasks that need to be done and go over the kind of paperwork that you need before any huge projects begin. Let's get our hands down and dirty and discuss what you need to do:

What is the Condition of Your Rental Property?

To pick up where we left off in the last chapter, you should already have a good idea of what condition the rental property is in. At this point, you'll already know what needs to be fixed. Also, you'll know what needs to be upgraded such as appliances.

The more thorough and accurate the inspection was, the better you'll be able to know what kind of repairs and upgrades are needed.

Adding Value to Rental Properties

There are various projects that you can do to add value to your rental properties. We won't delve into a lot of it since we'll be discussing more in the next chapter. But if you seem to have no idea how to increase the value, we've got you covered.

These are some suggestions, but if you want to get creative you are more than welcome to. After all, it's your property. You do what you gotta do.
Here are the suggestions that we recommend:

Landscape your garden

To begin, we'll start from the outside. Nothing is more beautiful and inviting quite like a garden. You might have a green thumb and put something together to make the property look beautiful from the outside. Because of this, you may prefer a tenant to be someone who might have a green thumb.

They can take care of the garden for you because they care about the flowers and keeping them beautiful. On top of that, you can also increase the 'curb appeal' of your home. Neighbors and others passing through will see that your property will stand out better than the rest of the neighborhood.

Consider evergreen plants or even colorful flowers if you so choose.

Go green

Believe it or not, we're not talking about gardening here. We're talking about energy efficiency. Think about it, if you go green, think of the utility expenses that you'll pay month after month.

You'll actually be spending LESS on utilities as an expense (regardless if it's you or the tenant). And that will definitely give your cash flow a bit of cushion. Plus, your tenants would save some money every month on utilities themselves if push came to shove.

So, going green is a win-win for both of you.

Consider remodeling

Throughout your inspection, you might have considered the idea of remodeling a specific area of the house. It could be the kitchen, the bathroom, or any place else. No matter what, remodeling an area will considerably increase the home's value.

But if you have no clue on which area you want to remodel, the most popular choice is usually the kitchen. This will include replacing the cabinets, re-painting the walls, and even making a few upgrades on the appliances.

Turn the garage into a little something

They say the garage is for cars and even storage space. But what if we just think outside of the box on how to use it? So, what would be a good way to use the garage while adding value at the same time?

You can convert it into an extra living space if you want to. And it could also mean that you can add a little extra income as well. This would be the perfect set up if your tenants were roommates as opposed to a family with a few kids.

You could add on to the currently existing property if you so choose. The real question is: what would be considered an extension? Would it be an extra bedroom?

What about a bathroom? What if you don't have a garage? Ah ha...you can build a garage and use it to convert it into extra living space.

Talk about a double whammy! That's killing two birds with one stone, if we do say so ourselves. But in all seriousness, if there is a way to build an extension then figure out how much it will be to get it built.

Setting A Budget for The Fix

Stating the obvious: doing these projects to increase the value of your property will not come cheap. It never does. But you knew this right from the beginning.

Having a budget handy to get the repairs done from start to finish will be important. This is why it's recommended to accompany the home inspector during the inspection process to get a good idea of how much you'll need to spend (ballpark estimate).

Here's what we suggest for a budget, so you know what to spend money on:

1. The essentials

What constitutes as the essentials? These can include plumbing, heating, electrical, or anything that requires repairing, replacing, or upgrading. Also, you'll want to keep in mind that some states will have different laws in terms of repairs and whether or not you need some kind of guidelines you need to follow. Specifically, these are guidelines that meet the health and safety standards of a potential tenant.

2. Curb appeal

You might already have a good idea on what you want to do on the outside. So, something like a garden or the like might be what you want to consider. After all, at least 30 percent of tenants will consider curb appeal as one of their main factors in deciding whether or not they want to rent the property or not.

At the same time, about a quarter of tenants would be willing to repair some of the exterior of the property such as the fence, driveways or walls (at least for a reduction of rent if at all possible).

3. Vacancies

Needless to say, the property will be vacant for many weeks before there is a tenant that moves in. In the meantime, it should give you a good cover while you are fixing up the place. Keep in mind that there is no set timeframe as to when your first tenant will move in.

Also, you'll want to keep your eye out for any external events that take place. These include a change in mortgage interest rates or massive job losses in the area (like the closure of a large employer). When in doubt, budget low in this regard (but not too low to the point where you may be drowning in a sea of losses).

4. Building codes

Even before the hammer hits a nail or fire up any power tools, there's one thing you need to make yourself aware of. You'll want to get a building permit for your project. This can be done by going through your local government agency that handles these (typically code enforcement or the like).

Keep in mind that there are fees that vary, and you must follow the safety standards in accordance with the local ordinances.

5. The interior repairs

What are the repairs that are needed? Do the pipes need fixing? Does the roof need a little tender love and care?

How about repainting the walls? It's all up to you at this point. You can make notes during or even after the inspection.
These can be minor repairs or major, urgent repairs (depending on what the inspection has unveiled). Be sure to double-check what else needs to be repaired before doing any major projects.

This repair budget should not be confused with your repair/maintenance reserves

Before moving further, this is a budget that is for initial repairs. This should not be confused with the amount of money you set off to the side every month regarding repairs and maintenance. Yes, things happen.

So as a reminder, don't forget to set off 10 percent of your total rent income that will be your repair and maintenance reserve.

Fixing It Yourself or Hiring Professionals, Make Your Choice

Would you be willing to do the repairs yourself or would you get a professional to get the job done for you? We'll be taking a look at the pros and cons of each so you can choose which route is best for you.

Let's compare:

The pros of doing it yourself

It saves you money: Clearly, without the use of a contractor you'll be able to get the work done yourself and save money that would otherwise go to a professional. Enough said.

Perfect for small projects: If the projects are small scale, then they are easy enough to do by yourself. This includes painting the interior, installing linoleum or vinyl flooring, or even building a wood deck.

They don't take a long time to do: It depends on your daily schedule. You might have a work schedule and it might take a few days as opposed to a weekend. Regardless, the project itself won't take a ridiculous amount of time to do unless you allow it to happen.

The cons of doing it yourself

Not suitable for large projects: Not only is tackling a large project solo a monumental task, but it's also unsafe to do. You could risk serious injury or even death depending on the project that needs to be done.

The pros of hiring a professional

Great for large projects: Does the bathtub need to be replaced? Do you need hardwood or ceramic tile floors? Or what about replacement windows? This is where the professionals come in. There's a contractor for any large project you can think of.

High-quality projects: When it's professionally done, the quality will be way better compared to doing it yourself. Therefore, the repairs and renovations will last longer than usual. Years or decades likely.

Quick to get approved for permits: A contractor will quickly get approved for a local permit to work on a project on your property. Unlike doing it yourself, you may need to wait a bit or pay out of pocket. For contractors, it's just another business expense.

The cons of hiring a professional

It can be expensive: Sure enough, professional contractors can be expensive. It will depend on the contractor and also the area they focus on. To help mitigate any unwanted costs, don't be afraid to shop around and ask for any recommendations. Again, your real estate network may also refer you to contractors (but they may not be the best decision due to affordability).

Set a Realistic Schedule

Setting up a schedule for the whole entire project is a must. If the project will take days, make sure that the schedule focuses on that one specific area of the house. You cannot go all over the place for the entire week (i.e.: part of the kitchen one day, part of the bathroom the next, and so on).

You'll want to keep it simple and straightforward. How long will the project take by estimation? Schedule those days straightforward.

Once that part of the property is complete, move on with the other part that needs repairing. When should demolitions be scheduled? When will the repairs start?

To get a good idea of what a construction schedule looks like, check out this article and you'll see a couple examples of them.

The Paperwork Involved for A Fix (In Case You Are Doing A Big Fix)

In the event of a big fix, you are going to need some of the following papers to ensure you are doing the job properly and legally. Let's take a look at what you need:

Permits (Electric, Plumbing, Etc.)

If you are planning on doing any work regarding the plumbing and electricity, you may need a permit for it. Requirements may vary depending on the location you are in. If you are working on a property that is in a state that is different from yours, remember that you must adhere to the requirements in the property located in that state.

Contract agreements

This will be an agreement between the contractor and the property owner. The terms and conditions set forth by the contractor will be laid out here.

Statement of Work (SOW)

This piece of paper provides you with the scope of the project. This will determine the amount of work that will be needed.

General conditions

This will provide you with the obligation and the rights on how the project should be executed. Included in the general conditions are what you can claim for overhead costs and your rights as a property owner.

Special conditions

This is an extension of the general conditions if and when needed. The special conditions must be specific depending on the job or project. This is part of the paperwork that you need to pay special attention to if some conditions are included.

Bills of Quantities

This will include a list of materials and trades that are included within the project. This is an optional part of the paperwork and the contractor can choose not to use it.

Drawings/Mockups

These drawings or mockups are the most recent design of the project that you want done. These will also be due to the contractor prior to the beginning date for construction.

Construction insurance

This will be useful in the event if something happens during a construction project. This may include mistakes being made, ill-fittings, and other issues that may arise while the work is being done.

Construction schedule

As mentioned earlier, a construction schedule will be useful since it determines how and when the project will be completed. There may be a construction schedule needed for any multiple room projects. Make sure that there is a construction schedule for each room that you want remodeled or constructed.

Final Thoughts

Before any repairs and renovations begin, it's better to plan them all out. This way, you'll want to decide what needs to be worked on and in a timely manner. Also, you want to make sure that you have the accurate budget to pull off the job.

You do have the choice to do it yourself. Yet, some larger projects may not be easy enough for one person to do all alone. If push comes to shove, be sure to contact a contractor that focuses on a certain area like kitchens, bathrooms, or residential remodeling or repairs.

The key here is to add more value to your rental property. This will help you command a higher rental rate for your tenants. At the same time, you can also sell the property at a higher price when the time comes.

Chapter 8: Fixing Houses While Keeping in Mind That It's for Rental Properties

You managed to purchase a property that needs some fixing up. First off, congratulations. It might have been tough to get the deal done on your end...but here you are.

This chapter will focus on the repairs and renovations that could be needed in your new property (assuming it's some kind of fixer-upper). We'll also be focusing on similar tasks should you consider the idea of adding value to the property itself. Either way, we'll be covering various tasks including demolition, excavation, landscaping, and everything in between.

Some of the tasks that we'll be discussing in detail may be a do-it-yourself task or may require a professional contractor to get the job done. However, if you decide to travel the DIY route, we'll provide you with tips and guides on what you can do with certain projects such as remodeling the kitchen, changing the floors, and even adding additional square footage to your new property.

Keep in mind that this isn't your own home that you are working on. This is for a rental property that will help you generate income in the future. The more work you put in, the more valuable your property is going to be.

In turn, the more valuable the property, the more enticing it will be for a tenant. And you can generate plenty of income if you repeat this process with multiple properties. Now, we are getting into the fun stuff.

Let's start tearing stuff down, building it back up, and show you how to get the hard work done:

Having Fun with Demolition

First and foremost, let's focus on demolition. Specifically, we'll be focusing on the interior as opposed to the outside of the property. Before moving any further, allow us to note the following:

Safety notice: *During a demolition or any other project involving the repair and renovation of your properties, always wear the necessary protective gear to prevent serious injury or even death. These include safety glasses, hard hats, gloves, overalls, or any appropriate attire.*

Now that we have that safety message out of the way, let's talk specifics in terms of demolition. What will you plan on tearing down? Are you looking to tear down a wall, a complete room, or the entire interior?

Your choice will also mean higher costs. For example, if you are planning on tearing down one wall (without reconstruction), that will be low in cost. However, those costs go up when you want to demolish a room or the entire interior ($2,500 is the average for room demolition while the entire interior is estimated at $10,000).

For this reason, you want to consider your options in terms of what's staying up and what's going down. Keep in mind that different types of removal like tile, floor, wall and so on will be charged on a square foot basis. For example, floor removal could range from $2 to $5 per square foot.

Don't forget, there are labor costs that you want to factor in as well. Consider $20 an hour as an average starting point. The price range for interior demolition will run anywhere between $500 to $12,000 depending on how much needs to be torn down.

Before any demolition occurs, be sure to get a permit (if applicable). If you are planning on removing things off the property, get estimates from contractors or consider costs when done by yourself.

How many dumpsters will I need?

Considering that you'll be disposing a lot of material, you're going to need dumpsters. How many you're going to need will depend on how much you're taking down. It will also depend on the kind of debris that you are throwing out. For example, if the house is 1,000 square feet and you have about 135 cubic yards of debris to remove, you'll need three and a half 40-yard dumpsters.

Keep in mind that the dumpster charges will depend on the weight of the debris that is being thrown out. So, consider talking to your local sanitation or waste management facilities and shop around for prices.

What to dispose and what to recycle?

During the demolition process, you'll want to consider what you need to throw away in the dumpster and what needs to be recycled. Obviously, you'll want to dispose of materials like old or even rotting materials that may hurt the structural integrity. Harmful materials like asbestos must always be removed safely (and should also be done by professionals).

As for what needs to be recycled, there are more than 70 percent of building materials that can be recycled. These include but are not limited to the following: beams, doors, lumber, and windows. Also, you should consider recycling sinks, tubs, glass from windows, nails, and even copper pipes.

Make sure everything is disconnected

Prior to demolition, it is important to make sure that the project is done safely. This includes disconnecting the electricity, sewage, gas, and water. Also, you want to close off the area, so no one steps on the property by complete accident and ends up in danger.

Excavating an Area

This should not be something you do if there are minor repairs that need to be done around the house. However, there are instances where excavating is necessary. Such examples include landscaping and also adding a swimming pool with the intent to increase the value of the property.

Excavation uses specialized machinery that shifts the earth, rocks, and other underground obstacles that need to be removed prior to construction. Nine times out of ten, a professional will handle this (unless you have access to excavation equipment). Once again, you should check to see if you have any licenses or permits to do an excavation (or consult a contractor that does have the proper approval).

Before any excavation can be done, there's always the precaution of surveying the area. You'll want to know exactly where excavation and construction will be done. Keep in mind that surveying the area will be beneficial since there is no guarantee that blueprints will be accurate for safe digging.

On top of that, you'll want to reduce the number of potential problems as much as possible. And you also want to reduce any community downtime that may arise due to an excavation project. Also, be sure to have the soil professionally tested before any construction occurs.

Landscaping

If you want to increase the curb appeal and the overall value of the property from the outside, consider landscaping. As a newbie to real estate, you don't need to go all out. You want landscaping projects to be as low-maintenance as possible.

Plus, if a tenant wants to do landscaping themselves, you don't want to put them in a position where they have to put in a lot of work. Especially when all they want to do is relax. So, don't pressure them into doing so much.

In this section, we're going to talk about some of the basics of low maintenance landscaping. We'll also discuss some of the 'do's and don'ts'.

Low maintenance landscaping ideas

As mentioned before, landscaping your property doesn't have to be a lot of work. You want to keep it as simple and low maintenance as possible. So, let's give you a few ideas to work with:

- **Weed control:** Instead of pulling weeds, consider applying a protective weed barrier to ensure that they are not growing all over the place (and at an alarming rate). Applying mulch to your yard will also keep the weeds at bay as well.

- **Consider hardscaping:** If you want to lessen the maintenance level as much as possible, hardscaping may be an excellent solution. You can remove plants on the property and replace it with walkways, patios, or borders. The less surface area containing plants, the better.

- **Add a small garden:** This is completely optional. But it would make the home a lot more attractive to tenants and even the neighbors. As long as the garden is tended to on a regular basis by you or the tenant, then it will certainly be an excellent landscaping addition.

The 'Do's' and 'Don'ts' of Landscaping

Let's take a look at some of the things you should and shouldn't do if you are landscaping the property:

DO:

- **Keep a neutral theme:** A neutral theme should be fine. Leave the personalization up to the tenant.

- **Consider plants or shrubs that are native/local:** If you are planning on adding some plants or shrubs, make sure they are native to your local area. This will help you save money and preserve biodiversity in the process. On top of that, it won't require a lot of maintenance as well.

- **Make shade a priority:** In the summertime, too much sun can be a bad thing. Especially when it comes to certain plants. Therefore, they'll need plenty of shade to counteract the amount of sun they're getting every day. Pay attention to the plant labels so you know how much sun a specific plant needs.

DON'T:

- **Overdevelop the yard:** Quality matters. Not the quantity. So, don't go overboard in terms of the pavement or hardscaping.

- **Don't personalize it:** To tie in with keeping a neutral theme, don't personalize the landscaping to your liking. Remember, this is a rental property that you own. It's not your primary residence.

- **Restrict yourself:** Even with planting new plants, don't feel like you're restricted to your current layout. You can move and replace plants if need be and set them up in different areas of the property. Don't be afraid to play around a bit rather than feel like the plants need to stay in a specific area.

Replacing or Repairing the Roof

During your inspection, the roof should have been inspected thoroughly along with the rest of the property. If there are any holes or flaws, they need to be repaired as soon as possible. Replacing the roof in its entirety can also be an option.

Water leakage from the roof due to rain or snow may lead to water damage (which leads to mold growth). And that alone will be a recipe for disaster if left unchecked. One thing to be aware of is if the roof needs work, then that's a project that needs to be left up to the professionals.

Should I repair or replace the roof?

Of course, there's a difference between repairing the roof and replacing it. So, when is a good time to do either or? Let's take a look first at when repairing the roof should be the best option:

When to repair:

- **If there are leaks around the pipe boot or chimney**

- **Nail pops**

- **Damage from trees**

- **Weather damage**

- **Shrinkage**

- **Splitting**

- **Poor install**

- **Cracking or blistering**

- **Granule loss**

- **Punctures or holes**

- **Ventilation issues**

Keep in mind that repairing the roof will help you save a ton of money compared to replacing it all together. On top of that, you'll also be expanding the longevity of the roof. Not to mention, it will increase the curb appeal.

However, matching shingle colors is one of the greatest challenges for repairing a roof because they may be hard to come by.

When to replace:

- **If the roof is worn**

- **The roof is too old**

- **Major vulnerability to future damage**

Replacing the roof will likely occur if it's wearing or showing signs of advanced age. Also, major vulnerabilities that are exposed will also lead to damage in the future. The best preventative measure at that point would be to replace the roof.

When replacing a roof, you'll have peace of mind knowing that a crisis will be averted. Yet, roof replacements can be noisy and even costly.

Adding Square Footage

One of the best ways to add value to your property is adding more square footage. We'll be taking a look at some of the best ways to do that so you have a good idea of what you can build should you want to add more space beyond the current layout.

When adding square footage, it's also possible to save money in the process. Let's take a look at some ideas on how to add square footage to your rental property

1. Build into the backyard

The backyard is usually a great place where you can add more square footage. This includes a patio or even expanding a room like a kitchen or a dining room. Not only does this give you the opportunity to expand, but a little bit of extra square footage in this manner can definitely help with bumping up the rent.

2. Build a greenhouse

A greenhouse is a nice way to add more square footage. At the same time, it will also give you plenty of space to grow a garden on the inside. You'll want to make sure that the greenhouse is properly equipped with the right kind of drainage system.

You'll also want to use the proper materials that will provide your plants with the appropriate climate. And finally, be sure that your greenhouse is in compliance with any HOA rule (if such are applicable).

3. Think big...or small

Whether it's adding another level or adding a small patio to the back yard, a nice sized expansion might be just what you need to give your property a little more square footage (and extra value in the process). You can build a small deck, a large pavilion in the backyard, or add another level to the home with new rooms.

When adding another level, this gives you a good opportunity to add more bedrooms or bathrooms to the property. That will give you plenty of opportunities to build upgraded bathrooms and bedrooms right from the start. The better they look, the more valuable your property is.

Changing Floors

Changing the floors can be done by yourself or a professional. The way it works is that the old flooring will need to be lifted (depending on the material). And in its place, a new floor will be installed. However, flooring comes in different materials. So, the installation process will differ. Also, it's important to consider which type of flooring is best.

It wouldn't make a lot of sense if you installed a carpet in the kitchen and linoleum in the living room, would it? Of course not.

The Dos and Don'ts of Flooring

Yes, there are some flooring 'dos' and 'don'ts'. And it's important that you follow these when you are doing the project yourself. Let's take a look at the 'Do's" first:

DO:

- **Know your budget:** This cannot be said clear enough. You'll want to find the best flooring that you can afford in terms of quality and style. Don't have your heart set on a specific type of flooring only to find out it is double your budget.

- **Know your flooring needs:** Your needs will far outweigh your dreams and wants for flooring. Think about it: would it be smart to put a hardwood floor in an area that will always get dirty? Probably not. But you want something that is durable and easy to clean, regardless of where it is in your house.

- **Know which floor is best for each room:** There's always a natural match for floors and the appropriate rooms. For example, a carpet would go well in a bedroom but never a bathroom. Or a tile floor would go well in a warmer room of the house, not a colder one. Get the idea?

DON'T:

- **Be afraid to ask the professionals:** You don't have to be a flooring expert to do a DIY project. But if you are worried about doing it wrong, then consider asking the professionals for advice. Alternatively, you can hire professional flooring experts to do the job for you.

- **Install a floor where it might not be appropriate:** A hardwood floor would be nice in just about any part of the house. However, it would not be wise to install it in a high traffic area like a doorway. Also, it might be weird just installing a carpet in a place where you typically install linoleum or vinyl.

What floors to consider

Choosing floors can be a hassle. But if you know which flooring will work best (and where to install it), you should be in good shape. Let's take a look at the flooring options you have:

Carpets

Carpets are excellent for insulation and will help reduce energy bills. It will also reduce a lot of noise as well. These are great for bedrooms or even upper-level rooms. They will not work well in bathrooms, basements, entryways, hallways, or kitchens.

Tile

These are available in stone, porcelain, or ceramic. They are durable, water resistant, and can be cost effective. But the cleaning and maintenance can be a real pain.

You can install these in basements, bathrooms, kitchens, or rooms that are humid in climate. If your property is located in a colder climate, avoid installing them altogether.

Hardwood

Hardwood floors come in different species of wood. Cut into planks, these are nailed over the sub-floor. Easy to clean and has a long lifespan, these floors will be best for bedrooms, dining rooms, living rooms, or a home office.

These hardwood floors won't fare well in bathrooms since they are susceptible to water damage. These floors may be difficult to install. So, you may want to consider a professional installation if possible.

Laminate

This will be a good option if hardwood is out of your price range. And it can be much easier to install as well. This will go great in dining rooms, bedrooms, living rooms, or offices.

Like hardwood floors, laminate is not appropriate to install in bathrooms because of possible water damage. At the same time, laminate should not be installed in kitchens or basements.

Vinyl

Vinyl is water resistant, cost effective, and easy to install. This kind of flooring is perfect for the do-it-yourselfer. These will usually go nicely in bathrooms or kitchens.

However, you may want to be aware that this floor type is not durable and may be susceptible to mold or mildew if enough moisture gets underneath it.

Linoleum

If you are looking for something that is environmentally friendly, linoleum might be the best choice. It's affordable, easy to install, and easy to clean. Only install these in dining rooms and kitchens.

One major con to be aware of is that it can be prone to dents and tears.

Remodeling the Kitchen

The kitchen is where the magic happens in the culinary sense. While your tenant may not be a professional chef, they will love seeing a kitchen that is brand new and very stylish. If you truly want to give your property a bump up in value, one of the best ways to go about doing it is remodeling the kitchen.

When remodeling the kitchen, most of the work goes into removing and replacing the appliances like the refrigerator, the stove and oven, and even the kitchen sink. This will depend on what you're planning to do.

With every good remodeling project, you want to put together a budget, so you'll know how much you're spending. You can compare things like refinishing the cabinets versus replacing them or choosing one type of countertop over the other. Most of the time, repairing and remodeling will always be more cost effective than replacing things.

Kitchen remodeling tips that will save you money

Don't get us wrong. But kitchen remodeling does not come cheap. However, you can soften the blow of your wallet.

These tips below will show you how to go about saving money while making your kitchen look brand spanking new. Let's take a look:

1. Do it yourself

If you want to save money, doing it yourself is the best option. That means no contractors or professionals throughout the entire project. However, the one caveat is that if this is your first time remodeling the kitchen, you may have no choice but to hire a contractor.

But for subsequent properties (should you acquire them), this will be the best possible option.

2. Get down and dirty

Get a sledgehammer and get to work. It might be fun smashing the crap out of an old kitchen. Plus, it pays to do that since you'll be saving money. Remember to get the right permits to use a dumpster (if applicable), do your demo during the day, and notify your neighbors ahead of time for any noises and the like.

3. Get multiple bids and negotiate

There can't be one general contractor in your area that is interested in a project. There may be several others. Get a list of contractors that you're considering and start negotiating with them.

Do not accept the first offer whether it's the lowest or not. Get an offer that will give you the best quality that you can afford. Never skimp on quality just because you want to save a few dollars.

You might get a beautiful countertop that usually is a lot in value for a fair price just because you asked.

4. Get your appliances during special holidays

If you want to get a good deal on appliances, there is no better time to get them than during a holiday sale. Memorial Day, the 4th of July, etc. there will be special sales. Also, the prices of appliances like refrigerators, stove and oven sets, and others will be at their lowest price.

For example, refrigerator models from various brands will dip down at around the 4th of July and around Black Friday/Cyber Monday. However, the best time to do remodeling is the former. That's because in the winter months, you'll lose a lot more money due to vacancies.

Also, you'd be remiss if you didn't get your appliance from major stores like Home Depot, Best Buy, or even Lowe's.

5. Reuse materials if need be

We're tempted to throw a lot of stuff away during a remodeling. But the best way to save money is to find out which materials can be reused and go down that road. Instead of throwing materials away, you can consider repainting or refacing kitchen cabinets.

Another thing to reuse is light fixtures. So long as they are in good condition and not too old, you can keep them around longer rather than replace them.

6. Time your renovations just right

The timing of your renovation should not conflict with peak rental seasons. So, it would be ideal to start your renovations in the spring and have them wrapped up right around the summertime or thereabouts.

If there is a tenant that wants to get out of a lease early and you're planning on doing some property renovation, you can allow it. This way, that will grant them their release while fulfilling your interest in renovating the property and getting more in rent from the next tenant. Talk about a win-win.

7. Consider installing an island counter

An island counter would be perfect for a kitchen. It would be the perfect place to prepare food or even install a dishwasher when there is no other place to install it. Plus, it would make a great centerpiece for any renewed kitchen.

8. Give your tenants a gift

Once you have a new tenant that is about to move into the rental property, leave them a nice welcoming gift for the kitchen. This can include a kitchen set, cleaning products, and so much more. This will help them save money while you help jumpstart what will be a trusting relationship between you and them.

Expanding Closet Space

Having a closet and storage space might just come in handy. And you might have tenants who hate the idea of having to deal with a lot of clutter. But why not give them a little more than they want?

Expanding closet space might be a good idea. Because your tenants may have stuff that they want to store away. They may even have a lot of clothes or linens.

But how can it be done on a tight budget? Let's take a look at a few tips:

- **Install central shelves or lazy susans:** If you want to maximize storage in a kitchen, you can consider installing central shelves on an island or install lazy susans in a corner cabinet. This will not only save you plenty of space, but it will also make your rental property look even better.

- **Bathroom cabinets:** You can build a bathroom cabinet that can be attached to the tub or shower. Or you can install a medicine cabinet with a mirror for more space. Giving your tenants more options to keep things organized will be way better than having them fend for themselves.

- **Closets:** One of the issues with closets is that they have wasted space. So why not consider the idea of installing an organizing system to ensure that the space is used to your advantage? For a master bedroom, consider the idea of expanding space for a walk-in closet. That will give tenants the ultimate opportunity of privacy and organization all in one space.

Painting It with New Colors

Painting the property isn't too difficult. But there are some challenges that present itself such as choosing the right colors. Will you need to paint the interior or the exterior?

Or will it have to be both? Either way, the goal with painting your property is to improve the overall value while giving it a boost in curb appeal. If you are planning on doing some repainting, let's discuss some of the things you'll want to do before you dip the brush in the bucket.

Exterior painting

First and foremost, you want to check to see if the exterior is in good shape. During your inspection, here's what you need to look for:

- **Is the paint bubbling, peeling, or chipping?**

- **Is the caulking cracked?**

- **Is the stucco damaged?**

- **Are the current colors fading?**

If you see any positive signs of this, that's when you know that the exterior will need to be painted. You can do this by yourself or have a professional contractor do it for you. Depending on your needs and your budget, choose the best option that's right for you.

How often should exteriors be painted?

The short answer: it depends on the material. Let's take a look at the different materials and how often you may need to paint them:

- **Brick:** Every 10 to 12 years

- **Aluminum siding:** 6 years

- **Wood siding:** 5 to 7 years

- **Stucco:** 6 to 8 years

Choosing the right type of paint and colors

Another one of the more challenging things about painting your property is choosing the colors. Or maybe even the type of paint. Whether you are painting the interior, exterior, or both you'll want to choose the right kind of paint based on your needs rather than wants.

Here are some tips that you should follow:

Choosing the right colors

When it comes to choosing the right colors, it's important that you steer clear from bright colors, camouflage, or even colors that resemble national flags. The reason why is because they do not have mass appeal and it might turn off tenants.

This means you'll have to go with an attractive, but neutral color. Consider choosing one of the following colors: grey, beige, off-white, or tan.

Choosing the right type of paint

There are five different types of paint finishes. You'll want to choose the right one depending on the interior materials or the room type. Here are the options for finishes and what makes them great:

Flat or matte: This finish is non-reflective and will conceal plenty of surface flaws. This is great when you want to fill cracks and other imperfections. Use this kind of paint for low traffic areas of your home such as bedrooms.

Eggshell: It's soft and velvety. But it isn't glossy. This will work well in rooms that have a medium amount of traffic like living areas, sunrooms, even bathrooms. Compared to flat finishes, this will hold up a lot better.

Satin: This has a bit more shine than eggshell. And it can be used for medium to high traffic areas of the property such as entryways and living areas. These can fare better in kitchens because of the amount of moisture that can be produced from there. This kind of paint is easy to maintain and may show application flaws after the fact.

Semi-gloss: This is by far one of the most durable finishes. And it's easier to wash should stains be present. This is perfect for medium to high traffic locations in your property. And it will work great with most surfaces such as woodwork, moldings, trims, doors, and windows (among others).

Hi-gloss: The most durable and washable paint of them all. This will be perfect for high-use surfaces.

DIY vs a professional: When to choose?

If you want to save money, the clear option is to do the painting yourself. However, if you are planning on painting the exterior of the property, you may want to consider a professional since the project will be a bit more complex.

Interior paint jobs are mostly done by do-it-yourselfers. So, if you want to make it easier on yourself, consider doing the inside of the property (assuming the exterior is in good shape).

Other Repairs and Upgrades That You Should Consider

By now, you already may have had some ideas on what needs to be repaired and upgraded. There might have been a laundry list that you put together during the initial pre-offer inspection. Now would be a good time to double check what else is needed?

For example, does the plumbing need repairing or upgrading? How are the pipes looking? Is the shower, sink, and toilet working well?

Also, what could you do to improve the curb appeal of the property? And how can you improve it while on a tight budget? Remember, simplicity is what you want so you don't let it eat into your cash reserves.

With that said, let's take a look at some ideas that you should at least consider:

- **Paint the front door:** Is the color boring? Is it not that appealing from the outside? Then consider the idea of painting it a color that will match the exterior nicely. White will usually match well with any color.

- **Replace the mailbox:** Is the mailbox falling apart? If so, replace it.

- **Make your street numbers stand out:** If the exterior has no street numbers, get them. Make sure they stand out nicely. Make it fresh and modern. It takes 15 minutes to install and no more than $15.

- **Improve the garage doors:** You can paint them, fix them up, or install materials to make it look more appealing. A tenant may use the garage door as an indicator of how the rest of the property will look.

- **Light up your front path:** Why depend on a single lamp post or a floodlight? Consider lighting up your front path like a runway using solar-powered lights or spotlights. Add a few of them in your garden beds as well.

Preparing the Property

Whether it's a showing or prior to moving in, you'll need to prepare the property, so it looks like things are in working order and clean. This means spending time checking everything around the property. Here are some tips that you need to follow in order to prep the property:

Make sure everything is working

Make sure that the phone and Internet connections are in working order. Next, test the heating and cooling systems to ensure that they are working properly and warming or cooling the property correctly. Also, check the locks to ensure that they secure the doors properly.

Since privacy is important, see if you have curtains that cover the windows. Alternatively, you can use blinds or shades. Lastly, check to see if the smoke detectors are installed and working.

Clean the place if needed

Everything should be spotless. The floors should be vacuumed, the sinks, toilets, kitchen counters, and everything else dusted and wiped down. Also, check to see if corners are free from cobwebs.

Make sure that the outside is presentable. The gutters should be cleaned. The grass should be mowed (and no weeds are included).

If there are broken lights, tiles, windows, and latches, fix them as soon as possible. These repairs should take anywhere between a few minutes to a few hours (depending on what needs to be repaired).

Final Thoughts

Fixing up properties for the purpose of increasing the value of your rental properties will be one of the smartest things you do. Especially if your goal is to get a tenant onto the property and collect rent from it.

Demolition may be needed if you need to do some remodeling projects such as the bathroom or the kitchen. Just make sure that you have the right kind of paperwork to get it done. It might also be a fun do it yourself project if you get the work done safely.

Also, keep in mind the kind of flooring that you'll need for each room in your property. Remember that some types of flooring will only be fitting for some rooms, but not all of them. You really don't want to put a carpet in the bathroom or a tile floor in the bedroom, no?

If needed, you can consider the idea of repainting some rooms of the property (or even the outside if you must). Remember to choose neutral colors that will stand out and make the place look nice. There are projects that can be done as a DIY project while others may require a professional to get it done.

However, if you are planning on getting a professional to do the projects for you, keep in mind how much money you have in your budget. Sometimes, doing it yourself is the best route so you can save money.

Lastly, be sure that everything is in good shape prior to presenting the property to potential tenants. Make sure everything is clean, working properly, and your presentations will go forward without any issue.

Chapter 9: What You Need to Know and Do to Finally Start Renting

By now, you have reached the point where your rental property is ready to go. You're finally ready to start renting it out to your first tenant. This chapter will be focused on what you need to do prior to fulfilling your vacancies.

We'll be answering the question of how much you should charge for rent? Also, you need to be aware that your rental property vacancies won't fill themselves. So, it is important to know how to market and advertise (without being a marketing wizard).

You'll learn how to choose the right tenants and do so while abiding to the Fair Housing Act. When you have whittled it down to the final candidates, you'll want to present the property to them, so they know what the property looks like and what they'll be paying for.

People will start applying to fulfill your vacancies. And it will be up to you on how to fulfill them. We'll also discuss rental contracts and how they work.

Lastly, we'll also discuss what to do next when you have chosen a tenant and they finally move in. This is a big step in your real estate investing journey. And you probably could not be more excited. Now, let's dive right in and get to the good stuff:

How Much Should You Charge for Rent?

Before moving any further, let's give you a brief reminder: you'll want to choose a rental rate that will keep your cash flow in the green rather than operating at a loss. Also, you want to keep in mind of the expenses that you will be paying every month for the property itself. So how much should you charge exactly?

It will depend on several factors. For one, there's the location. You could be closer to the downtown area and charge a high enough rental fee because of its walkability, close proximity to points of interest and more. Whereas, if you're in the suburbs, the rent may be lower.

By now, you should have a good idea of what the average rental rate is for an area. However, if you are in a highly populated city, your rent may be more expensive compared to lesser populated areas (Ex: Los Angeles will command higher rates than properties in Cleveland).

If you live in states like Oregon, New York, California, District of Columbia, New Jersey, or Maryland, you'll want to be aware that there are rent control laws. This means you can dictate how much you can charge and how much you can increase in the future.

Also, you can follow what is known as the '1 percent rule'. This will allow you to take the property's value and charge 1 percent of it as rent. For example, if the property you have purchased is $250,000, then one percent is $2,500.

Security deposits are an amount of money (which typically is a month's rent). This is something the tenant will pay for on top of the first month's rent. This will be used to cover any damages and repairs that the tenant is responsible for.

If a tenant moves out, they can have the security deposit returned in its entirety or partially depending on any damages that have been incurred. Also, keep in mind that there may be laws that can determine whether or not security deposits will be used in certain situations. So be sure to remind the tenant to take good care of the property or risk losing their deposit or at least part of it.

Start Advertising

As we've said early on, a tenant just cannot waltz into your rental property and plant their stake there. Nor will a vacancy fulfill itself. So, it's time to start advertising your property.

Advertising addresses a problem (someone is looking for a place to live). And you have the solution, (your rental property). However, in some forms of advertising, you'll need to exclude certain types of tenants like those who have a bad credit history, pay their rent late, or anything that may cause certain problems for you.

What are some of the best ways to advertise your rental properties? Let's take a look at a few places where you can start:

- **Online ads and listings:** We live in an age where online ads like Facebook and Google are geocentric to the point where you can only show it to people who live near a certain area. The more laser focused it is on a certain area, the better it will perform. But it's not always a guarantee that you may get a ton of leads. But it's focused on a certain age group, gender, and the like. Also, you can depend on websites like Apartments.com, Craigslist or the like.

- **Classified ads:** Yes, landlords still like to go old school. So, you can post a classified ad in the local newspapers or certain guides that offer 'Buy, Sell, or Trade-Ins'. Keep in mind that ads of specific spaces will be charged by space. Meaning a small ad will be financially sound compared to a larger space ad that commands a higher rate.

- **Flyers:** Flyers with photos of the property will usually get a bunch of eyeballs. You can place these flyers in high traffic areas like community bulletin boards, supermarkets, laundromats, college campuses, and more. Make sure the photos are clear, colorful, and gives someone the exact details of what the property looks like.

As for what to include in your advertising, it's important to eliminate the potential 'problem tenants'. Speaking of which, we'll be talking more in depth about them right now.

Pick Your Tenants, Never Randomly Accept or Choose One

It would be a mistake to randomly draw a name out of the hat and give that person your rental property. If you need to choose the right tenant, you'll need to be thorough. For this reason, you'll need to do the following when performing a background check:

- **Credit history:** The better someone's credit history is, the more likely they'll pay on time and be financially stable. There may be a certain credit score that will be considered a cut-off point where you can automatically reject applicants. Hey, it's kind of the same as applying for a loan. Bad credit? Instant rejection.

- **Criminal history:** Your rental property may be in a neighborhood that is considered safe. However, you want to pay special attention to this section. And you want to double check if your applicants are telling the truth. There may be certain crimes that will automatically disqualify them from renting from you (i.e. -- domestic violence, drug crimes, sex crimes, etc.)

- **Rental history:** This will give you a good idea of whether or not they'll pay on time or if they're going to be a good tenant to deal with. Rental history will give you a list of references (such as past landlords) so you can confirm if they are a good person or someone who can frustrate you.

- **Employment History:** Can the tenant hold down a stable job? How long have they been with their current employer? This will be good indicators that they will be able to pay you for as long as the lease is intact.

To note, you have the choice to choose the applicants yourself or go through a property management firm that can handle all that heavy lifting. It can be a daunting task, but you'll need to use your better judgement here in terms of who should occupy your rental property. You want them to be someone that you can trust, not someone who is going to be difficult to deal with for as long as possible.
You may face difficult decisions in choosing a tenant because they might be considered 'model tenants'. But at the end of the day, someone is going to be moving into your property.

Be Mindful of The Fair Housing Act

The Fair Housing Act was a law that was established in 1968. This law was created to limit any discrimination practices that involves housing. This was intended to give Americans an equal opportunity whenever they are looking for a place to live without the fear of being discriminated against.

As a landlord, it is up to you to give applicants a fair chance. Whether they are a minority, someone who is LGBT, or a non-citizen of the United States, it is incumbent upon you to give them consideration if they apply. They should not be automatically disqualified because of their race, orientation, or the like.

Those protected by the Fair Housing Act are based on the following factors:

- Color
- Disability
- Family status
- Nationality (including foreign nationals)
- Race
- Religion
- Gender

While sexual orientation is not one of the factors, we encourage you to consider going through the selection process as if it were. They should be treated and looked at the same way in terms of how they qualify. Focus on their credit history, rental history, and the other factors listed in the previous section.

If you are consistent with the screening process, this could protect you from any potential accusations of discrimination. One rule of thumb is to assume that everyone is working for the Department of Housing and Urban Development (or HUD). Treat everyone with respect and dignity and perform the regular qualification checks as usual.

Presenting the Property to Possible Tenants

If you have whittled your list down to some of the last few candidates, it's time to show them the property. This may be something to include in your tenant selection process for a couple of good reasons. For one, you may have a potential tenant that might not like something about the property itself (like the paint color of all things or lack of walkability).

Depending on the tenants, you can show them relevant areas of the property. For example, if the tenants are a family of four, you can show them the bedrooms where the kids will sleep. If it's a young married couple, then you can show them some of the features like the kitchen and living room space where they can entertain guests and have dinner parties.

Common questions that tenants ask

During the showing, expect the tenants to be asking you some questions. These are common questions to which you will have answers on the fly. Your answers may be a 'make or break' deal for potential tenants.

Let's take a look at some of those questions:

'Do you allow pets?'

If you allow pets, explain what kind of pets are allowed. Also, you'll want to mention a pet fee if you choose to implement one. And you'll want to explain how it's charged.

Some landlords charge a flat fee or based on the pet's size. A tenant with a chihuahua would pay a lesser fee than someone with a husky. However, this may depend on the type of rental property.

Also, keep in mind that if the tenant has pets, you may command a higher rate to cover any pet related damages. If you do not want pets on the property, say so. Some potential tenants would never give up their pets just for the sake of moving into a property.

'Can I pay ahead up front and move in as soon as possible?'

This may sound like a good idea for both the landlord and tenant. However, this might be more of a red flag. Why is that?

This could be a sign that something may be negatively affecting the tenant on their end at some point in the near future. And they'll use this tactic to persuade the landlord to take more cash than usual. But this is a risky move that may constrict your cash flow rather than help it.

On top of that, the tenant may cause problems to the point where you evict them. And prepaid rent will make the situation more difficult. At this point, you should state that you do not accept prepaid rent.

If someone says that they are in a hurry and asks to pay the rent and move in the same day, the answer should be 'no'. They have to go through the application process like everyone else. Plus, it won't be fair to anyone who may want to see the property other than that prospective tenant.

'Will you consider a short-term lease?'

This will depend on the property you own. You may have apartment buildings that accept short-term lease tenants (or month by month). However, some of your properties will have long-term leases like apartments or single-family properties.

If you require a long-term lease, state that the lease minimum is 12 months, but recommend that if they want to stay longer than that, they can. If you do have vacancies that involve short-term leases, do not be afraid to make those recommendations to the potential tenant.

While you do own the property per se, it would be wise to address yourself as the 'property manager' instead. However, you are welcome to say that you are the owner as you so choose.

The short answer: no. It should be the first of every month. No ifs, ands, or buts. Moving on.

Another question with a short answer: no. The reason being is that if the tenant leaves and the other person still resides on the property, they are not technically a legal tenant. Therefore, you'll need to let prospective tenants know that anyone over the age of 18 must fill out an application, pass the screening requirements and be on the lease. No exceptions.

What to Do When People Start Applying

Once you have tenants interested in applying, they'll do it using a regular paper form or online (depending on which will be easier for both you and the applicant). Also, you want to be clear on whether or not there are application fees.

During the application process, you want to require that tenants procure a copy of any identification including a driver's license, state identification, or a passport. Anything with their photo on it will be a plus.

If the application is all digital, you'll want them to send scanned copies of their ID. From there, you or the property management company that you hire will screen each application. What should be included in the application besides identification:

Here are some things to include in your rental application:

- **Photo ID**

- **Name**

- **Address**

- **Phone number**

- **Email**

- **Employment and income information**

- **Past addresses**

- **Pets (if any)**

- **Background information**

- **Rental history (and landlord references)**

- **Personal and professional references**

- **Emergency contacts**

- **Credit checks**

Aside from this information, you want to make sure that they are going to be reliable tenants that pay on time. As such, you can request their previous W2 or pay stubs dating back to a previous time period. Also, you'll want to ask if there are any additional tenants over the age of 18 (in this case, you may require them to fill out an application as well).

When should you approve an applicant?

So, when is a good opportunity to approve an applicant? Consider the following:

- If they have good to excellent credit

- No felonies on their criminal record

- No bankruptcies or evictions

- Favorable responses from professional, personal, and landlord references

- Meet's any pet criteria

Keep in mind that they can be rejected if they do not meet some of the requirements listed above. However, if you have found someone with a better application, be sure to inform them in the best way possible.

While it's not considered an outright rejection, sometimes you have to swallow hard and make tough decisions. However, be sure to keep them in mind while they are still looking for a place. You may have another property that might better suit them than the original.

How Do Rental Contracts Work?

Rental contracts are written agreements that will be signed by both you and the tenant. There are two kinds of contracts that you can offer depending on the property: month-by-month or lease agreements.

Rental agreement

A rental agreement (or month-by-month) is perfect for short-term leases. If you have apartments that accept tenants on a month-by-month basis, these rental agreements can be renewed every month or can be allowed to expire.

A rental agreement can also be modified every month. A tenant and you will discuss any changes if need be.

Lease agreement

Lease agreements will focus on the long term. At minimal, you'll be looking at 12 months. However, some tenants may be willing to stay on at least longer than that.

After the old lease has expired, you can consider changing the terms. However, the tenant may not agree to the changes and may decide to not renew. So, consider talking about possible changes to the lease before the old one expires.

What's included in an agreement?

The following is included in a rental or lease agreement:

- **Tenants who are residing on the property (over the age of 18)**

- **The term of the tenancy (month-by-month or lease length)**

- **Rental rate plus security deposit**

- **Whether or not pets are allowed**

- **The responsibilities of the tenant in terms of utilities**

- **Permission for the landlord to access the property for repairs, maintenance, and inspections.**

- **Additional rules of the tenancy**

- **Damage policy**

- **Signatures (NOTE: The tenant must sign first before you do! Keep a copy for your records and encourage the tenant to keep a copy as well)**

When A Tenant Moves In

When a tenant moves in, you'll want to do one final inspection of the property before moving day arrives. It's also important to welcome them to their new home and cover as many bases as possible as far as what they need to know about their property and what actions they need to take going forward.

Here are some tips on what to do when your tenant moves in:

- **Provide them with your contact information:** Communication between you and the tenant is key. You want to encourage them to keep in touch with you regularly. If something happens to the property, you must inform them no matter how late in the night it is.

- **Give them a welcoming gift:** If you want to make a lasting impression on your tenants, leave them a few nice gifts. This can include cleaning products, decor, things they can use in the kitchen, bathroom products, and others. Your tenants will be happy that you went the extra mile to get them some goodies.

- **Provide your tenant with two sets of keys:** If there is one sole tenant, then two sets of keys will be enough. This will ensure that the tenant will not have to worry about being locked out of their apartment or house. If there are storage units on the property, be sure to give them a set of keys to access it.

Final Thoughts

Finally, you are able to rent out the property to a tenant. At this point, preparing the paperwork such as the contract or agreement will be one of your top priorities. Meanwhile, you might want to get started on advertising your vacancies.

When meeting with tenants, keep an eye out for any red flags. If you are good at picking up on things, you can make a decision in your mind to determine whether or not the person would make a great tenant or not. Once everything looks good, you can then give the tenant the lease agreement so they can sign, and they can move right in.

Chapter 10: Business Is Business, Don't Think Otherwise

In this chapter, we're going to focus more on the administration end of your real estate business. We'll be talking about what you'll be doing in terms of your day-to-day tasks. This chapter will give you the ins and outs so you can build your business from the ground up.

You'll learn what an LLC is and what other business structures you can form in your business. We'll also discuss how you can put together your business advisory team. These are people who will help you set up your business and manage it wisely.

Speaking of managing, we'll discuss tips on how to manage your time wisely. And you'll learn how to become a business leader while becoming an effective investor at the same time. You'll learn how to develop systems while applying the relevant technology.

Lastly, we'll discuss what you'll need in your office. After all, you need a workspace to set up meetings with sellers, business partners, and those who are relevant to your success. Keep in mind that business is business, and it shouldn't be anything but that.

You're in the business of giving people a place to live while bringing in income to provide more property options for your tenants. So, it really shouldn't be considered a hobby of sorts. Let's get to it:

LLC (Limited Liability Company) and Other Business Structures

Typically, you're going to consider setting up an LLC or a Limited Liability Company. This will give you sole proprietorship of the company. At the same time, it will give you liability protection and ensures that you won't be double taxed (unlike some business structures).

One of the best things about an LLC is that you are not liable for any business debts. On top of that, your business finances will be separate from your personal finances. Should anything happen in terms of legal issues, the business finances will be affected while your personal finances will not be subject to anything.

Depending on the state you live in, LLCs may have a limited lifespan. If a key figure of your business were to leave or join, you may need to dissolve or reform the LLC. For more information on how your LLC will work, take a look at your state's guidelines and laws.

There are other options to structure your business aside from an LLC. Let's take a look at the following business structures and what their advantages and disadvantages are:

- **Sole proprietorship:** Aside from LLCs, this is one of the most common business structures. This is owned by one person. A sole proprietor will not produce a separate business entity. And therefore, business assets and liabilities are not separate from each other. Unlike an LLC, if your business goes into debt your personal finances may be affected as well.

- **Partnerships:** There are two kinds of partnerships: general and limited. A general partnership comprises two or more people while a limited partnership requires one general partner and one limited partner to start. While general partnerships are taxed at the personal income level, they have control and responsibility for the business. Meanwhile, a limited partner owns a portion of the company without taking any risks or responsibilities.

- **Corporation:** There are different types of corporations that you can form including a C Corp. In the eyes of the law, corporations are independent legal entities. Corporations are double taxes, meaning you pay income taxes twice. And they require a lot of recordkeeping and reporting in accordance with tax requirements and regulations. If you are new to the real estate business, refrain from forming a corporation as this might be complex.

- **S Corporation:** An S Corp is where profits and losses are passed through the personal income of the owner. Therefore, they are not subjected to a corporate tax. The owners and shareholders of an S Corp are taxed. If you want to incorporate without the double taxation, an S Corp may be a good decision.

Create Your Business Advisory Team

Your business advisory team are the people you want to get in contact with each time you need assistance with a certain area of business. This includes the financial aspect of running a business and even those who are willing to help you understand the risks and complexities of real estate.

Who should be a part of your team? Here's a list of who you should include:

1. Accountant

No one knows numbers better than an accountant. In fact, they will give you the lowdown on how your company is performing financially. They will also help you decide whether or not the property you are interested in acquiring might be worth the investment.

They'll crunch your numbers, so you don't always have to. They will also help you prepare for purchasing a property and ensuring you have the budget to make the sale final. They will also handle the financial statements for the banks and handle any tax related business.

2. Banker

Having a banker as part of your advisory team is key. That's because they'll help you secure financing for any property acquisitions and even the expenses that go along with your real estate business. You may need something like a contingency fund for unexpected expenses, renovations for newly acquired properties, downtime for location changes, and more.

3. An attorney

Yes, real estate businesses will be dealing with the legality of things all the time. Everything from tenant contracts to taxes. This will be your legal advisor should there be any concerns regarding what you'll want to do in order to solve a problem (such as evicting a tenant). If you have any tax issues to contend with, a tax attorney knowledgeable with such laws will be of help.

4. Contractor

Most of the time, your properties will need a little fixing up. So, it would make sense to have a contractor that is known for doing plenty of renovations and repairs for residential properties. When looking for a contractor, be sure to get references from past clients before making a decision to bring them on.

5. Appraiser

An appraiser is someone you can contact whenever you want updated figures for a property's value. They can be very helpful especially if you plan on upping the rent in between tenants or selling the property outright. After they give you an estimation on the value, you can decide where to go from there.

6. Building inspector

This is someone who will inspect the property thoroughly so they can determine what may need to be fixed or replaced. This might be someone you have already worked with from the beginning when you first began to acquire properties. One reason why they are so important is because they see issues with the property that no one else does. They'll give you a good idea on how much you'll be spending on repairs.

Managing Your Time

If there is one thing any business leader should do, it's manage their time wisely. We'll be taking a look at a few tips to help you maximize your time management, so you don't feel overwhelmed about the tasks at hand. Here are four things that you should do:

1. Always make notes

Sometimes, we forget things. Even the most important things. That's why you should write them down at the beginning and end of each day.

If it's something you really don't want to forget, write it down anyways. A relapse in memory happens. And it saves you a lot of time rather than wasting thinking about what it was.

Make sure that your list and notes are organized nice and neatly. That way, you can cross off one thing on the 'to-do' list before moving onto another.

2. Stick to the to-do list

When putting together a to-do list, you'll want to plan and prioritize everything. The tasks that require the most importance and urgency are done first. Following that, take a look at the tasks that are important, but not as urgent.

To give you a good understanding of how to organize and put together a task list, check out the 'Eisenhower Matrix'. It's a system that will allow you to separate tasks based on the importance and urgency. Remember, the tasks with the most importance and urgency are done first every single time.

3. Delegate any tasks if needed

There are larger tasks that need to be done. However, it might be too large for one person to do. That's where delegating comes into play.

You can delegate the small manageable tasks to those you employ. Meanwhile, you focus on the more important tasks that are related. For example, if you need to collect rent checks, you should consider collecting from tenants from letters A-N while another person collects checks from names O-Z.

Be sure to delegate any tasks so they are done quickly and efficiently each time.

As a business leader, you should always stay in contact with those you've employed. This is one more reason why maximizing and managing your time is important. You want tasks done quickly and efficiently.

Being in constant contact while also delegating any tasks to your workers will be the norm, you'll want to communicate with them on how the tasks must be done. Make sure the tasks are manageable for them and nothing is too complex. Don't be afraid to answer questions they may have.

Looking for More Talent

Obviously, there's a lot of work that needs to be done in a business. So, your best solution would be hiring the right people. As long as you have the budget to hire talent, there is nothing stopping you bringing in a few extra hands.

When is it time to hire the right kind of people? Let's take a look at some scenarios:

When you have several tenant applications

If and when you have several tenant applications to field through, it may seem like an overwhelming task for you. That's where hiring a property management company comes into play. Not only will they be knowledgeable in the application process, but they will be able to help process the applications and determine which applicants are considered qualified tenants based on the criteria set forth.

Repairs are needed on a property

The damage may have been no fault of the tenant. Or maybe it was. Either way, hiring a contractor to fix the damage will be key.

However, this will depend on what needs to be fixed. Remember, contractors should be a part of your advisory team when you're running your real estate business.

When administrative tasks are piling up

In any business, there are administrative tasks that will need to be fulfilled. And you can't do everything all at once. That's when you'll need to hire administrative assistants and the like.

They can do everything from booking appointments, connecting important people like clients and contractors to you, and everything in between.

There will come a time when you want to add another piece of property to the portfolio. That's where you can hire someone who can scout out something that may be up for grabs. From there, that person will relay the information about the property such as the number of bedrooms and bathrooms, how much it's going for, and so on.

They can also assess whether or not the property may be worth acquiring based on walkability, its close proximity to points of interest, and so on.

Evolving Your Skills and Becoming A Better Investor and Businessman

Being a business leader while being an effective investor at the same time will be vital in real estate. Not only will you be employing your most reliable employees, you'll also be looking out for more opportunities to further your business growth.

That's why it is always important to evolve your skills constantly so you can keep the business up and running for as long as you can. Here are some tips that will help you become better skilled at being an excellent business leader and investor:

Build a competent staff

When it comes to hiring the right people, they need to be knowledgeable at what they do. If necessary, there may be people who will need to be trained. As such, they must be willing to learn and know what they are doing without making a lot of mistakes.

Hire people who should clearly understand their roles and responsibilities. Identify their strengths and consider them for positions that will help them put it to good use.

Set SMART goals for your team

Setting Specific, Measurable, Attainable, Relevant, and Time-Bound goals are what makes business leaders great. As long as they are in alignment with the company's work and strategic plans, those goals can be accomplished.

Reward your staff for a good performance

As an employer, it would be incumbent upon you to reward your staff for a good job performance. However, you must also know how to hold anyone accountable for doing less than their best.

You can't always win every investment opportunity there is. And you cannot be emotionally attached to them either. Sometimes, a missed opportunity is a blessing in disguise.

You will eventually find opportunities to grow your portfolio. And you also will need to accept the fact that the next opportunity may not come as quickly as the last one.

A true business leader is someone who can solve a conflict at any time. He or she will look at the problem from different angles and find a creative solution. If there is tension between two employees, a leader can set each of them off to the side, listen to them, and come up with a solution based on what they hear.

The ability to resolve conflict in business will separate the true business leaders from those that may not be cut out for it.

Developing Systems and Applying Technology

In business, you'll want to keep everything organized and working like a well-oiled machine. That's why you'll want to invest in software that may be beneficial for your real estate business. Take a look at some property management software that is available on the market.

For example, if you want something that will be great for DIY landlords, you can use Tenant Cloud. If you want something that is easily customizable, then Avail would be an excellent choice.

Also, you want to consider investing in software that will allow you to automate those small, mundane tasks. You can't spend the entire day doing small menial tasks when you have other priorities to focus on.

While you're at it, consider investing in a software that will allow tenants to interact with you and even send their rent payments online. Not only will it be easier for them to pay the rent, it will be easier for you to collect it without going door to door.

Your Office, and Everything You'll Need in It

In today's business world, you have two choices for your office. You either rent a small space out or have a home office. If you don't want to spend a lot of money on office space, you can operate an office right out of your own home.

It would be nice to have an office since you'll be meeting with tenants, contractors, fellow investors, and those who you'll be interacting with on a regular basis. You don't need to go all out in order to impress clients and potential tenants.

At the same time, you'll want to use your office as a place where you can work and be free from distractions. This is your headquarters for your real estate business. But you won't need a lot of space if you have just a few people working for you.

What you need for your office

When putting together your office, it's important to have the following things: a computer (linked to high-speed internet, a desk and a chair, paper shredder, printer, filing cabinet, and a fire-safe box. Just the basics will be enough to ensure that you operate like a business without all the bells and whistles.

Final Thoughts

Your rental properties are all part of the business. You'll be making more than enough money to grow it even more if you so choose. When it comes to the formation, consider a business type that works best for you.

As a beginner, you may want to start off as an LLC since it provides you with a much easier structure compared to corporations. Remember to manage your time wisely and focus on priority tasks while automating the tasks that seem to be mundane and tedious.

You'll also want to delegate any tasks that you may not want to do to other employees. They may include taking calls and messages, scouting out properties, preparing the paperwork for tenants, contractors, others, and more. Don't forget to put together your business advisory team so you have a group of go-to people to consult with whenever you run into any problems.

Chapter 11: Keeping the Properties in Perfect Condition and Interacting with Your Tenants

As a landlord, you will be saddled with responsibilities to ensure that your property is in good shape. At the same time, you also want to make sure that the tenants who occupy it are happy as well. In this chapter, we'll discuss what your roles, responsibilities, and rights are as a landlord.

While you are responsible for managing the property as you see fit, the tenant is responsible for following the lease agreement as outlined. One shared responsibility that both you and the tenant should have is communicating with each other on a regular basis.

That's because things like property damage can happen at any time. Or they may have some questions or concerns about the property itself. Either way, keeping the lines of communication open both ways will be essential.

Even your property managers (should you hire them), must also be willing to communicate with tenants on a regular basis. After all, the property must undergo routine inspections and maintenance (if needed). If the property is in good shape, the tenant is happy and so are you.

We'll also talk about how you can handle maintenance and repairs along with difficult or bad tenants. You'll also learn how to collect rent when the time comes. There are advantages and disadvantages to becoming a landlord, but we'll help you handle them in this chapter.

Also, we'll discuss specific tenant-centric situations such as when a tenant dies or if they outright abandon the property without warning. Lastly, we'll discuss what you need to do once a tenant moves out of your property.

If your goal is to keep your tenants happy, keep reading:

Your Role, Responsibilities, and Rights as the Landlord

Let's take a look now at the roles, responsibilities, and the rights that you possess as a landlord:

Warranty of Habitability

It is your responsibility to provide a place for a tenant that is habitable. This means that the conditions must be favorable for them to live in. This includes making sure that the structural integrity of the property is in good shape, keeping the HVAC, heating, water, and plumbing running properly, and complying with codes and regulations in accordance with local, state, and federal laws.

Also, you must fulfill any repair requests that are made by the tenant. You can do the repairs yourself or delegate the task to a handyman or contractor. Lastly, the property must be peaceful, quiet, free of hazards, and free of any invasive pests.

A secure dwelling

Safety is paramount for a tenant. That's why you want to make sure that the locks on the property are in good working condition before a tenant moves in. No matter how safe a neighborhood can be, home invasions can happen anytime and anywhere.

You want your tenants to have peace of mind knowing that their locks are good to go (even when they are sleeping or away). Likewise, the landlord should also be responsible for ensuring a crime-free property by doing a criminal background check on every tenant application.

Making one wrong choice by moving in a tenant that may be a threat to the neighborhood should be the last thing you ever do. Especially if there's a chance they may re-offend again (depending on the crime). Assume that every property in the neighborhood is yours and make it your responsibility to keep the others safe.

Making repairs

If you don't have any repair skills, you can always employ the services of a handyman or a contractor. If you have basic repair skills, then you can opt to use them. Things can and will break on the property (whether by fault or no fault of the tenant).

Tenants must put in a request for repairs if need be. The landlord must fulfill that request as soon as possible. This is one of the major reasons why the responsibility shared between the tenant and the landlord is communication.

However, if the damage is done by the tenant, you may be more inclined to defer the responsibility to the tenant to repair the damage. Which means the tenant will need to take care of the repair at their own expense (or the security deposit).

Maintaining the property

The property must be maintained regularly. Which is why regular inspections are important. If and when an inspection is needed, it is important to make sure that you let the tenant know ahead of time (just so there are no surprises).

Meanwhile, you can also go out of your way to do small tasks to make the property look good. If there is a garden, tend to it when needed. If there is a need that appears to be fulfilled and the tenant doesn't notice, bring it up to them so they know what's going on.

Every month (specifically on the first), rent is due. Which means you'll need to collect it from your tenants by rent check or any method of payment. If you have multiple tenants, this may be a difficult thing to do.

If you have multiple tenants, you may employ the responsibilities of a property management company to collect the rent on your behalf.

As a landlord, you have the right to evict a tenant. It should be under the condition that the tenant broke the lease agreement in a grave violation. For example, a landlord can evict a tenant if the property is known for a place where illegal drugs are being sold.

If a lease agreement is broken by a tenant, it can result in an eviction. The question is: where will you draw the line? Typically, illegal activities that may draw constant police attention just might be the start.

Communicating with Tenants

As stated earlier, you and the tenant have a shared responsibility. And that is to keep the lines of communication open between each other. The reason being is because things can and will happen anytime.

The both of you must communicate regularly and be transparent with one another. When the tenant first moves in, it's important to go over with them their rights and roles. What should they be reminded about?

Let's take a look at what the tenant is responsible for:

- **Keeping a line of communication open:** Enough said.

- **Report any damage or need for repairs promptly:** It doesn't matter if it's 5pm or 5am. If there is damage or a repair that is needed, it is the tenant's responsibility to give the landlord a heads up. That way, the issue is addressed quickly and thus the property is habitable once again. If the damage is caused by the tenant, it will be their responsibility to have it fixed at their own expense instead of yours.

- **Follow the lease agreement:** It's all there in writing. They have a responsibility to follow the agreement as it is seen fit. No illegal activity. Pay the rent on time. Maintain a healthy and safe environment. The list goes on and on. Just make sure that the tenant honors the agreement.

- **Keep the door open:** To ensure that the lines of communication are open, have an open-door policy intact. This will benefit both you and the tenant. On top of that, it will place a high priority on tenants that want to be valued. Whether they have questions about the lease, rent extensions, or whatever it is, be willing to listen and have an answer.

- **Respond to repair requests ASAP:** We cannot stress this more, if the repair requests are made by a tenant, it is your responsibility to have them fulfilled quickly.

- **Have multiple lines of communication open:** It doesn't always have to be done by phone. Make sure that you and the tenant can communicate via text/SMS, email, or in-person. The more ways you and your tenant can communicate, the better.

- **Be honest and transparent:** Honesty and transparency goes a long way. And it's also a two-way street. This will lead to a healthy, long-term relationship with each other. Not only that, but a tenant will also need to be honest if they want a good rental reference from you.

- **Alert the tenants prior to any pre-planned activities:** These include repairs, regular maintenance, and showings. You'll want to let your tenants know ahead of time to ensure that the tenant's right to privacy is not violated.

How To Handle Inherited Tenants

Inherited tenants are currently existing tenants from the previous property manager. This may happen down the road whenever you acquire additional properties. So already, you might have a new addition to your cash flow without doing a lot of work to fulfill vacancies (if any).

How do you handle inherited tenants, even though they might not know who you are? Let's take a look at the following tips:

Note that you are handling someone else's issues

Truth be told, the issues the previous landlord is dealing with may also be yours. This includes dealing with tenants who may become a source of frustration for you. That is why it's important to gather all the information and intelligence you need (in a non-invasive way) on the tenants that reside on the property.

However, if you want to avoid any bad tenants or the like, it's important to consider taking this next tip to heart.

Just like due diligence, you want to know the kind of tenants you are dealing with before you buy the property. Looking before you leap comes in different ways. When you are touring the property, be sure to talk to as many tenants as possible.

They may already be aware that their current landlord may be selling the property. Plus, there may be no better time to establish the lines of communication with the people who could potentially become your tenants. From there, you can tell which ones will be good and which ones may be a cause for trouble.

Let them know about any potential rule changes

With new landlords comes the idea of new changes in rules and policies. And for this reason, you're going to expect some pushback from tenants. It may almost end up getting to the point where the tenant may violate their lease and get evicted (which may not be the smart thing to do).

If there are any changes that you plan to make, be sure to go over it with your tenants so you can get some feedback from them. Implementing changes without warning will lead to angry tenants. In other words, don't make your first impression on them a bad one.

Handling Maintenance and Repairs

One thing you need to ask yourself is should you handle the repairs and maintenance or not? The short answer: it depends. If you have one property and have basic repair skills, you can do it yourself.

However, if you lack the repair skills or if you have multiple properties, then you'll want to delegate those repair and maintenance responsibilities to the property management company. At the same time, you'll want to employ a handyman and have contractors on speed dial should any needs arise.

Keep in mind that if you plan on doing repairs and maintenance yourself, you may need the proper certification and the like in order to perform them. If this seems like you're going to jump through so many hoops, then it would be a better idea to defer all maintenance and repairs to those who already have the certifications and the like.

With that said, here are some other tips and considerations to keep in mind:

- **Always have a budget:** Repairs and maintenance will always come in a timely or untimely manner. Regardless, you'll need the money to pay for it. That is why your expenses for the month must include setting aside an amount of money to cover any incidental costs.

- **Let your tenants know ahead of time:** If and when repair requests are being made, it is your responsibility to let them know when the handyman or you will be arriving to make the repairs needed. This will give the tenant notice that the landlord will enter the property (regardless if they are at home or not). Also, this will give the tenant an opportunity to tidy up the place if needed.

- **Schedule inspections periodically:** You and the tenant must be aware that the property must be inspected to ensure things are in good shape. And that's where you need to let the tenant know ahead of time of when an inspection can take place. No need for surprises or anything of that nature.

What to Do When Faced with Difficult or Bad Tenants

A difficult or bad tenant will be one of the biggest problems you'll run into. Not to mention, it's one of the most stressful. What will you do in an effort to deal with them accordingly?

Certainly, evicting them would be a solution. However, it has to be within a legal reason to do so. You cannot simply evict a tenant just because you can (considering the laws and regulations discouraging this).

What constitutes a difficult or bad tenant? This could be someone who may be committing illegal activities on the property such as selling drugs. Or this could be someone who could be making a lot of noise to draw the ire of their neighbors.

Even if you are dealing with a difficult tenant, you must take the following into consideration in a professional manner:

Lay down clear rules

It's your property and it's your rules. Those rules must be honored by the tenant. At the same time, those rules must be outlined in the lease agreement.

If the lease agreement is violated, that can give you the opportunity to evict the tenant if it is warranted. You want the tenant to make sure they understand and be aware of these rules. This way, they won't use the 'I misunderstood the rules' excuse.

Use any line of communication possible, including digital

Whether it's by phone, text, or social media, you want to communicate with the tenant as best as you can. Whether they respond to you or not will be in their court. Also, make sure that the lines of communication stay open no matter what. One last thing, keep a record of every bit of communication between you and the tenant. This way, should any legal issues arise, you can use this in your case if it ever goes to court.

Be patient

Yes, we know that difficult tenants can be a pain in the...well, you know. But no matter what, you'll want to be patient with them. Again, the way you handle the situation may be brought up in a court of law should things go into a legal battle.

Set deadlines

Rents are due the first of the month. The leases expire at the end of a specific month after a period of time (i.e. -- 12 months). Simple as that.

And you want the tenants to respect and meet those deadlines in a timely manner. If for some reason the tenant may have missed a deadline, give them breathing room such as a grace period.

Begin the eviction process if all else fails

If you have exhausted every possible option there is. And the tenant seems to give you grief. At this point, you know what to do.

If the tenant has repeatedly broken the lease agreement, it will be in your legal rights to evict them off your property. If they miss rent payments, refuse to move out after the lease expires, or violated the terms, those are grounds for eviction.

Law enforcement may need to get involved if needed. Especially if the tenant is doing something illegal on the property (and on a regular basis).

Preventative measures

Screening tenant applications and checking for references is always the best line of defense in keeping bad tenants out. That's why you want to go as deep as possible when looking through every application. When you hear of anything about a difficult tenant and you notice a pattern through other references, that's a no brainer to deny the applicant.

Why a tenant must move out, if needed

- **Missed rent payments:** Simply put, if a tenant cannot pay their rent on time constantly and always delays them, you know it will hurt you financially. If they frequently miss payments and grace periods, that's when you need to evict them as soon as possible.

- **Illegal activities:** Safety is your number one priority. And you want to be considerate of the neighbors that live nearby. Once again, assume that every neighboring property is yours. And you are responsible for the safety and security of the inhabitants. Law enforcement may need to be involved if push comes to shove.

- **Lease expiration:** The tenant has the responsibility to renew the lease or allow it to expire. In the event of the latter, they must be prepared to move out the day of the lease expiration. Otherwise, if they occupy the property beyond that, it may be an issue that you need to work out. If they refuse to leave, you must get law enforcement involved since the tenant is technically trespassing.

Everything You Need to Know About Collecting Rent

Collecting rent may seem like a simple task to do as a landlord. However, it's not as easy as you think. That's because not every tenant that resides on your properties will pay on time, every time.

This section will show you everything you need to know about collecting rent including the best practices. You'll also learn what to do if a tenant does not pay rent or you receive a bounced check. We'll also discuss grace periods and extensions.

Tips on collecting rent on time, every time

Set up online payments: In today's digital world, automation is king. Especially when it comes to collecting rent. The best way to collect rent is by working with the tenant to where it can be set up digitally. This way, the rent will be paid for by the tenant every first of the month. There is plenty of software and apps that you and the tenant can use to take care of this.

Collect in person: Collecting in person is never out of the question. Especially if you or the tenant are not so technologically inclined. However, if you have more than one property, this process will be difficult. You don't want to be driving from one location to another and then another all day long. Not only that, but you also don't know if the tenant is going to be around when you're there. Alternatively, a property manager can collect the rent on your behalf.

Drop box: Because of the likelihood of in-person payments not being done regularly, a drop box might be the next best solution. This will work to your advantage if the property is a multi-family home. This can also work if you have a few properties of your own. If you do have a drop box, make sure it has the proper security like a security camera so you can deter and prevent theft from occurring.

Checks by mail: If you really want to go old school, consider accepting the checks by mail. If you are uncomfortable giving tenants your home address, then set up a post office box and have the tenants send you the checks that way.

What happens if a tenant misses a rent payment?

Missed rent payments will happen. And if that does, it would be up to you on how to handle it.

One way to do this is provide a grace period for the tenant. This allows the tenant to pay the rent within that period without a late fee. For example, you can allow a grace period for 15 days.

After that, if the tenant pays the rent, they may be subject to a late fee. If you issue an eviction notice after that grace period, remind them that the notice will be null and void if the payment is made (plus a late fee).

One thing to keep in mind is that a missed payment may be due to circumstances on the tenant's end. They may have lost a job, got robbed, or something may have occurred beyond their control. This is one good reason why both tenants and landlords should communicate regularly with each other.

What if a rent check bounces?

One such situation that can take place is a rent check being bounced. And this can hurt your bank account in a few days. That is why it is important to implement a policy in the lease that will ensure that the tenant 'shall pay' a fee should the rent check be returned due to insufficient funds.

Depending on your state, you may also sue the tenant to reimburse any losses if a rent check bounces.

When a Tenant Dies

If a tenant dies whether on the rental property or elsewhere, you have your rights to handle such a situation. However, there is a certain protocol that you must follow. Here are the steps that need to be taken should a tenant pass away:

1. Get a written notification

This written notification should be procured by the tenant's next of kin or the executor of their estate. Either way, the landlord will find out about it. This notification shall be required in order to begin the termination of the lease via the legal channels.

2. Secure the property as soon as possible

From there, you'll want to secure the property as soon as possible. This will prevent unauthorized individuals from entering the property and attempting to remove the deceased tenant's possessions. At the same time, you'll want to consider using the emergency contact or next of kin as the designated person to receive any possessions that will be removed from the property.

If the tenant has died on the property and you were notified, be sure to notify the authorities and the emergency contact. Be sure to follow any local or state laws that are applicable to securing the property or the possessions of the deceased tenant.

3. Return the security deposit

After the property has been vacated and the deceased tenant's possessions have been removed, do a check of the property. Check for any damage, wear, tear, or the like. Once complete, you can return the tenant's security deposit (or a portion of it) to the next of kin or the executor of the estate.

4. Go through the legal channels to terminate the lease

Just because a tenant dies, doesn't mean the lease is terminated automatically. This will also depend on the type of lease. If it's a month-to-month lease, the death will serve as a thirty (30) day notice and thus allow the lease to expire as is. However, if it is a long-term lease, then the landlord can allow the lease to end early.

In the event of the latter, please contact your attorney to see what can be done so there is no burden placed upon you or the deceased tenant's family. From there, you can also prepare the property for the next tenant.

Dealing with Abandonment

There will be tenants who will up and leave the property for no apparent reason. They'll just outright abandon it and never return. In the event that this does happen, it's important to take the right action.

At this point, you'll have to perform a protocol that can last as much as 8 weeks. First, you'll want to serve a first warning notice to a tenant. You will request that they pay rent within an eight-week period.

If there is no response after a couple of weeks, issue a second warning. If the tenant does not respond after the second, issue a third and final warning on a much noticeable area of the property. The third warning must be issued at least 5 days before the 8-week period set in the first notice has expired.

If the tenant does respond to the notices, the procedure will end. However, if the tenant does not return, you are within your legal right to enter the property under the one of the following conditions:

- The property is in a condition that is considered insecure

- If there are any damages or dangers to the property (including electrical and gas appliances)

During the abandonment process, you'll want to get in contact with the tenant's emergency contact in an attempt to locate them. At the same time, check to see if they are actually still paying rent. Lastly, check the utilities to ensure that they are in good working order.

If the property is indeed abandoned, you'll want to consult with any local and state laws that allow you to enter the property and remove any possessions that belong to the tenant. Make sure that they are stored properly and send a notice of storage to the tenant or the emergency contact.

What to Do After A Tenant Moves Out

When a tenant moves out, usually they'll do it with prior notice. At that time, you can advertise the vacancy immediately. This will ensure that it can be fulfilled as soon as possible (and when the old tenant moves out).

On the day of the move out, you and the tenant should go over the property one last time. Check for any damages, malfunctions, or the like. After the inspection is complete, you can hand over the security deposit (either in full or partially if there is any damage or wear).

The tenant must hand over the keys to you on the day they move out. After the tenant has left, be sure to change the locks before the new tenant moves in. And for good measure, inspect the property once more to see if everything is in good condition and working properly.

Final Thoughts

Your tenants will be good to your properties if you choose the right ones. Keep in mind that each of you have roles and responsibilities. And you both need to do your part to ensure that the property is in good condition.

Both you and the tenant must communicate regularly. Also, you'll want to notify the tenant ahead of time if you plan on being on the property for inspections or maintenance. When dealing with bad or difficult tenants, you'll want to ensure that they have broken the lease agreement in some way prior to evicting them.

If a tenant dies or has abandoned the property, you'll want to follow the specific procedures outlined for such events. Either way, this may also require you to consult your attorney to ensure that you follow any legal protocols and procedures. When a tenant is about to move out, your job is to make sure that the vacancy is fulfilled as soon as possible.

That way, when the old tenant moves out, you can prepare the property for the new one. And the whole cycle starts all over.

Chapter 12: Establish Your Real Estate Network Even If You Are Investing in Rental Properties

As someone who invests in rental properties, you are technically involved in the world of real estate. So, it wouldn't hurt for you to establish your network. Imagine having a robust network of real estate professionals that you can work with in various situations.

You may know someone who is looking to purchase a house. They may be looking for a certain property and you might just know the person that sells it. Aside from that, this is a network of people you can provide value for.

We'll talk about how you can build your network in the real estate world and where you can find them. We'll also discuss the importance of real estate clubs, what they are, and why joining one is a must. By the end of the chapter, you'll also learn how to build a database of not just real estate professionals, but also tenants, agencies that will connect tenants to property managers, and more.

When it comes to building networks, you'll want to make sure that your ability to communicate and build relationships is on point. You'll learn the ins and outs of those in this chapter. Ready to build your real estate network for the better?

Let's get crackin':

Networking in The World of Real Estate

If you want to be successful in real estate, then it's best to build a network that will help you out. Especially if you are looking to connect with real estate professionals and others who may be associated with them. The first thing you need to ask is where you should begin.

Let's take a look at a few places where you can start building your network:

Online databases

Today, almost every real estate professional in the world has some kind of online presence. To begin, you can take a look at online databases. You can whittle down the location, the type of real estate business they do, and so on.

From there, you can get their contact information and send them a message. Even though you are someone who invests in rental properties, you at least know enough of the language that the real estate professionals speak. But don't say a lot of it just to impress them or bend over backwards.

Social media

Yes, social media is a great place to connect with real estate professionals. Most of them may be found via LinkedIn or Facebook. You may also connect with real estate professionals in dedicated social media groups.

You can find groups that are focused on local real estate professionals and even those in a much larger region. Either way, join as many of these social media groups as possible.

Networking events

If there are any networking or industry events in the area, you'd be insane not to go to them. This will give you a good opportunity to meet with local and regional real estate professionals face to face. This will also give them a chance to get to know you in a different way as opposed to exchanging phone calls and emails.

Real Estate Investing Clubs

A real estate investing club might be something that you're interested in joining. You can join one yourself so long as you have your own money to invest in. People who are retired, students, wealthy business owners, and everyone in between can join these clubs.

Typically, a real estate investor club is small in size. Usually, you'll have five to ten people in a single club. All of which have the same investment goals even though there are not legal limits or minimums to deal with. Members of these clubs pool their money together and will make investment decisions as a group.

You can see if you can join an existing club if there is one in your area. However, if you so desire, you can create one. This is one of the reasons why you should always be building a real estate network, even if you invest in rental properties.

In fact, you could get other real estate investors in your network to join you. And from there, once it's established, you and the rest of the club can begin to make investment decisions using the money that you all have pooled together.

Creating Your Database

If you're going to build a network, you're going to have to put together a database. This way, you'll know who is who and you'll be able to connect with them so long as you have the right contact information. On top of that, you'll have a list of people that you can use to connect one person to the other that is in your network.

For example, if you have an old tenant that wants to rent a property from another landlord, you can make the connection from there. This will make it easy on the tenant because you serve as a rental reference that can put in a good word for them.

Your databases should be kept separate, first and foremost. Second, your databases should be assigned with the following labels:

- **Buyers**
- **Sellers**
- **Tenants (past and present)**
- **Real Estate Agents or agencies**
- **Brokers**
- **Contractors**
- **Bankers and financial professionals**
- **Attorneys**

Whenever someone in your network (or outside of it) may need something, you'll know exactly who to connect them to. You can give that person value just by leveraging your real estate network. Even if it's a tenant that does not plan on renting from you, you can always refer them to other landlords as a gesture of goodwill.

Also, having a database of buyers will also serve as an excellent backup plan for rental properties. Because you might have someone who might be willing to rent a place if things fall through with a previous tenant. Or, if you are ready to sell a rental property, you can find a good buyer who will be willing to pay a good price for it.

Any way you slice it, there's always more than one way to leverage your network. And having neat, nicely organized databases with their own labels will be just the start. Use them to your advantage and you will be known as that person who is the ultimate connector.

Imagine being the go-to person and having them access your network of people. There could be property investors looking to get in the business and wanting to connect with you as well. So, things seem to come full circle because at one point, that new property investor was you.

Establishing Your Presence and Building Relationships

If you're planning on building your network, it's better to establish a presence both online and/or offline. Without it, no one will know that you exist. In today's technology driven world, an online presence is a must.

But that doesn't mean you shouldn't leave out the idea of building an offline presence. Let's take a look now at the ways you can build an online presence:

4 Ways to Build Your Online Presence

Start a website

To start, you should consider building a website if you want to establish a good online presence. That way, when people search for landlords or real estate professionals in their local area, they'll be able to know that someone exists.

You can also include things like a blog and even a listing of your currently vacant properties. As for the blog aspect of the site, don't talk about your personal life or anything like that. Instead, use the blog to provide some kind of value.

For example, you can write blog posts that are targeted towards tenants who may be looking for a place to rent but don't know how to fill out the application properly. Another post would be dedicated towards how they can automate their rental payments. Using the blog to provide some kind of value to tenants and real estate professionals alike will help you stand out more.

Social media

Social media seems to be building up by the day. And as a real estate investor, you can even use it to show off your properties that are available. Your potential tenants may be looking for a place and are using every channel imaginable to find something.

You could set up a Facebook page and post pictures of a vacant property so prospective tenants know what they are looking at. The posts should be straightforward, to the point, and contain clear, easy to look at photos of the property.

You can also use social media as a way to get in contact with potential tenants should they have questions about the property, the application process, and so on.

There will come a time where vacancies need to be fulfilled. And you'll want to advertise your properties both online and offline. You can use paid advertising such as Facebook or Google ads.

The cool thing about paid advertising is that it will help get more eyeballs on the property and even some click throughs. You may even get online applicants using this method. Especially if all the potential tenant has to do is apply online (or even in person).

If you really want to put yourself out there, don't stop with a website or social media. You can sign up for local directories and databases. Some of them may require a fee to be on the list for a period of time (while others like online databases may not).

Building an offline presence

Flyers

As mentioned before, flyers are a great way to put yourself out there. One of the best times to do this is whenever you have a property that has a vacancy that is waiting to be fulfilled. Remember to post these in high-traffic areas in your locale.

Classified/Newspaper Ads

Classified and newspaper ads will usually give you a space for cheap. You can pay for a small space or pay even more for something larger.

Communication Is Key

Networking requires one thing: communication. And nothing but communication. That's because you are talking with fellow investors, real estate professionals, tenants, and everyone that is involved in the process in some way.

It takes strong communication skills to succeed in the real estate business. And the same can be said about building your network. Let's take a look at some of the following tips that you'll need in order to make communication worth it in building your network:

1. Stay friendly and professional

Needless to say, effective communication in networking must always be friendly and professional. You want to sound like someone you can trust (while being that person that can be trusted by someone). Also, it's good to maintain a positive mental attitude while communicating with others.

2. Emphasize with people and their needs

If there is one thing that you absolutely need in terms of being an excellent communicator, it's having empathy. A client may have concerns about acquiring a property. A potential tenant may have concerns about the area that they are living in.

The list goes on and on. And it's important for you to understand their concerns while listening to exactly what they are dealing with. Plus, when you listen, you'll be able to come up with ideas and solutions on the fly.

The same goes when people are having frustrations that people are facing in the market. Don't be afraid to ask questions about the issue that's facing them. For example, ask someone who may be buying a house about what they are looking for in an agent.

If you are talking to tenants, ask them what they are looking for in an ideal rental situation? There are questions that are tailor made to any person you talk to when it comes to real estate.

3. Always follow-up or call back

The ability to follow up or call-back goes both ways. Don't be the person that calls once, talks to someone, and is never heard from again after that. Not only will that leave a bad impression, but that won't fare well with others who want to communicate with you.

If you are promising to call someone back, do good on that promise.

4. Ask questions

Seems simple enough, right? Ask questions that may address any issues a client may have. Ask questions to an attorney about a certain process that works with leases.

When talking with buyers or sellers, ask relevant questions such as 'what are they looking for in an agent?'. If it's someone selling a house, ask them what is motivating them to sell.
The deeper you dig, the more you'll learn to understand others who may be in the same situation in the future.

Final Thoughts

Even if you invest in rental properties, you are still part of the real estate ecosystem. This means you can still build your real estate network from the ground up. And make sure you have one that is well-built so you can connect one person to the other if needed.

Be sure to meet with real estate professionals and everyone else who may also be involved with the process. Establishing long-term relationships with people in your network will pay off in the long run. Who knows...someone may also look to you for advice on real estate investing as well.

Remember, if you want to build a strong real estate network, having strong communication is your number one asset. Without it, you'll more than likely be going nowhere. Another thing to place a lot of importance on is your presence both online and offline.

People need to know that you exist. That way, they can contact you with questions, concerns, or if they just want to rent a property from you. The ability to communicate and be visible is just a couple of keys to success in real estate.

Chapter 13: Marketing Your Way on Rental Properties

Without marketing, nothing would ever be sold. Or even rented for that matter. That's why the best thing to do when you need to fulfill a vacancy on your rental property is to get the word out.

This chapter will be dedicated to just that. We'll be talking about the real estate market in general. From there, we'll also talk about your marketing plan and how to execute it. In today's world, a lot of real estate investors will likely go the digital route.

However, you're going to learn how to implement some nice 1-2 punches using a combination of digital marketing and traditional marketing. Plus, we'll give you some marketing tools that you can use to your advantage.

Simply put, the first thing that you need to realize is an effective marketing campaign needs to start by knowing where the 'starving crowd' is. Where do they hang out? What exactly are they looking for?

You cannot simply just spread-out flyers and digital ads without knowing some insights and information about the market itself. Let's get right into the action so you have a marketing plan that you can put together and hit the ground running with it:

The Real Estate Market

First, we'll be taking a look at the real estate market. It's true that it consists of buyers and sellers. However, what kind of market is it?

It could be a seller's market or a buyer's market. The best way to tell which is which is based on the conversations you hear. Another way of finding out is evaluating the market.

You can evaluate the market based on these two steps: analysis of the city and the neighborhoods within the cities of interest. How do you make an accurate analysis of both? Let's start with the city analysis:

City analysis

To get a good idea of whether or not a city has a robust real estate market, we'll have to look at the following:

- **Job market:** If the job market is on the upswing, chances are there's a growing demand for housing. This is a good sign, especially for those investing in rental properties. There are major cities that serve as major hubs for several industries. Even the suburbs of these major cities would be ripe for rental properties.

- **Tourism:** Some cities will have a thriving tourism industry, and some may not. In a tourist centric city, this is a hotbed for Airbnb properties. That's because people will eschew the traditional find a hotel idea and find a place to crash like a spare bedroom or an apartment.

- **The price to rent ratio:** If you want a true market analysis number to work with, the price to rent ratio will be your best friend here. This will help you determine the demand for rental properties in the area. The higher the ratio, the more renters there are than homeowners.

- **Property taxes:** Property taxes are one of the most common expenses that investors face. However, the lower they are, the better. Keep in mind that larger cities will command higher property taxes compared to properties in the suburbs.

Neighborhood analysis

While analyzing the neighborhoods of a city, you'll want to see what's close by (i.e. — a one mile radius) and take notes. How far are the available rental properties from a grocery store or a school? Is it closer to a medical facility?

Typically, you'll want to find a rental property that is close by to some amenities that are easily accessible. To take it a step further, get a list of major employers for the area. What's the average commute time for residents in that neighborhood?

If you want to go a little deeper, there are heat maps that you can find on various real estate websites. These heatmaps will help determine which areas are valuable and which are not based on factors like walkability, commute time, and so on.

You can also whittle it all down using data such as listing price, average rental income, cash-on-cash-return, and more.

Your Marketing Plan

This is where you want to put together a killer marketing plan. As mentioned before, the first rule of marketing is knowing where the fish are. In other words, you need to know where you can find the 'starving fish'.
Even if you know where the starving fish are, you still need to get the offer and the message right. Otherwise, it will fall flat. With that said, we'll be sharing with you the following tips that will help you put together and execute a marketing plan that can work to your advantage.

Let's take a look at what you need to do:

1. What is your marketing philosophy?

Your marketing philosophy should be simple. You're looking at this as an investment rather than an expense. This should be your marketing philosophy to begin with.

At some point, you know that you're going to generate leads and potentially applicants that may become tenants. Now, let's discuss your goals and objectives.

2. What are your goals and objectives?

This is where you want to sit down with your business advisory team and discuss what kind of goals you want to set for your marketing strategy. This includes evaluating the levels of growth and your current position in the market space.

Next, you'll want to make a list of marketing goals. Then choose the top three to five goals that you feel are most important and go from there. Be sure to choose the goals that are actually measurable and hold yourself accountable towards them.

3. Setting your strategies

This is a step that you do not want to skip. Because strategy is a lot better than just tactics. As the old saying goes, tactics without strategy is like a car without a steering wheel.

Your strategies could be increasing awareness for your brand, generating leads, or increasing your sales overall. Since you're going to be fulfilling vacancies, you want to focus on lead generation since you want to generate interested applicants.

4. What are the tactics you want to use?

Make sure that your strategy and tactics do go together. Tactics are specific actions that you need to take in order to achieve your goals. For example, if your strategy is generating leads, what kind of actions are you going to take?
Are you going to take a digital approach and see what sticks? Or are you going to start out with a more traditional marketing approach? Or why not both?

If you want to generate awareness about how a tenant can be approved for an application, you can write a blog post on your website about the pertinent information they'll need to add when applying. The strategy is generating awareness and the tactic is posting something on your site that will get someone to take action.

See where we're going with this? With the right strategy comes the right tactics that will make it work.

5. What is your budget?

Your marketing budget must be enough to where you're able to fulfill the goals and objectives of your company. At the same time, you want to determine how soon you want to fulfill these vacancies. Aside from money, your time and resources will play a role in marketing your rental properties.

Before the marketing plan is executed, consider the amount of time and manpower it will take. Evaluate this with your team regularly to determine its progress and whether or not adjustments have to be made, if necessary.

Traditional Marketing

The good news about traditional marketing: it has not gone the way of the dinosaur due to the Internet. The even better news: there's less competition that you'll have to deal with. And it is still as effective today as it was before the Internet had ever been introduced to the world.

What exactly are the traditional ways of marketing your rental properties? Let's take a look at them:

- **Classified ads:** You find them in newspapers and local guides where people are looking to sell things. The more money you spend, the greater the space. Plus, you can advertise in local or large regional periodicals and newspapers.

- **Flyers:** You probably see them every day at supermarkets, banks, drug stores, and so on. One of the reasons why flyers stand out is because you can give people a preview of what the property looks like.

- **Business cards:** You can leave business cards on bulletin boards or leave them at local businesses where your ideal market hangs out. Or you can talk to the manager of a business and ask about leaving a stack of business cards and hand them out whenever someone mentions about finding a place.

- **Signs/billboards:** If you have a property already acquired, you can use signs or billboards indicating that a place is for rent. From there, the call to action is simple: apply now.

- **Direct mail:** Indeed, direct mail still works. You can send it to a list of people who are looking to sell their homes and want to spend less money on living expenses. Or you can do a direct mail campaign with the goal of generating awareness. You buy the home they're selling and explain what your plans are with it.

- **Word of mouth/referrals:** This is one of the best reasons why you should always be building your network. Someone may be looking for a place. And someone within your network may serve as the bridge for that person to connect with you. Never count out word of mouth or referrals as a way to fulfill your vacancies.

Digital Marketing

Digital marketing is targeted, and laser focused. It's not as broad reaching as traditional means. However, the issue here is that the competition can be fierce. But mixing some traditional with digital never killed anyone.

Let's take a look at some digital strategies that you can employ:

- **PPC ads:** These include Facebook ads, Google ads, or even banner ads. PPC ads charge per click. You can set it to where a specific demographic, local area, gender, and so on can see it while the rest that are outside of the target market cannot.

- **Social media:** Simply put, social media is being used a lot. And you can use your fan page or business page to post listings to your followers. The goal here: get your followers to share your vacancies with those who may be interested in finding a place.

- **Website:** A website may be a great place to do some digital marketing. Specifically, if you are using blog content to provide value to potential renters or even home sellers. This will also help establish your online presence and let people know that you are the real deal.

Marketing Tools

There are plenty of real estate marketing tools out there (both free and paid). What can you use based on your budget and your goals? It's important to explore your options so you know which ones will work for you.

Let's take a look at some of the tools you can use:

Facebook/Google Ads

This is a paid tool depending on the budget you set. You can set your ad budget to $5 per day if you want to and it can still generate leads. However, the higher the budget, the more people you'll reach.

You can advertise your vacancies on real estate listings or even multiple listing services (MLS). Your properties can be listed on Zillow or Apartments.com (and similar sites). Use these listing sites to optimize your listing data and also get reviews that will be useful to you whenever you have more vacancies available.

Social media

Social media is free to use (unless you are using their ad platforms). Yet, you can market your properties at any time. Or for a small amount of money, you can 'boost' your post so you can get more eyeballs without having to rely on the ad platforms.

Email marketing

Your website will have an opt-in box that will allow people the opportunity to stay in the know about local properties that are up for rent. But having them give you their email address won't be easy. So, offer something in exchange such as a free guide for potential renters or house sellers. Something that will be valuable for them. From there, you can send regular newsletters and emails about property vacancies and other information that is relevant and valuable to your target market.

Postcards

We're not just talking about those postcards you send on vacation. These are small postcards that you can buy for cheap. A stack of 100 will be $10 or less (depending on where you get them). Using a mailing list of home sellers, you send them a personalized postcard indicating your interest in the property. In fact, direct mail is most effective because no one ever spams a physical mailbox (other than bill collectors).

Final Thoughts

Your marketing strategy will require a starving market, the right message, and possibly the right 'offer' (in this case, your rental properties). Your marketing message should target the right people while being able to 'exclude' those who may not fit the profile of your ideal tenant.

To make it effective, consider doing a mix of both traditional and digital marketing. However, you want to consider how much your budget will allow. Before you execute your marketing strategy, know what your goals are.

Once you have a goal in mind, find the right strategy and tactics that will help you reach them. It may take time, resources, and money. But when done right, you can generate leads and get the right tenants to rent from you.

Chapter 14: Building A Long-Term Wealth and Passive Income with Rental Properties

One of the reasons why many people become real estate investors is to make money. And that's one of your goals (assuming you have picked up this book). It is possible to build long-term wealth and even passive income with rental properties.

However, as we've said before in the beginning, this is not a get rich quick scheme. This will take time to get you to your financial goals. At this point, we're pretty sure that you understand this.

In this chapter, we'll be talking about the basics of handling your finances. Also, we'll explain why achieving long-term wealth and passive income is possible with rental properties. But the thing is, once you have it going to where it generates passive income, it doesn't stop there.

We'll talk about what else you need to do now that you have the income you want. Also, you'll learn how to generate more income while keeping expenses low. Lastly, you'll learn that managing real estate taxes is still something that you need to keep an eye on (especially when there always is a potential for change).

Now, let's talk about the financials:

Learn the Basics of Handling Finance, and Develop It from There

Basic finances may seem simple to do. You take the income, minus the expenses, and you get a profit or a loss. With real estate, the concept is the same but it's a little different. Here's what you need to know about basic finances involving real estate:

Keeping personal and business finances separate

This must be rule number one in business finance. Keep your business bank account separate from your personal account. This means that all your business income and expenses must be subtracted from your business bank account.

Also, keep all receipts and paperwork in a separate file folder that indicates all things business. The same must go for your personal finances. Doing this properly will not only make things easier on you, but when tax time comes, you'll also get some sweet deductions for your business.

Open separate accounts for your rental properties

To ensure that everything is kept separate, make sure that you open separate bank accounts. Specifically, you want to open one up for each rental property. This will keep the income and expenses separate from the other properties (and keep things well organized).

You'll get profit and loss statements, easily reconcile your bank account, and be able to file taxes easily without doing a lot of number crunching. You'll easily identify which bank account is tied to your rental property by organizing them by file folder, account number, and so on.

Always track expenses

It cannot be stressed enough. Track every single dang expense that goes towards your rental properties. It will help you out during tax season. And it will give you an accurate account of everything.

Since you must keep financial records of every rental property in a separate folder, be sure to make a note of which expense is tied to whatever property that it went towards. For example, write down the address of the property so you can positively identify it.

Also, remember what your expenses are in terms of your rental properties. These include your marketing and advertising, property management fees, repairs and maintenance, and more. These are known as your operating expenses.

Automate some tasks

There are some tasks that are so tedious and simple to do, they can be automated. When doing this with numerous rental properties, it can get to a point where it can consume your entire day. For this reason, you can automate the tasks, so you don't have to do the same thing all day long.

If there's a small task, automate it. This will free up a lot of time so you can focus on other business priorities.

Prepare ahead of time

In business, a lot of people are forecasting their income and expenses. This is why it's important to always check on lease agreements and when they are due to expire. Also, you want to make forecasts that are based on certain situations (such as whether a tenant renews a lease or not).

Either way, prepare ahead of time for any changes in income and expenses (whether a tenant moves out or new tenants are moved into a property you recently acquired).

The tax forms that you need to familiarize yourself with are W-9 and 1099 forms (among others). A W-9 form is a contractor's tax form that determines the type of business that you are. A 1099 form will be used for those who are self-employed (and make over $600 or more from their business).

These are basic tax forms that you'll want to use when the time comes to file them. If you have any questions or need to know any additional tax information, then talk to a tax expert or a CPA.

Hire a CPA

A CPA is someone you should already have in your network (and your business advisory group). These people crunch numbers like no one's business. And they will give you advice on how to handle your finances.

They'll also analyze your financial performance based on the properties you own and the business finances as a whole. They will also help you during tax season when the time comes to pay them.

Achieving Long-Term Wealth Is Definitely Possible

It's possible to achieve long-term wealth. But as we've said before, it takes time to get there. At the same time, it also takes properly managing your finances, the property itself, and everything in between to get there.

The key is doing it properly. You need to make sure that the income and expenses are calculated accurately. Second, you want to keep your tenants happy. And third, you need to be smart with the properties you want to invest in.

It will take one wrong move to further delay your progress (or blow it all up entirely). Here are some tips to achieve long-term wealth with rental properties:

Make sure to pay off everything on-time, every time

You can pay off loans and that will take care of one expense that you'll no longer pay for. Once your debt is paid off, you don't have to worry about losing a ton of money.

Always start out small

We all start somewhere. It might as well be from the ground level. With real estate, starting out can be as small as a single-family property.

From there, you can build your way up and acquire another property and repeat the process as many times as needed. The more properties you acquire, the more income you'll have. Sounds simple enough, right?

However, this is something that will take time. So, don't rush into buying another property when you know that you're going to need a little extra cash first and foremost. Your next property acquisition may be even more challenging than the last (so will things like repairs and the like).

Simply put, the best way to generate long-term wealth with rental properties is holding onto your rental properties. Don't sell them at all. Even if the properties don't have a mortgage anymore since you paid them off, you can enjoy getting a little extra money in your pocket.

It's as simple as that. When you see that bump in income after paying off some expenses, you'll be feeling pretty good.

Turning It to Passive Income

Passive income is a lot of fun to have. Especially when you're earning a lot of money per month from your rental properties. And it's actually fairly easy to do once you know how to do it properly.

What you do with your passive income is entirely up to you. You can build a retirement fund, go on vacation, achieve financial freedom, and so on. The sky is pretty much the limit.

With that said, here are some tips to keep in mind while you are looking to generate passive income:

Have enough cash flow: Pretty much self-explanatory. If you have enough cash flow, you'll be able to generate passive income for each property. But remember, the market can change course over time. And because of that, the numbers can and will change.

Screen your tenants properly: Whether it's you or the property managers you hire, you want to make sure you screen and choose the right tenants. These are people who are reliable, willing to stay on for the long-term, and won't cause any trouble. A bad tenant is actually worse than no tenant at all, so screen wisely.

Collect rent promptly: The lease agreement should be clear enough to both you and the tenant. The rent must be collected on time and every time. Even though you might be the most laid back and chill person on the planet, you have to draw the line somewhere in terms of collecting rent. This way, it doesn't give tenants the opportunity to take advantage of you and skip out on rental payments.

What's Left for You to Do?

Just because you have money rolling into your bank account, doesn't mean that's it. It doesn't mean sit back and relax. There are some things that you need to do while you are generating income from your rental properties.

Here are some things that you should do:

Check the properties regularly: Communication is important. So always check on the properties on a regular basis. Talk to the property managers and the tenants. Check to see if everything is fine. If there is a problem, address it promptly.

Avoid legal trouble: Legal issues can arise at any given time. That's why it is important to check the properties regularly and listen to your tenants if something is wrong. Also, be mindful of the privacy of your tenants. If you need to go to the property for inspection or maintenance, let them know ahead of time rather than make a surprise appearance.

Honor the lease agreements: This seems easy enough. You honor your end of the agreement and the tenants should honor their end. You cannot just evict someone from the property just because you don't like them.

Keep the property safe: Safety and security is important for your tenants and their neighbors. Make sure each property has working locks, so it prevents any burglaries or invasions of any kind. At the same time, check to see if the properties are not a place where crimes can be committed (like the production and sale of illegal drugs).

Generating Extra Income and Reducing Expenses

This is the goal we all want, right? Extra income and less expenses. It's possible to get it done.

But the question is: how? Let's start with reducing expenses. There are plenty of ways to go about doing this.

Here are some examples on where you can reduce expenses:

Fulfill vacancies quickly

The expenses add up when there are vacancies. Granted, once they are filled, those temporary expenses used to fulfill them will be off the books until the process needs to be repeated. Therefore, a fulfilled vacancy means more income and less of an expense.

If there are renovations that need to be done, do it whenever there are vacancies. This might be easy to do if you are renting out single family homes. From there, once the renovations are complete, this will give you a great window to increase the rent before the vacancy itself is fulfilled.

You must never increase the rent while there are tenants that are occupying the property. You don't want to put them in a financially precarious position where they feel like the need to make more just to make rent every month.

Consider energy saving methods

You can save energy and a whole lot of money at the same time by doing some small tasks. These include cleaning the HVAC filters regularly, sealing any cracks around the windows and doors, keeping the temperature of the water heater down to a minimum, and installing LED light fixtures.

Also, you can install low flow shower heads and high-efficiency washers to save money on water. Efficiency is one of the best cost-effective ways to save money whether you are a property owner or a tenant.

Consider alternative services

There may be a waste management service that provides less pickups for less money. This may be better than the other guy that does weekly pickups, but commands a high price. There may be a lawn care company that does mowing every month as opposed to every other week and charges you less for it.

Consider what might be the best alternative services to save a bit of money while keeping quality in mind. In other words, don't allow the property to let itself go just for the sake of saving extra money.

Don't Forget to Manage Real Estate Taxes

If there is one thing you should never forget to do, it's the real estate taxes. If you forget to do them, not only will you fall behind financially, but you'll also find yourself missing out on a ton of awesome benefits and write-offs.

What are some real estate tax deductions you will possibly qualify for? Let's take a look at some of them:

Cost for repairs, maintenance, and upkeep: Yes, it pays to fix and maintain your properties. And that's why it's so important to keep a record of your expenses that are aimed towards it. The amount of sales taxes that you pay on all things repair and maintenance will definitely help you out in the long run once tax season comes. And you can even save a ton on your tax bill.

Utilities: Some utilities you have to pay for, and others will be the tenant's responsibility. Consider which utilities will be beneficial for your tax bill and go from there.

Mortgage interest: The interest that you pay on your mortgage will yield one of your best tax deductions yet. So, if you are paying off a mortgage, be sure to keep a record of how much interest you're paying on it. Also, if you have a mortgage insurance premium, you can get a tax deduction on that as well.

Travel expenses: You might have property on one end of town or in a different state. Either way, the travel costs such as gas and the like for going to and from your properties can count as a deduction on your taxes.

Property tax deductions: Don't forget, paying your property taxes on time will yield towards extra relief on your overall tax bill.

Final Thoughts

Building your long-term wealth and your passive income via rental properties is possible. As long as you are taking the necessary steps, you'll be able to generate the amount of passive income and wealth you so desire. One thing to go about doing this is increasing your income while keeping expenses low.

Also, be sure to keep your business and personal expenses separate from one another so you avoid as much confusion as possible. Plus, keeping everything separate will make tax season a lot less frustrating. Remember, you can enlist the help of a CPA to help keep your finances in order.

Just because you have income rolling in the bank, doesn't mean you should just sit back and relax. You still have to take care of the business side of things such as checking on the properties and ensure that they are maintained. Not only that, but you also want to keep the tenants happy and listen to any issues they may have.

Remember, this is still a business that you need to tend to regularly. Sure, you can enjoy your financial freedom. But neglecting your business will lead to that financial freedom fading away.

Chapter 15: If and When You Really Need to Exit, Here's What You Must Learn

Let's say you have amassed quite a bit of wealth over time. You've worked hard to put together a solid portfolio of rental properties. And now, it's time to move on and enjoy yourself.

In this chapter, we're going to be talking about exit strategies. When is a good time to exit? What should you do before executing your exit strategy?

There is more than one type of exit strategy that exists. And we'll be taking a look at each of them, so you'll know which one works best for you. There are also some mistakes that you need to avoid so the exit is smooth and seamless rather than filled with problems.

At this point, you have achieved your financial goals. Now, it's time to cash out and enjoy life after real estate. So, let's talk about exit strategies and everything you need to know about them:

What Does It Mean to Exit?

To exit means to sell your rental properties if you want to move on with something else. In short, you are removing yourself from an investment deal. You could already be making money and decide that you've made enough to retire on.

Or maybe, you want to use a portion of the wealth you've amassed and use it to invest in something outside of real estate. With exit strategies, there's always an end goal. But still, it's important to plan it before executing it.

With this in mind, when should you consider an exit? You might not even be thinking about it during the time when you purchase the property. But at some point, once you already have a few properties under your belt, you might be thinking about the long-term future.

Yes, dealing with the rewards and risks of real estate for a long period of time can take a toll on people. And some landlords may feel burnt out by it all. Or, you may decide that it's time to wind down and start a new chapter in your life.

If you're young when you're starting out, you might be making plenty of money, and even retire at say age 40 or 45. From there, you can spend time with family or do some small ventures to help propel your retirement plan. If you are someone in your 30s or 40s, maybe you are looking to generate income from rental properties as a way to support your family for the long-term.

But when the time comes to exit, you'll think back and say that you've built something meaningful. You hate to let it go. But you are cashing in your chips and want to focus on what's next in your life, whatever that may be.

Things to Consider Before Exiting

Before executing your exit strategy, you'll want to take a few things into consideration. Because you want the exit to be as smooth and issue-free as possible. What needs to be done before you finally are able to get the properties out of your hands?

Let's take a look at the following:

Why now (or soon)?

The biggest question is why are you exiting now than perhaps later? This may be a personal question or perhaps you have other business plans and responsibilities that may require your full attention.

Are my properties in good enough shape?

Before letting go of any property, you'll want to make sure that it is in good condition. Just like someone selling a house, they don't want to sell it to anyone who may be buying a piece of junk. So, you want to be considerate and sell it to someone who is getting a good property for what it's worth.

Just remember, if the property appears to be worn or in need of repair, you may be selling it for a lot less than what you paid for. And that will give you a loss rather than a gain.

What does the current market look like?

How is the market looking at the moment? Are people looking to buy houses? How many people are selling their properties at the moment?

If the demand is healthy enough, you may move forward with your exit plan. However, you also want to check the supply as well. You may fare better in selling the property if there aren't a whole lot of properties up for sale at the same time.

If the market shows low demand and high supply, then you may want to hold off on your exit strategy until later on.

Will you sell the property to a homebuyer? Or will you sell it to another investor? At the end of the day, the buyer will do whatever they want with it.

This is entirely up to you. But if you see it still has the potential as a solid rental property, then by all means, sell it to a fellow investor. However, if you feel like a single-family home might just be a place that can be bought outright, then sell it to someone who wants to find a home.

Is there any depreciation of the value?

Depreciation can kill an exit strategy dead. And it might take time before you recoup your losses by way of repairs or renovations. If the property value somehow depreciates, figure out what is causing it.

Also, find ways to increase the value so you can sell the property, even for a reduced price if it comes down to it.

Do the maintenance costs cancel out the profits?

If the maintenance costs cancel out the profits, odds are it won't fare very well for anyone looking for a property that they're looking to rent out. At this point, it might be ideal to sell the property outright to a potential homeowner. If you are intending on selling it to an investor, be sure to find ways to cut down on maintenance costs so it's not a burden that is shouldered upon the new owner.

Are there any issues affecting the cash flow?

As an outgoing owner, you want to be considerate of your fellow investors. If there is an issue regarding the cash flow of the property, figure out what it is and find an alternative solution. For example, you may be spending too much on a certain expense.

Therefore, it would be wise to make adjustments on said expenses to ensure a positive cash flow for the new owner.

Learning Exit Strategies

We'll be taking a look at some of the common exit strategies that property investors can use. Since each differs from the other, we'll take a look at how each one works. From there, you can decide on which exit strategy will work for you best.

Let's take a look at the following:

Fix and Flip

This is basically an exit strategy that is already implemented before you even buy a property. To explain this, you are purchasing a property (specifically a fixer-upper), repairing and rehabbing it, and then flipping it for a larger profit.

Since the property value has no place to go but up, you'll walk away with a nice tidy profit. You buy the property at below market value and sell at the purchase price plus repair costs. For example, if you buy the property at $100,000 and it costs you $75,000 to repair the property, then ideally you sell it at $175,000.

Buy and Hold

This is usually one of the most used strategies. The way this works is you purchase the property and hold on to it for as long as possible. When the property value appreciates and you have built up enough equity, that's when you can sell it for a higher profit if you so choose.

Selling it outright to a homeowner

If you have a single-family house or a townhome, then you have the option to sell it to a homeowner outright. This means the property will no longer be considered a rental property and will therefore become a private residence.

Before going down this route, be sure to make sure that the neighborhood that you're in has more homeowners than renters. If there are more renters than homeowners in the area, this kind of exit strategy will not work.

Selling it to an investor

So, it comes full circle. One investor selling his property to another. You know exactly what will happen here and why the buyer is purchasing it.

Make sure the property is in an area where more people are renting as opposed to home-owning. The demand for homeowners and rental profits are different depending on the area that you're in.

The 1031 Exchange

The 1031 Exchange is named after a part of the tax code (1031). The way the 1031 exchange works is where you swap one property with a 'like kind' property. If the exchange meets the 1031 requirements, there will be either no tax or limited tax that will be due around the time of the exchange.

In some situations, you may trade in a like-kind property and end up getting something in return that has far greater value. But don't count on that always being the case. Keep in mind that there is also a time slot in which the exchange must occur.

First, there is the 45-day rule. The sale of the property must occur within the first 45 days in order to qualify. You must designate the replacement property to the intermediary in writing with the correct address.

However, there is an additional rule known as the 180-day rule. If there is a deal, it must be closed within 180 days. This occurs in the event of a delayed exchange.

Wholesaling

A wholesale deal is when a real estate investor acts as a middleman between the buyer and the seller. However, it's you that is the seller. So therefore, you are not the middleman in this setting.

The seller will have a purchase price like normal. However, the buyer must plan on purchasing it at a price higher than the listing price. The wholesaler will get the difference.

For example, if a seller's listing price is $250,000 and a buyer gets it for $275,000 then the wholesaler gets $25,000.

Refinancing

Suppose you cannot sell to a homeowner nor an investor. What could possibly be the issue? The best solution would be to refinance the property.

Before you go down this road, make sure that your finances are in good shape. For example, make sure that your monthly rent is covering all expenses. Double check both your net operating income and your operating expenses.

After refinancing your property, try and sell the property again and see what happens.

Avoid These Mistakes

Your exit strategy may hit a snag if you make some of these mistakes. Before you sell your properties and ride off into the sunset, here are some things you need to be aware of so you can prevent making these mistakes:

Don't leave the place in bad shape

Simply put, you don't want to leave the property in worse shape than you found it. You worked hard enough for it to be a good rental property. Why let it go to waste?

Plus, you'll be screwing yourself out of a good deal if you allow the property to fall apart. Also, don't use it as an excuse to get out when you know full well that it is your responsibility to keep it clean and well-maintained.

Leave the new investor with bad tenants

If you are selling the property with current tenants still occupying your property, be sure that the tenants are aware of the changes and what may follow. Be sure that they are still willing to pay the rent and follow the lease agreements.

The last thing the new investor wants is to deal with an inherited tenant that will end up being a headache.

Take care of unexpected maintenance issues

Make sure that you perform one final inspection to see if there are any 'surprises' that need to be fixed. Because a need for repairs and maintenance may pop out of nowhere. Be sure to nip it in the bud and take care of it before the property changes hands.

Final Thoughts

Your exit strategy may take place years down the road. Or it may be a quick repair and flip. Either way, it's good to have one planned even before acquiring the property itself.

Consider your exit strategy options and choose which one will work for you best and why. And always avoid the mistakes listed above to ensure an orderly and proper transition of ownership between one investor or owner to the next.

Conclusion

There you have it. You have just learned the ins and outs of building your rental property empire. At this point, you have either followed some of the steps already outlined or have yet to get started. Either way, no time is better than now to begin your journey towards making money with real estate.

You now have a basic understanding of the process of acquiring properties. You understand how there are various ways to receive financing. And you also have a process where you can repeat the process over and over again if you want to.

Remember, building a rental property empire is never easy. You know that it will take a few people to help get you there. These people are your mentors, your advisors, your partners, and your friends in the business.

It's important that you get your finances in order before making the first step if needed. If you haven't already, that should be the first thing you do. Soon after that, see what options are now available for financing.

After you've made a preliminary decision, you can then look for properties using the strategies and tactics outlined in Chapter 5. You also now have the know-how to make a good offer so you can land the property of your dreams. You don't have to be a master wheeler and dealer to get a good deal on a property.

Once the keys to the property are in your hands, you'll want to make some decisions on how to fix up the place before you rent it to a potential tenant. The more repairs and renovations you put together, the more value you'll add to the property.

Fixing up the property may require some DIY and professional contractor work. But you'll want to double check to see what fits in your repair and renovation plans before spending money on it. After the place looks nice and brand new, you can then rent it out to your ideal tenant.

This is a process that will get repeated over and over again as many times as you please. It can be with single-family homes, apartment complexes, townhomes, and more. It's a process that can be a challenge with every property you acquire or an easy one.

As always, be sure to build your real estate network from the ground up. Plus, you want to maintain it as best as you can. Communicate regularly with people in your network and connect those who are in need.

If someone is looking for a home loan, direct them to the loan officers you know. If a fellow real estate investor is looking for a contractor that remodels kitchens, give them a name. Your network will help you become the 'it person' to go to whenever something real estate related needs to be addressed.

Your tenants are the lifeblood of your rental property business. Without tenants, you will lose more money than you make. And if you don't get along with your tenants, they won't put in a good word for you if someone is asking for a place to rent.

Be sure to be on good terms with your tenants and be willing to handle any conflicts or repair requests whenever it's needed. With happy tenants, they'll be more than happy to help you out in looking for newer tenants when they move out.

At the same time, if you have vacancies to fulfill, get the word out. Because these vacancies can fill themselves. It's up to you to find the right tenant based on the application criteria.

When looking through applications, you want to make sure that they meet your requirements. Do background checks and make sure that they are the person that will give you an easy time rather than a hard one. Because tenants can cause trouble, damage the property, or have ridiculous demands.

It is possible to build long-term wealth with your rental properties. And you can earn plenty of passive income. However, treat your rental properties like a business rather than a hobby.

You still need to handle some of the other tasks such as maintaining the property, keeping the tenants happy, and making sure that everything is in good working condition. The properties are still your focus even if you are making plenty of money.

If you want to make as much money as possible, find ways to increase your income while keeping expenses low. There are plenty of ways to go about doing this. Find the best way without financially pinching your tenants.

And if you're ready to wrap it all up, be sure to have a good exit strategy in mind. You may fix and flip, buy and hold, or exchange it for a like-kind property via the 1031. Either way, choose an appropriate exit strategy that works for you.

After all this work you've put in and the actionable steps you've taken, you're well on your way to making money with rental properties. It doesn't get more satisfying knowing that you are on the path to absolute financial freedom.

What you do with the extra money you make is up to you. But don't let money change you in the slightest. Those who do will get complacent and may not care about their properties, thus allowing them to fall apart and lose tenants in the process.

What's your greatest takeaway?

What are some great takeaways that you've learned from this book? Were there some things that you never knew about before reading this? What stuck out to you as most interesting?

We love to hear from you. Also, one more thing. We encourage you to keep this eBook as a reference guide.

Because if you are stuck on something, you can always refer to a specific chapter in the book. Don't let this be one of those books that you read once and be done with it. Oh, and we encourage you to share this book with someone who might be interested in rental properties as well.

Resources

4 Types of Real Estate and How to Profit from Each. (2021). The Balance. https://www.thebalance.com/real-estate-what-it-is-and-how-it-works-3305882

5 Popular Types of Rental Properties. (2021). Best Rent. http://www.bestrent.vn/5-popular-types-of-rental-properties/

15 Step Real Estate Due Diligence Checklist. (2021, March 16). Financial Wolves. https://financialwolves.com/real-estate-due-diligence-checklist/

1031 Exchange Rules: What You Need to Know. (2021). Investopedia. https://www.investopedia.com/financial-edge/0110/10-things-to-know-about-1031-exchanges.aspx

A. (2019a, January 30). *How To Prepare My Property For Rent*. Madeleine Hicks Real Estate Brisbane. https://madeleinehicks.com.au/how-to-prepare-my-property-for-rent/

A. (2021a, February 12). *Loan to Cost vs. Loan to Value - Definitions*. HM Capital. https://hardmoola.com/loan-to-cost-vs-loan-to-value/

Agent Image. (2019, October 31). *Real Estate Marketing Strategies to Boost Your Online Presence and Turn Leads to Conversions*. Best Real Estate Websites for Agents and Brokers. https://www.agentimage.com/blog/5-real-estate-marketing-strategies-to-boost-your-online-presence-and-turn-leads-to-conversions/

Aiello, J. (2019, October 28). *How to Prepare Your Unit for a New Tenant*. Apartment Management Resources | Zumper. https://www.zumper.com/manage/resources/how-to-prepare-your-unit-for-a-new-tenant/

Aiello, J. (2020a, February 13). *What To Do If Your Rental Property Needs Repair*. Apartment Management Resources | Zumper. https://www.zumper.com/manage/resources/what-to-do-if-your-rental-property-needs-repair/

Aiello, J. (2020b, February 13). *What To Do If Your Rental Property Needs Repair*. Apartment Management Resources | Zumper. https://www.zumper.com/manage/resources/what-to-do-if-your-rental-property-needs-repair/

B. (2020a, June 25). *20 Top Real Estate Investors Reveal Their Secrets for House Flipping and Wholesaling Success!* 7 Figure Flipping. https://7figureflipping.com/20-top-real-estate-investors-reveal-their-secrets-for-house-flipping-and-wholesaling-success/

Benson, A. (2020, October 26). *How to Make Money in Real Estate*. NerdWallet. https://www.nerdwallet.com/blog/investing/make-money-real-estate/

Brumer-Smith, L. (2020, February 10). *6 Ways to Earn More From Your Rental Property*. Millionacres. https://www.fool.com/millionacres/real-estate-investing/articles/6-ways-earn-more-your-rental-property/

Brumer-Smith, L. (2021, March 4). *Building a Cash Buyers List for Your Real Estate Investing Business*. Millionacres. https://www.fool.com/millionacres/real-estate-investing/building-a-cash-buyers-list-for-your-real-estate-investing-business/

Bryant, C. W. (2020, January 27). *How Foreclosures Work*. HowStuffWorks. https://money.howstuffworks.com/personal-finance/debt-management/foreclosure.htm

C. (2019b, August 8). *Top 5 Tips for Effective Communication in Real Estate - MyBayut*. A Blog about Homes, Trends, Tips & Life in the UAE | MyBayut. https://www.bayut.com/mybayut/tips-effective-communication-real-estate-clients/

Carson, C. (2016, December 21). *6 Reasons I Prefer Creative Financing to Bank Financing*. Coach Carson. https://www.coachcarson.com/6-reasons-i-prefer-creative-financing-to-bank-financing/

Chandler, D. (2018, October 3). *Multifamily homes: Make your house pay for itself*. Mortgage Rates, Mortgage News and Strategy : The Mortgage Reports. https://themortgagereports.com/27635/multifamily-homes-make-your-house-pay-for-itself

Chang, J. (2021, March 16). *How Much to Charge for Rent in 2020: A Landlord's Guide | BiggerPockets*. The BiggerPockets Blog | Real Estate Investing & Personal Finance Advice. https://www.biggerpockets.com/blog/how-much-to-charge-for-rent

Corporate Finance Institute. (2020, April 23). *Real Estate*. https://corporatefinanceinstitute.com/resources/careers/jobs/real-estate/

DIY Plumbing vs Hiring a Professional - BFP Bay Area. (2017, June 28). Benjamin Franklin Plumbing, Inc. https://bfplumbingbayarea.com/blog/diy-plumbing-vs-hiring-a-professional/

Do you have an accountability partner on your side? (2016, July 15). Inman. https://www.inman.com/2016/07/15/do-you-have-an-accountability-partner-on-your-side/

Esajian, J. D. (2021, February 26). *BRRRR Strategy.* FortuneBuilders. https://www.fortunebuilders.com/brrrr-strategy/

First-Time Home Buyer Checklist | Property Inspection & More. (2021). Mr. Handyman. https://www.mrhandyman.com/tips-ideas/checklists-resources/first-time-home-buyer-checklist/

Foy, N. (2020, April 16). *The Ultimate Guide to Financing Real Estate Investment Purchases.* Under 30 Wealth. https://under30wealth.com/the-ultimate-guide-to-financing-real-estate-investments/

Frankel, M. C. (2021, February 4). *How to Make Money in Real Estate.* Millionacres. https://www.fool.com/millionacres/real-estate-basics/investing-basics/how-to-make-money-in-real-estate/

G. (2019c, September 3). *How to Evaluate a Real Estate Investment.* Above the Canopy. https://www.abovethecanopy.us/how-to-evaluate-a-real-estate-investment/

G. (2019d, September 3). *How to Evaluate a Real Estate Investment.* Above the Canopy. https://www.abovethecanopy.us/how-to-evaluate-a-real-estate-investment/

Gerardo, P. (2019, September 17). *You want to fire your real estate agent. Can you do that?* Mortgage Rates, Mortgage News and Strategy : The Mortgage Reports. https://themortgagereports.com/37074/fire-your-real-estate-agent

Gerardo, P. (2021, March 2). *Avoid these 7 mistakes when making an offer on a house*. Mortgage Rates, Mortgage News and Strategy : The Mortgage Reports. https://themortgagereports.com/38667/avoid-these-7-mistakes-when-making-an-offer-on-a-house

Hall, B. (2021, March 16). *Is Renting to Family a Good Idea? Beware of the "Personal Use" Trap*. The BiggerPockets Blog | Real Estate Investing & Personal Finance Advice. https://www.biggerpockets.com/blog/renting-to-family

Hamed, E. (2018, March 11). *Buying a Rental Property Below Market Value*. Investment Property Tips | Mashvisor Real Estate Blog. https://www.mashvisor.com/blog/buying-a-rental-property-below-market-value/

How can I look for rental housing? (2021). Settlement. https://settlement.org/ontario/housing/rent-a-home/find-rental-housing/how-can-i-look-for-rental-housing/

How Much Money Do You Need To Invest In Real Estate? (2021). Investopedia. https://www.investopedia.com/financial-edge/0712/how-much-money-do-you-need-to-invest-in-real-estate.aspx

How the Fair Housing Act Prevents Discrimination. (2021). The Balance Small Business. https://www.thebalancesmb.com/what-is-the-federal-fair-housing-act-2125014

How To Advertise Your Rental Property: Step-By-Step Guide. (2020, October 19). RentPrep. https://rentprep.com/tenant-screening/advertise-rental-property/

How to Build And Maintain Cash Reserves For Your Rental Property. (2021). Real Life Planning. https://reallifeplanning.com/blog/how-to-build-and-maintain-cash-reserves-for-your-rental-property

How to create the right team of commercial real estate advisors. (2020, September 12). BDC.Ca. https://www.bdc.ca/en/articles-tools/money-finance/buy-lease-commercial-real-estate/how-get-right-team-commercial-real-estate-advisors

How to Hire a Handyman for Rental Property. (2018a, December 21). Rental Resources | RentPost. https://rentpost.com/resources/article/hire-a-handyman-for-rental-property/

How to Hire a Handyman for Rental Property. (2018b, December 21). Rental Resources | RentPost. https://rentpost.com/resources/article/hire-a-handyman-for-rental-property/

How To Use Rental Income To Build Long-Term Wealth. (2018, September 15). VerraTerra. https://www.verraterra.com/how-to-use-rental-income-to-build-long-term-wealth/

Huber, J. (2021, February 9). *Should I Repair or Replace My Roof?* Huber & Associates. https://www.huberroofing.com/blog/2018/4/13/should-i-repair-or-replace-my-roof

Income, P. (2020, May 12). *Use Leverage to Purchase Properties*. Passive Income M.D. https://passiveincomemd.com/use-leverage-to-purchase-properties/

Investing in Rental Properties for Beginners. (2021). Realty Mogul. https://www.realtymogul.com/knowledge-center/article/investing-rental-properties-beginners

Jan, O. A. (2019, June 10). *Real Estate Valuation.* XPLAIND.Com. https://xplaind.com/726953/real-estate-valuation

K. (2020b, June 25). *How Rental Property Financing Gives You Investment Leverage.* HomeUnion. https://www.homeunion.com/how-financing-a-rental-property-gives-you-leverage-in-real-estate-investments/

K. (2020c, June 25). *How Rental Property Financing Gives You Investment Leverage.* HomeUnion. https://www.homeunion.com/how-financing-a-rental-property-gives-you-leverage-in-real-estate-investments/

Landlord and renters insurance. (2021). Understand Insurance. https://understandinsurance.com.au/types-of-insurance/landlord-and-renters-insurance

Landlord Characteristics and Responsibilities. (2021). The Balance Small Business. https://www.thebalancesmb.com/what-is-a-landlord-duties-and-responsibilities-2125057

Lee, M. (2020, November 11). *DIY Flooring: Should I Install My Flooring Myself or Hire a Professional? | BuildDirect® Blog.* BuildDirect Blog: Life at Home. https://www.builddirect.com/blog/diy-flooring-should-i-install-my-flooring-myself-or-hire-a-professional/

Leusin, Y. (2019, March 2). *Owning Rental Properties: 4 Challenges and Their Solutions.* Investment Property Tips | Mashvisor Real Estate Blog. https://www.mashvisor.com/blog/owning-rental-properties-challenges-solutions/

Lofgren, L. (2021, March 1). *The Best Property Management Software – 2021 Review.* QuickSprout. https://www.quicksprout.com/best-property-management-software/

Lucas, T. (2018, November 30). *What happens when my real estate offer is accepted? [Video]*. Mortgage Rates, Mortgage News and Strategy : The Mortgage Reports. https://themortgagereports.com/45667/what-happens-when-my-real-estate-offer-is-accepted

Luxon, B. (2020a, November 4). *Key Figures For Evaluating An Investment Property*. Landlord Studio. https://www.landlordstudio.com/blog/key-figures-for-evaluating-an-investment-property/

Luxon, B. (2020b, November 4). *The Landlords Guide To Successful House Hacking*. Landlord Studio. https://www.landlordstudio.com/blog/the-landlords-guide-to-successful-house-hacking/

Marrs, M. (2020, June 24). *35 Easy & Effective Real Estate Marketing Ideas*. WordStream. https://www.wordstream.com/blog/ws/2015/04/16/real-estate-marketing

Martin, E. J. (2018, October 19). *How do I finalize my offer to buy a home?* Mortgage Rates, Mortgage News and Strategy : The Mortgage Reports. https://themortgagereports.com/39613/how-do-i-finalize-my-offer-to-buy-a-home

Martin, E. J. (2019, September 17). *What is "recording" when closing on a home purchase?* Mortgage Rates, Mortgage News and Strategy : The Mortgage Reports. https://themortgagereports.com/37838/closing-real-estate-recording-fees

Martin, E. J. (2020, September 3). *Understanding a real estate contract or purchase agreement*. Mortgage Rates, Mortgage News and Strategy : The Mortgage Reports. https://themortgagereports.com/37569/understanding-a-real-estate-contract-or-purchase-agreement

Maughan, J. (2018, January 17). *How to Handle Inherited Tenants*. RentPrep. https://rentprep.com/facebook/how-to-handle-inherited-tenants/

Merrill, T. (2020, November 13). *A Beginner's Guide To Starting A Real Estate Business*. FortuneBuilders. https://www.fortunebuilders.com/a-beginners-guide-to-starting-a-real-estate-business/

Miller, M. (2018, June 13). *Is It Time to Hire Employees for Your Real Estate Investment Business?* 5 Arch. https://5archfunding.com/blog/is-it-time-to-hire-employees-for-your-real-estate-investment-business/

Miller, P. (2019, September 17). *Home closing: What you need to read, what you can skim*. Mortgage Rates, Mortgage News and Strategy : The Mortgage Reports. https://themortgagereports.com/39671/home-closing-what-you-need-to-read-what-you-can-skim

Mizes, B. (2020, April 24). *How to Overcome the 5 Challenges of Owning Rental Property*. National Landlord Association (NLA). https://www.nationallandlordassociation.org/how-to-overcome-the-5-challenges-of-owning-rental-property/

Moran, G. (2015, November 19). *8 costs to consider when buying a rental property*. Hsh.Com. https://www.hsh.com/finance/real-estate/costs-to-consider-when-buying-rental-property.html

N. (2021b, March 19). *Bank loans*. Nav. https://www.nav.com/business-financing-options/bank-loans/

Patel, K. (2018, February 5). *5 Key Numbers to Know for Any Kind of Real Estate Investment*. Copyright (c)2004-2021 BiggerPockets, LLC.

https://www.biggerpockets.com/member-blogs/10401/70423-5-key-numbers-to-know-for-any-kind-of-real-estate-investment

R., A. (2020, August 20). *Top 5 Tenant Communication Tips for Landlords*. DialMyCalls. https://www.dialmycalls.com/blog/top-5-tenant-communication-tips-landlords

Ragan, B. (2021, February 23). *Should I Repair My Roof or Replace It?* Bill Ragan Roofing. https://www.billraganroofing.com/blog/should-i-repair-my-roof-or-replace-it

Real Estate Definition. (2021). Investopedia. https://www.investopedia.com/terms/r/realestate.asp

Real Estate Taxes 101: Rental Property Tax Deductions. (2020, September 9). HomeUnion. https://www.homeunion.com/how-to-claim-real-estate-taxes-and-deductions/

Rental Property Renovations to Attract Tenants. (2021). Dumpsters. https://www.dumpsters.com/blog/renovating-a-rental-property

Rentometer: How to Increase Storage Options in Small Rental Properties. (2021). Rentometer. https://www.rentometer.com/articles/how-to-increase-storage-options-in-small-rental-properties

Richey Property Management, LLC. (2021). Richey Property Management. https://www.richeypm.com/rental-application-process

Roeling, T. (2021, March 16). *Tenant Abandonment Guide for Landlords*. TurboTenant. https://www.turbotenant.com/blog/tenant-abandonment-guide/

Roos, L. A. O. D. (2021, February 10). *How Buying a House Works*. HowStuffWorks. https://home.howstuffworks.com/real-estate/buying-home/house-buying.htm

Santarelli, M. (2021, March 11). *How To Make Money In Real Estate And Get Rich In 2021?* Norada Real Estate Investments. https://www.noradarealestate.com/blog/how-to-make-money-in-real-estate/

Scott, J. (2021, March 29). *Real Estate Investment Analysis: Step-by-Step Guide*. The BiggerPockets Blog | Real Estate Investing & Personal Finance Advice. https://www.biggerpockets.com/blog/real-estate-investment-analysis

Screening to Get the Best Tenants for Your Rental Property | Mynd Management. (2021). MYND Management. https://www.mynd.co/knowledge-center/screening-to-get-the-best-tenants

Should You Be Investing in Real Estate? (2021). The Balance. https://www.thebalance.com/real-estate-investing-101-357985

Siddons, S. (2021, February 12). *How Real Estate Investment Clubs Work*. HowStuffWorks. https://home.howstuffworks.com/real-estate/buying-home/real-estate-investment-clubs.htm

Six Types of Problem Tenants – and How to Deal With Them. (2020, June 9). Propertyware. https://www.propertyware.com/blog/six-types-of-problem-tenants-and-how-to-deal-with-them/

Solutions, R. (2020, April 22). *How to Make an Offer on a House*. Daveramsey.Com. https://www.daveramsey.com/blog/how-to-make-an-offer

Solutions, R. (2021, February 24). *How to Find a Real Estate Agent*. Daveramsey.Com. https://www.daveramsey.com/blog/how-to-find-a-real-estate-agent

Syrios, A. (2021, March 16). *13 Ways To Increase Rent & Value To Your Rental Property | Blog*. The BiggerPockets Blog | Real Estate Investing & Personal Finance Advice. https://www.biggerpockets.com/blog/13-ways-increase-rent-add-rental-property

T. (2013, September 26). *10 Ways for Landlords to Avoid Tenant Legal Claims*. Anco. https://www.anco.com/blog/10-ways-landlords-avoid-tenant-legal-claims/

T. (2021c, January 28). *Landlord Tax Tips: Hiring Family Members is a Win-Win*. AAOA. https://www.american-apartment-owners-association.org/property-management/latest-news/landlord-tax-tips-hiring-family-members-is-a-win-win/

Tenant Vacating Checklist for Landlords. (2021). The Balance Small Business. https://www.thebalancesmb.com/sample-move-out-checklist-for-landlords-and-tenants-2125000

The 5 Best Real Estate Marketing Tools to Use in 2019. (2021). EZ Texting. https://www.eztexting.com/blog/5-best-real-estate-marketing-tools-use-2019

The Big List of Real Estate Scams, Fraud, and Misleading Tactics. (2021). Kris Lindahl. https://www.krislindahl.com/real-estate-scams-fraud-and-misleading-tactics.php

The dos and don'ts of landscaping on rental properties. (2021, March 8). Total Landscape Care. https://www.totallandscapecare.com/business/article/15042222/the-dos-and-donts-of-landscaping-on-rental-properties

The Homeowner's Guide to Interior Demolition. (2021). Hometown Demolition. https://www.hometowndemolitioncontractors.com/blog/homeowners-guide-to-interior-demolition

Time Management Tips for Busy Property Managers. (2021). Renters Warehouse. https://renterswarehouse.com/education/time-management-tips-busy-property-managers

Treger, T. (2020, February 24). *Real Estate Due Diligence: A Simple Guide for Investment Properties*. Financial Poise. https://www.financialpoise.com/real-estate-due-diligence/

Turner, B. (2021, March 16). *The 11 Most Common Questions Asked by Tenants—Answered*. The BiggerPockets Blog | Real Estate Investing & Personal Finance Advice. https://www.biggerpockets.com/blog/11-common-questions-asked-tenants-answered

Undecided About DIYing or Hiring a Pro? This Chart Tells All. (2021). The Spruce. https://www.thespruce.com/remodel-myself-or-hire-pro-1822421

Warden, P. (2019a, March 8). *Open houses: What's their role in the home-buying process?* Mortgage Rates, Mortgage News and Strategy : The Mortgage Reports. https://themortgagereports.com/37900/open-houses-whats-their-role-in-the-home-buying-process

Warden, P. (2019b, September 17). *How to get out of a real estate contract*. Mortgage Rates, Mortgage News and Strategy : The Mortgage Reports. https://themortgagereports.com/37472/can-you-back-out-of-an-offer-to-buy-a-home

Weber, J. L. (2020, February 10). *How to Make a Construction Schedule*. ProjectManager.Com. https://www.projectmanager.com/blog/make-a-construction-schedule

Welles, H. (2019, August 22). *5 Ways to Communicate Better with Challenging Tenants*. Rental Housing Journal. https://rentalhousingjournal.com/5-ways-to-communicate-better-with-challenging-tenants/

What to Consider When Self-Managing Your Rental Property. (2021). Wilmington For Rent. https://www.wilmingtonforrent.com/blog/what-to-consider-when-self-managing-your-rental-property

White, S. M. (2018, June 12). *What to Do If a Tenant Dies in Your Rental Property*. RentPrep. https://rentprep.com/property-management/tenant-dies-your-rental-property/

Why Reserve Funds Are Important When Managing A Property. (2021). Lofty Real Estate. https://www.loftyrealestate.com/property-management/why-reserve-funds-are-important-when-managing-a-property/

Wilson, C. (2019, April 1). *Real Estate Negotiation Tips for Home Buyers and Sellers*. Homesnap. https://blog.homesnap.com/real-estate-negotiation-tips-for-home-buyers-and-sellers/

Building Your Real Estate & Rental Property Empire: 23+ Beginners Property Investing Strategies & Tips For Creating Wealth & Passive Income, Managing Tenants, Flipping Houses, Air BnB& More

By Unlimited Potential Publications

Table of Contents

Introduction

First off, congratulations on getting this book in your hands. There's a reason why you now have a copy of this. You have interest in investing in rental properties.

It's true that there are plenty of streams of income out there. And real estate investing is perhaps one of the best of the bunch. However, we're not talking about investing in large parcels of land or skyscrapers.

Our focus for this book are rental properties. Why this kind of property in particular? Well, think about it for a moment.

Imagine having passive income month after month. Enough to do what you want at any given time. You can invest in a new business venture, spend it on something you please, or even invest in more properties and add more cash to your bank account.

Not only that, investing in rental properties is perhaps one of the best ways to get into real estate investing itself. You'll be able to get a ground floor level look at how real estate actually works. From the buying process to fulfilling the vacancies and everything in between, you will learn exactly how to acquire rental properties that you can own and have income every month via rent payments from your tenants.

What you will learn in this book

You're going to learn a lot of valuable information. Not only will you absorb it, but you will apply what you've learned as well. Consider this book as your instruction manual to a successful career in rental property investing.

We will show you how to take certain action steps including how to form a team of trusted people that will help you become successful. And we'll also show you how to acquire your first rental property (and multiple properties as well, if you're up for it). You'll also learn a great way to acquire property using a proven system that can give you the best return on investment yet.

Not only that, you will also learn some of the ins and outs of real estate. You will learn some of the basic terminology and then some. You will also understand how financing properties work. And you will even learn how to build a robust network that consists of real estate agents, property managers, contractors, attorneys, and more.

You will also find out which courses of action are better for you. For example, are you planning on managing the property yourself or hiring a property manager to oversee it for you? Also, what kind of tenants will you want living on your properties?

This may sound like a lot of overwhelming stuff. But rest assured, learning how to invest in rental properties while making money in the process is fun to do. Sure, there are some things that you need to do that will require time, money, and effort.

But in the end, it will be worth it.

Overview of what you'll learn in this book

Cutting to the chase, here's what each chapter will cover:

Chapter 1: You will learn about the perks and joys of investing in rental property. You'll learn about how you can enjoy being an investor in such properties like single-family homes and apartment buildings among others.

Chapter 2: This chapter will show you that there are plenty of options in terms of rental properties. Whether it's residential or commercial properties, you'd be surprised what kind of properties are available for you to buy and rent out.

Chapter 3: Building your rental property empire won't take a one-man show. You're going to need to form a team of people that you can trust so you can get the ball rolling. This is an important chapter that should not be skipped.

Chapter 4: This chapter will go over the risks of investing in rental properties. Where there is reward in investing, there are a set of risks as well. If you are willing to take the risks, you can move farther along in the book.

Chapter 5: Knowing what a good rental property is takes time. And you'll soon come across one. In this chapter, you'll learn how to do some analysis and determine whether or not the properties you want will actually yield a return on investment.

Chapter 6: Once you have the know-how to analyze and run the numbers, then you can find the properties that are worth investing in. Using online and offline tools, you'll be able to find your first rental property in no time.

Chapter 7: This chapter reminds you that when it comes to finding that rental property that you want to invest in, there is always analysis that needs to be done. Learn how to properly run the numbers so you can be able to confirm that the property you want is the right one.

Chapter 8: Financing is another hurdle that you want to jump over. There are plenty of options on how you want to finance the property. This chapter will show you everything you need to know about the kind of loans that exist and how you can be guaranteed approval.

Chapter 9: This chapter will cover a proven system known as BRRRR. Once you learn the power of this system and how it can work to your advantage, it can become your go-to method for acquiring properties and getting an excellent return on investment.

Chapter 10: Your first rental property may not be in your local area. It might be hundreds of miles away or in the next state over. Either way, this chapter will show you how to expand your search area so you can find the rental property of your dreams.

Chapter 11: Are you going to manage the property yourself or have a property manager do it for you. This chapter will weigh both options so you can make the best decision.

Chapter 12: The agreement is the most important piece of paperwork for both you and the tenant. Learn what needs to be included in a rental or lease agreement and make sure that both you and your tenant come out in a win-win situation once the agreement is set in stone.

Chapter 13: Finding tenants can be a challenge. Finding the right kind of tenants can be an even greater challenge. Learn how you can screen for these tenants and put together a system that will allow you to get the right people to move into your properties while avoiding all those other bad apples.

Chapter 14: It is your responsibility to perform tasks before, during, and after a property is rented out. You'll learn how to perform walkthroughs and inspections. Also, you'll find out what you are responsible for as a property manager and what the tenant is responsible for in terms of maintenance and repairs.

Chapter 15: If you're thinking about getting out of the rental property game altogether or just building your portfolio, it's important to have an exit strategy. We'll cover four of the best exit strategies that are at your disposal.

Before we move on

A few things to go over before we move on to the first chapter. One, this isn't one of those 'get rich quick' schemes. Building your wealth with rental properties will take time, money, and effort. If you want some 'get rich quick' thing, then you're wasting your time reading this book.

Second, understand that building your rental property empire will not take one person to do it all. There are plenty of things that you need to do. But with the help of the right kind of people, you'll be in good shape (and focus on the priorities of the business).
And finally, be sure to read through this book while taking notes at the same time. There's a lot of valuable information here that just cannot be glossed over. You'll want to apply everything you've learned and jotted down in your notes.

There is no easy path to building your rental property empire. But with hard work and dedication, the rewards are oh so sweet to have. Now, let's get moving and start with Chapter 1.

Chapter 1: The Perks and Joy of Investing in Rental Property

To lead off, we're going to be talking about the perks about investing in rental properties. There is no better way to generate monthly income than someone renting your property whether it's housing or even commercial rental properties (if you want to go down that route). However, it's always good to have people who are reliable tenants that pay on time.

In this chapter, we'll talk about the perks and joys that come with investing in rental property. As the old saying goes, it's better to look before you leap. In other words, you have to know what you're getting into.

So as a word of caution, you want to read this book in its entirety before considering the idea of purchasing your first rental property. Sure, the benefits of having them are awesome. But you need to come in well-informed and have a good understanding of how it all works.

This chapter will discuss what rental property Is and whether or not it can actually get you the passive income you want. We'll also talk about why it shouldn't be just a hobby and more of a business thing. We'll talk about the top four benefits along with the principles that you'll need to follow in order to maximize success.

Enough talk. We know why you're here. And we're excited that you're on board with the possibility of acquiring new property.

Let's get going:

What is Rental Property Investment?

Rental property investment is simply defined as property that is designed to get you a return on investment. Most of the time, that return on investment (ROI) will come in the form of rental income. However, another way to get a positive ROI is through the future resale of property.

However, you can get a good ROI that is generated through both means. You could have plenty of tenants sending you monthly rent every month. And when the time comes to sell, you could have more money in your pocket due to the increase in property value.

In plain English, this kind of thing is known as 'flipping'. In real estate, 'flipping' can be described as acquiring property that is sold at a low price. The reason why it may be seeling so low may be due to the low value of property and even the building being in poor condition.

Let's say that you purchase a piece of property that is a run-down and abandoned motel. You have plans on turning it into an apartment complex specifically for short-term stays (or corporate housing). You put in a good amount of money to renovate the abandoned motel and it takes you almost six months to a year to put it all together.

Now, let's say you have tenants who are professionals and executives who are in your area temporarily on business. You generate income by way of short-term leases and rent. Over time, the property value increases. After five years, you decide to sell it to another property owner who is interested in keeping the thing going.

You run off like a bandit with what might be 10 times the original investment (or a 10x ROI). That's flipping at work. And it's not just something you see on those house flipping TV shows.

Flipping will usually happen when you want to purchase property, renovate it, and sell it for more after a short period of time. Either way, the goal is getting a good return on investment. So whatever your goals are for investing in rental properties are, be sure to make a note of them.
Investment property can also be used for the purpose of holding on to it for future appreciation. Land is one of those types of property that you can invest in and it may increase in value over time for some reason or another.

What to know about investment properties

Investment properties are not used for the purpose of primary residences. These properties are designed to generate some kind of income. This income can come in the form of rents, royalties, dividends, and more.

If you intend to invest in property in the not so distant future, it's better to look before you leap (or as they say in the biz, do your due diligence). In other words, you want to do your due diligence on how to determine what may be considered the best and most profitable use of the property itself.

Will it be for single-family housing? Apartments? There are plenty of options to consider as you go.

In short, you want to figure out what would be the highest and best use of said property. Also, you want to keep in mind of the kind of property that you want to invest in. One thing to pay attention to is how the property is zoned.
If it's zoned for residential use, then your best bet is utilizing it for the purpose of living spaces such as apartments or single-family housing. Obviously, if it's zoned for commercial use, then it would be better fit for a place of business. But what if the property is zoned for both residential and commercial use?

This is where things get interesting. But it's important for you to weigh the pros and cons. What will give you the best return on investment going forward?

Once you are able to determine which approach will give you the best ROI going forward, that's when you'll use the property in that way. So if building an apartment complex for student housing yields the best ROI since it's close to a college campus, then that's when you can take the ball and run with it.

There are three types of investment properties that we'll be focusing on: residential vs commercial vs mixed-use. We'll be taking a look at a comparison between the three types so you'll know the difference between them. It will also give you a basic understanding of rental properties should you invest in more of them later on down the line.

Let's take a look at the following definitions:

Residential

Residential properties are rental homes. The intent is renting out these properties for those looking for a place to live, but do not want to purchase a home of their own. You rent out a property and charge a monthly rent to tenants. These properties come in the form of single-family homes, apartments, townhomes, condos, and other residential structures such as student housing.

Commercial

Simply put, commercial properties are for places of business. While most commercial properties are not aimed to provide some kind of residential use, there are commercially owned apartment buildings. But for the most part, commercial properties are more apt to house retail businesses or the like.

Compared to residential properties, maintaining and improving these types of properties will cost more. However, because of the rent you may collect on the property on a regular basis, the impact doesn't seem all that bad. Because the leases for commercial properties will yield higher rent rates, the maintenance and improvement costs are usually off-set.

Mixed-Use

A mixed property is defined as a property that is designed for both residential and commercial use. One such example of this is the following: let's say that you own a convenience store on the lower level. On the upper level, there is a one bedroom apartment that is also part of the property.

You can collect rent for both the business and the residential property itself. Typically, it's common for a business owner to own the property in its entirety. So for you to generate income from a small business while generating rent from a tenant who lives in the apartment above you might just be a win-win.

Generate Income Passively, How True Is That?

Do rental properties generate passive income? The short answer is yes. So long as you have a positive cash flow coming from reliable tenants that pay on time, you will generate passive income from your rental properties.

What exactly is passive income? Passive income is earnings that are received from a rental property. However, you can earn it by way of a limited partnership or if you are part of an enterprise and have no active role in it.

Passive income is taxable (as it is with active income). The only difference is how the IRS handles it. Passive income is one of three main categories of income (the other two being active and portfolio). And sure enough, rental properties are one of the main examples of generating such income in the first place.

To avoid any confusion, if you decide to own land and lease it out, the income you receive from it is not considered passive. It may be more apt to quality under active income (assuming you maybe owning more land in the future). However, a landowner can benefit from the loss rules that relate to passive income if there is a net loss from the previous tax year.

Understanding cash flow with rental properties

What is cash flow? This can be defined simply by two words: income and expenses. You take the income, minus the expenses and that's your cash flow.

The goal here is to net as much positive cash flow as possible. Aside from the income and expenses, you may be setting some money aside for the purpose of renovations or the like. But if you are someone who is a buy-and-hold kind of property owner, cash flow is the best way to determine your passive income.

Why should you have positive cash flow?

Stating the obvious, cash flow is what you want. There is no sense in holding onto property that is going to lead you to losing money. So what are the reasons why you need it?

Let's take a look at a few reasons:

- **Cash flow equals opportunity:** One great example of where cash flow creates opportunity is the ability to own more rental properties. The more you own, the greater the cash flow. Sounds simple enough, right?

- **Cash flow provides a safety net:** When you have positive cash flow, it helps to have a large enough reserve for those just in case moments. And we're not just talking about repairs that may be needed. We're talking about the 'just in case' moments in your personal life like medical expenses, car repairs, and the like).

- **Cash flow gives you freedom:** Think about it. When you have cash flow of your own, it's way better than working paycheck to paycheck. Not to mention, you won't be tied down by a schedule that has you working odd hours of the day. You spend time with family, friends, and you have so much time to yourself. However, the key is to balance out that time between focusing on the properties (if needed) with your personal life. 'Work' and life doesn't have to have some imbalance.

Cash flow is as follows: [Gross rental income] - [expenses and cash reserves]

So let's put this formula into action, shall we. In this example, let's say you own rental property that generates a monthly income of $1,500. Now, let's lay out the operating expenses for the month:

Operating expenses:

- **Property tax:** $200

- **Insurance:** $30

- **Mortgage:** $300

- **Property management:** $70

- **Vacancy reserves:** $25

- **Repair reserves:** $100

Total monthly expenses: $725

Cash flow: $1500 - $725 = $775

So in this example, your cash flow is $775. Not bad, right? However, let's take a look at some of the expenses up close such as the property management and reserves for vacancies and repairs.

For property management, you may want to set aside a percentage of the rental income for the expenses revolving around managing the property (such as mowing the lawn, plowing the snow in the winter, and so on). Also, set aside an amount of money that you will need to keep handy in case there are vacancies. Lastly, set a percentage of money that is needed monthly in case of repairs that need to be made as soon as possible.

What will hurt your cash flow?

There are a few factors that can play a negative role in your cash flow. It's important to know what these are so you can be able to reduce as much of the damage as possible. The following are the things you want to watch out for when tending to your cash flow:

- **Repair and maintenance expenses:** Yes, a necessary evil. Things break or deteriorate over time. As a property owner, you must be aware that these things will happen at any given time. So it would make sense to set off some money to the side each month that will cover these repairs and maintenance fees. Try not to make it too small for a percentage to the point where it can eat into your cash flow completely.

- **Tenant turnover rate:** The turnover rate for tenants will depend on various factors. The property may be falling apart or something that makes the tenant feel uncomfortable. For this reason, turnover rates can greatly reduce cash flow. Not to mention, there may be tenants who will leave without telling the property owner about what needs to be repaired. And that alone can really take a hit on your cash flow. Because of this, property managers and owners will often enact a 'new lease fee' for the new tenant to cover such costs.

- **Tenants who don't pay:** There will be times when a tenant will miss a rent payment. This could be due to financial hardship on their part. However, there may be tenants who don't even bother paying at all. If a tenant doesn't pay in full, it's detrimental to cash flow. However, those who don't pay at all means no cash flow. This means you'll have to pay extra to cover all the other expenses that you are already paying from income to begin with.

- **Property taxes and insurance:** Like repair and maintenance expenses, this is something that is a necessary evil. This is also one expense to watch closely. Your municipality or state may change the tax policy for some reason or another. Your property tax could go up or go down. In case of the former, this can hurt your cash flow. Insurance expenses can also increase at the discretion of the insurer.

- **Vacancies:** Vacancies = no cash flow. Simple as that. So it would make sense for property owners to set aside some kind of percentage of income to cover any expenses should vacancies exist. Consider it an additional insurance policy of sorts. People leaving is all part of the business. So the sooner you can fill the vacancy, the better.

How to maintain a positive cash flow

Now that you know some of the factors that can hurt cash flow, let's take a look how you can maintain it and keep it above water. These are some approaches that you should consider:

- **Increasing the rent:** Is increasing the rent a smart move? That depends. It may hurt existing tenants if you raise the rent (and can lead to them vacating). However, you can increase the rent so long as the spaces are vacant. If you want to set a rate that will be enough to generate positive cash flow, consider purchasing property that is underperforming (i.e -- if the rents are lower than the market average).

  A great way to increase the rent is by doing things that can increase the property's overall value. This includes but not limited to adding more amenities like a laundry center, air conditioning in all spaces, and more. Also, improving the property both inside and out will also help with increasing value.

- **Bring in long-term tenants:** One of the ways to ensure a positive cash flow is by having tenants stay on for the long term. Long term leases are defined as leases that last a year or more. However, you want to do your part to keep them happy and comfortable for the most part. The more you do that, the longer they will stay. One way to go about doing this is making sure that all repair needs are fulfilled in the quickest and most professional way possible. One more thing, resist the urge to increase the rent once the lease expires. It's nice to have more money in your pocket, but it's wise not to be greedy as well.

- **Consider preventative maintenance:** It's good to keep ahead of the curve when it comes to the common issues that can happen on your property. For example, take a look at your property for certain safety risks. What if there is a tree that is dangerously close to the property? A tree can fall onto a building during a storm and cause damage (not to mention any serious injuries in the process). Also, take care of things like gutters and HVAC units before they will be used frequently. Yes, there will be expenses for all of this. But better to spend now and prevent disaster than wait until it's too late (which by the way is even more costly).

- **File a property tax appeal:** As mentioned before, your municipality or state might raise property taxes. Most of the time, those increases will happen long before you even consider raising the rent. The government works fast and may usually tell no one about the increases until after the fact (unless you're keeping a close eye on things). You can appeal the property tax hike if you feel the increase itself was an unjustified move on their part.

- **Refinance the property:** This is something to consider from time to time. Conclust with the lender you are working with and see what the interests rates are for your mortgage. If they have reduced since acquiring the property, that's a great time to consider refinancing and lowering the mortgage payments. If you are successful, you increase your cash flow in the process. Win-win. But you have to double check the numbers before you make the move.

Be aware of the 1% rule

If you need to know whether or not a property will generate a positive cash flow, consider using what is known as the '1% rule'. How does this work? Let's take a look at an example:
Let's say you buy property that is priced at $150,000. The rent should be roughly $1500 a month for cash flow. As such, one percent of $150,000 is $1,500.

So, does this mean 'green light' and go? Not so fast. There are other factors and expenses that you'll need to consider.

Specifically, you'll want to pay close attention to the cost of the mortgage, property taxes, insurance, HOA dues (if such apply), and so on. Of course, you'll need to take into account what you need to set off to the side for reserves that are based on repairs and maintenance and in case there are vacancies.

One other thing to pay attention to is the cash flow per unit. Before going any further, it's important to note that finding properties that generate positive cash flow is no easy task. Even when the market is booming, it takes time and research to find the right property to settle with.

But don't get discouraged. You'll find a piece of property that might generate cash flow and is hidden in plain sight from the other investors. In a market that isn't so hot, you will have an easier time finding a property that gives you positive cash flow.

However, the problem with acquiring properties in a 'cool market' will equal rental rates that may not be high enough to move your financial needle in the right direction. The reasons why are two things: one, there is the property value itself and the rental rates that are considered average in that location.

Not Just A Hobby

When it comes to acquiring and maintaining rental properties, some people will say it's not a fun thing to do. Others consider acquiring rental properties for generating passive income as a hobby (and get paid in the process). However, you'll want to adopt a different mindset in regards to acquiring properties.

It shouldn't really be like a hobby per se. It should be treated like a business. But still, it should be fun to do. What's not so fun about making your own money when you don't have to answer to a boss or have to work hours that you don't want to work?

So why not treat it like a hobby? Well, here are some things to consider when making the distinction between that and a business:

- Hobbies are personal. Business is professional. Repeat those two sentences over a few times. That should be one of the many mantras you might adopt in your lifetime. In business, you want to be fair and professional with your tenants. You want to keep them happy and listen to whatever suggestions or issues they may have.

- When treating it like a hobby, you become lax. So if a tenant is frequently late on payments, you give them more chances than they should. That alone can cause a lot of recoil to the point where it hurts your cash flow. Not good.

- You want to keep boundaries in place. These are boundaries that your tenants must honor. You don't want to be lax on rental payments and then turn around and put your foot down. That will cause your tenants to drive you crazy. Because of this, property managers tend to get burnt out because of the added stress that piles on.

- Treating it like a business allows you to say 'no' when you need to. You can deny a tenant based on their credit history. You can deny them based on their history as a tenant. However, don't say 'no' to them just because you can. You'll need to have a policy in place that will allow you to say 'no' for that reason.

With investment properties, you should treat it like a business. Set the boundaries and the guidelines that will help your cash flow rather than hurt it. Yes, it's fun and fulfilling to have your own business and have your own cash flow.

However, there's a balance between having fun and being professional. And it can be done without consuming too much of your time.

What if you want real estate to be a hobby?

So what if you want it to be more of a hobby rather than a business? For one, you'll want to be part of a group. More importantly, you want to be part of a group of investors that trust each other to make the right decisions and choices.

The risks of investing are smaller when it's just you and a few others in one group (as opposed to going at it solo). Someone else can handle the day-to-day operations if you choose not to do it. However, it would be incumbent upon you to relay any information and feedback from your tenants to the group if and when such a thing occurs.

Remember, you can still earn passive income even if you treat property rentals as a hobby. However, you'll still need to incorporate some solid business practices since you have partial ownership and income as part of being a group of investors. Even better, it won't be a strain on your professional and personal life.

One great way to make real estate a hobby is investing in turnkey properties. With turnkey properties, the risk of losing your investment is out of the picture and in its place is guaranteed monthly income.

Hobby or business? What should you really do?

The ball is in your court at this point. However, we can make a couple of suggestions. Rest assured, we want you to come to the conclusion that regardless if you treat real estate like a business or hobby, it still can be fun and fulfilling.

Sure, there are some downsides to this. But they are necessary evils and that's just the way things go. If you can handle the day-to-day things of managing a property, go for it.

But you'll want to build a team of people that you can trust. This includes someone who handles your legal issues, a reliable contractor that can do property management, someone who inspects the property regularly, and so on. You don't need to fill all these positions at the outset (especially when acquiring your first property).
But just know that when it comes to managing multiple properties, you'll need to work with the right kind of people in order to keep everything in line. You don't need to do everything all at once when it comes to managing your property. And you surely don't want it to be a time suck either.

While you're at it, consider connecting with your local real estate groups before acquiring property. They will be happy to help you with whatever you need before you even acquire your first piece of property. Not only will this help reduce the risk of experiencing a lot of frustrations and headaches down the road, but you'll be pacing yourself and taking your time rather than rush into something.

Top 4 Benefits You'll Get In Rental Property Investment

So what kind of benefits will you get when you invest in rental property? That's what we'll be taking a look at. Not only will you be able to enjoy financial freedom of your own, these benefits are basically just the layer on the 'awesome cake'.

Let's waste no time and jump right into what else you can get out of the whole thing:

Better asset stability

When it comes to asset stability, real estate has the best. Unlike stocks, which are volatile and can change in terms of stability hour by hour and day by day, your real estate investments are pretty much insulated from all of that.

Not to mention, you get immediate returns on your investment (namely in the form of rent income). If the demand for rental property increases, that's also the perfect opportunity to get in on the action and shore up more property and up the rent before you fulfill vacancies. From there, you'll be able to get more returns on investment that are stable and consistent.

Tax benefits

How can you say no to tax benefits? If you want to get something good back from Uncle Sam, you can with the help of rental properties. There are many tax advantages that you can get just by purchasing investment property (depending on things like how much you pay in loan interests). Not only that, you get some sweet deductions in the process that can be used to soften the blow on some expenses (like urgent repairs and the like).

More diversification

Diversification is the key word when it comes to investments. You want to spread out your investments rather than have all your eggs in one basket. With purchasing property, you can be able to diversify across many types of property.

You may already have non-real estate investments to begin with. And since they might be a little more volatile, you'll at least have something more stable like rental properties. Not only that, you won't have to worry about the value of your overall portfolio.

Real estate for the win!

Protection against inflation

Want something to hedge against inflation? Rental properties are your best bet. With inflation, the price of rent and homes goes up.

Not only that, but when inflation rises, guess what doesn't? If you said mortgage payments, you are absolutely right. Inflation and the mortgage rate are two separate things.

However, the one caveat to pay attention to is that your other expenses can rise with inflation. For example, your property tax and insurance costs can rise along with the inflation rate. If there is one figure that you really need to pay attention to, the inflation rate should be that.

So far, the inflation rate is north of a percent. And US home prices as of 2021 have risen to nearly 5.5 percent. And let's not forget, there is an increase in demand for homes (which could be a good sign if you are looking to snag up some rental properties).

Key Principles That Would Take You To Success

What are the key principles that will help you become more successful at investing in rental properties? We'll be taking a look at them here shortly. Your goal is to build and manage an empire that will create more financial freedom than you never thought was possible.

Following these key principles (without cutting corners or skipping steps) will assure you possible success. Keep in mind that the results are not usually typical compared to one rental property investor to another. Some may find success in a short amount of time while it can take longer for others.

Timing and patience are two things you'll need to have in order to succeed in building your rental property empire. With that said, here are the following key principles to adopt so you can achieve your own success:

It starts with effective management

In order to be successful, you'll want to do a good job at managing your rental properties. Regardless if you have a property manager that is taking care of the day to day operations of one property, you are still the manager since you own it (meaning you have a say in terms of the property and how it operates).

At the same time, you'll want to keep the issues of property management at bay. You'll have untrustworthy employees, unreliable tenants that refuse to pay, and so much more. So you'll want to keep those to a minimum as best you can (without sucking the time and life out of yourself).

Remember, managing your rental properties is more of a business. So treat it as such or you'll find yourself drowning in a sea of negative cash flow. Also, it helps to keep an accurate count of things so you can be able to achieve and sustain success over time.

Increase your income

Sounds like a no brainer thing to do, right? Increasing your income by way of rental increases or just snagging up more property (among other ways) should be something to focus on. The more you earn, the better.

However, you'll want to make sure that your property is being rented at the market rate. To set the rent price below market rate would be a mistake (and a costly one at that). So don't miss out on all that money if you are planning on setting the rent at rates that are lower than what the market averages are.

What you're missing out will add up over time. Don't be that person that is kicking themselves for missing out on that six figure payday.

Decrease expenses as well

Obviously, if you are going to increase income you might as well decrease expenses as well. There are a myriad of ways to cut expenses so you can save money. However, one thing to pay attention to is the quality of service.
And we suggest that you do not sacrifice the quality of service for the sake of saving an extra bundle of cash. It comes down to the best quality that you can afford (without killing your cash flow). So what are some ideas and suggestions that you should consider?

Consider some of the following cost-effective ideas:

- Look for an insurer that will give you reasonable insurance rates

- If your property tax bill is too high, challenge it

- Consider installing water-saving appliances such as low-flow toilets (assuming you are paying for a water bill)

- Energy efficient appliances go a long way. If you have a laundry center on your property, consider investing in energy efficient washers and dryers

- Find a waste management company that can pick up large volumes of trash, but does fewer pickups (i.e -- Every two weeks or thereabouts)

- Place the responsibility of such expenses like utilities and the like to the tenant. It doesn't have to be a long laundry list, but something that can be manageable for their finances

Make sure you have the right people as your tenants

Screening for potential tenants will certainly be one of your best moves whenever you are managing your rental property. The bottom line is this: you want tenants who pay on time, won't cause too much of a headache, and just want to stick around for the long haul.

If you can't do the screening process, get someone who can trust. Find someone who is fair, knows the policy, and can be able to say 'no' to anyone because of what the policy states. For example, if a prospective tenant has had a history of late payments, that's a clear and resounding 'no'.

Surround yourself with people you can trust

We might have said this earlier, but will say it again. Surround yourself and choose the right people who will do a good job to keep your rental properties in good shape. This includes finding the right people who manage the property when you can't (such as collecting the rent on your behalf) and other tasks.

As your rental property portfolio grows, that's when you need to assemble the right people who will manage the property effectively and be reliable for any tasks you want done. Also, it's important to find the right people who will take care of the property and make it look good (like a property management company that mows lawns, plows driveways, etc.)

Don't get too emotionally invested

Certainly, it's a good feeling knowing that you will be able to invest in rental properties and get a nice amount of cash every month. It's a bad feeling if you tend to lose it all. Keep in mind that like most of how business works, there will be successes and failures.

When you experience some kind of failure, it's important not to get too negative about it emotionally. At the same time, there will be things that can go wrong. The last thing you want is to be stressed out about it.

Not only that, if you let your emotions get in the way, you may be making decisions that you'll soon regret down the road. Especially when those decisions show that they have a negative impact on your finances. Not only that, your tenants won't care about the work you've put into the place since you've purchased it (they care more about the byproduct of it).

Have a plan and execute it

As a real estate investor, it's always good to have a plan. To not have one is like flying blind in the fog. So it's good to have a plan for the long-term.

For example, let's say you have a goal to have a net worth of $10,000,000. How will you get there? Set the goals that will help you achieve that (both short-term and long-term).

Those goals should be reviewed on a regular basis so you know that you are on the right track. You'll know where you are at one point and be able to know where to go from there. Think of your plan like a roadmap to success.

You can't reach your goals if you don't have them set in the first place.

Final Thoughts

There are a lot of perks and benefits that go into investing in rental property. And yes, it can be fun as well. Yet, you should balance fun with business.

It can be a hobby depending on how things are structured. But we more or less recommend that you treat managing your rental properties like a business if you are serious about making money (and increasing your personal net worth). When investing in your first property, it's good to know a few things before diving in .

More importantly, know the difference between residential, commercial, and mixed use properties. If you are fairly new to the game, you should consider acquiring a residential property since they are mostly accessible to begin with. Plus, it's a lot easier to start out with for many reasons (such as the income and expenses that you need to deal with).

There are plenty of benefits to investing in rental properties. Having excellent asset stability, more diversification, a hedge against inflation, and a whole slew of tax benefits are some of the best. While there are plenty of benefits, remember that there are downsides to the whole thing.

Don't let these downsides like expenses, unreliable tenants, and the like discourage you. At the end of the day, you'll find that investing in rental properties and reaping the rewards are worth it. As long as you follow the key principles and execute on the plan you have set for yourself, you'll be in good shape for the long run.

Chapter 2: There Is More Than One Type Of Rental Property

In the previous chapter, we've talked about residential, commercial, and mixed use rental properties. As a beginner, we highly suggested starting off with residential properties because it is a lot simpler to work with compared to commercial properties (especially when it comes to dealing with expenses). In this chapter, we'll be focusing on some options that are within the residential property category.

Yes, you have plenty of opportunities all over the place. Not to mention, you could be able to acquire property and repurpose it for some kind of housing. However, it can depend on the location and even the return on investment that you'll receive in the process.

We'll be taking a look at options like single-family housing, multi-family apartments, town homes, and more. We'll also help you make the determination of which rental property will work in your favor. Each rental property does have their pros and cons (so we encourage you not to skip each section discussing a specific property).

Now, let's dive right in and see what you can be able to work with:

Options! Options! Options!

Think of the options that are at your disposal. We will be going over some of the most common residential rental property options. If you think there is a lack of them where you live, this could be due to two things: one, you may legitimately have little options to work with (possibly because you live in a small town) or you might not be looking hard enough.

There are rental properties that are hidden in plain sight. It is up to you to find them before someone else with an extra set of eyes does. Understand that with the options you have, you'll be able to know the difference between one type of property and the other.

In this chapter, you will know the difference between single-family housing and perhaps student housing. There are different types of rental housing such as assisted living facilities, halfway houses, income-based housing, and so on. However, these options below are some of our best recommendations.
Let's begin by taking an even closer look at single-family rental houses and how they can work to your advantage.

Single-Family Rental House

Just so we're clear, your first residential rental property doesn't have to be an apartment building. You can start off with one single tenant if you're more comfortable with it. However, this will most likely require a single-family house that is under your ownership.

A single-family rental property will be a house that you rent out to someone who may be living alone or may be living with a significant other (with or without kids). Also, there could also be a few people living together as roommates and want a bigger space compared to an apartment.

Like this and the other types of property will be looking at, we'll be going over the pros and cons of each. Single-family rental homes may be your cup of tea or it something else might be. Are single-family homes right for you?

Let's find out by laying out these pros and cons:

Pros of single-family housing

- **Longer leases:** One of the main goals for any rental property owner is having a tenant who can stay for the long-term. Long-term is anywhere from 12 months and beyond. So it makes sense considering that you can have a tenant who is reliable and pays on time for the long term. And longer leases equals a better ROI (be it monthly or annually).

- **Lower property taxes:** In the previous chapter, we suggested that you should consider keeping expenses reasonably low. With single-family homes, you pay less in property taxes compared to different types of property like apartment buildings. On top of that, commercial real estate is taxed differently compared to real estate that is zoned for residential use.

- **Lower management costs:** Keeping in continuation with minimizing expenses, a single-family home. When it comes to these types of property, the repair and maintenance costs will be relatively low. Once again, the expenses are not that bad compared to apartment buildings and the like.

- **Resale value can improve:** Let's say you have a tenant that is leaving because they purchased a home of their own. At the same time, you're thinking about selling the house to someone as well. You can sell the house for more than what you bought for it in the first place. The resale value will increase under the condition that the house is in a neighborhood that is thriving. Also, if the property is kept up well, the resale value could be even better. Your tenant may have put in some work or you might have some work put in before you consider selling it yourself.

- **HOA fees:** Payable HOA fees can be a damper on a rental property. This means you will need to pay some kind of monthly fee. This may be due to the amenities that are available in the neighborhood. If you want to avoid these kinds of fees, ask around the neighborhood where your target rental property regarding if an HOA exists.

- **Land size:** If you are looking to rent out a single-family home, there may be tenants who may decline the offer because of the land size. They might want more land (or perhaps an even larger backyard for the kids). That doesn't mean you can own a house that has a large amount of land as well. Sometimes, you win some and lose some because of the amount of acreage.

- **Vacancies mean lower ROI:** When a tenant vacates, that could mean a temporary decrease on your ROI (assuming you hold more than one piece of property). Once the lease agreement ends, the tenant can choose to renew or not. Keep in mind that when it comes to finding a new tenant, increased costs aimed towards fulfilling a vacancy will arise.

- **Initial sale price may be higher:** When buying a house for the purpose of renting it out, you may contend with higher prices. That's because the house itself can be renovated for the purpose of increasing the value. On one end, someone is focused on increasing the resale value (while the other is facing the necessary evil of having to buy it at a higher price). That happens all the time in real estate. But it is what it is.

For those who are renting a single-family house, there's a reason why they are going this route. Maybe they're holding off on buying a house in the future. They might need a large amount of space like a garage or an attic. Whatever the need, there is a good chance they'd be willing to pay rent for it as opposed to purchasing it outright.

Multifamily Apartment

A multifamily apartment is a residential property that contains more than one unit of housing. These include but are not limited to duplexes, townhomes, apartments, condos. With multi family homes, you can be able to generate a good ROI since you'll likely be renting these out to multiple residents.

In other words, one family can live in a downstairs apartment while another family lives in the apartment above. If you are looking to purchase a multi-family home as a primary residence, you are welcome to do so. From there, you can rent a vacant space to a family or someone looking for a living space.

This is what is known as owner-occupied properties. Regardless of how you approach multi-family apartments and housing, it's a great rental property to invest in. So what are the pros and cons of this property type?

Let's take a look at them:

Pros of multifamily apartments

- **Better cash flow:** Of course, you have a better cash flow (not to mention an even large amount of it) when you rent multifamily apartments. You could stand to make double the rent from two people renting separate spaces (one renting the downstairs, the other the upstairs at let's say $750 a month for each tenant)

- **Increased valuation potential:** Multifamily real estate does appreciate in value. At the same time, they can hold their own when things don't look so well in terms of the economy. While there really is no timetable on when you'll see an increase in value, they are bound to happen at one point in time or another

- **Keeps insurance simple:** Did you know that the insurance policy for apartment buildings can be a bit more complex? So if you are not one to wrestle with all of that, but want to rent out multiple units, then multifamily apartments may be your best bet. Not to mention, once you acquire more multifamily properties, they can all be simply covered under the same insurance policy. Plus, you deal with no further complications at all
- **Tax benefits:** Obviously, the recurring pattern for these rental properties are the tax benefits. So what will you get from renting out multi family properties? Your mortgage payments and the interest you pay on them may yield some tax benefits in the long run. You may also qualify for some pretty cool deductions as well.

Cons of multifamily apartments

- **Cost:** Yes, the cost for a multifamily apartment is going to be high compared to single-family housing. At the same time, you'll need to consider the location that you are in. The closer you are to a major metropolitan area, the more expensive it will become. If you are starting out and find multifamily units appealing, consider going a bit farther away from the city center

- **Management can be complex:** When dealing with multiple family properties, the juggling can get a little complete. There are tenants who have different expenses from the other. Some of them have different repair and maintenance needs. So keeping track of these things can be difficult at times. You can find a way to organize these and handle them on your own or have a property manager handle some of the operations to take the weight off of things.

- **They are a bit more competitive:** When it comes to investing in properties, you will run into some competition. The more appealing the property, the more competitive it can get. Multi Family homes are typically one of the most competitive properties out there. Why? For one, they are not dealing with so many units. So the costs will be less compared to an apartment building. On top of that, going at it along on your first try is going to be difficult. So it would be smart to team up with people who have experience in investing in this kind of property.

- **Regulations:** Depending on the kind of property you are investing and managing in, there's a good chance that you may run into some kind of regulations. The regulations set upon multi family homes are way different than single-family homes. Not to mention, those regulations may be stricter compared to the latter. That's why it is important to team up with someone who may be experienced (such as being part of a group investment). These experienced investors have been there and are aware of the laws and regulations that may be in place.

On the surface, multifamily properties will more than likely give you a nice boost in ROI. However, for the newbie, handling the common downsides that comes with it all can be a bit overwhelming. If you have never owned rental property, you'd be wise to steer clear from multi family homes until you have some experience under your belt.

Alternatively, you could become part of an investor group. But the entry to get in may not be easy. For now, put multifamily units on the backburner until you have a clear understanding of what you are getting into.

Student Housing

Student housing might be a great option for first-time investors like yourself. College students may be getting tired of the dorm life. So they may opt for some larger space.

Most student housing complexes will fare well in larger universities (think schools with a large student population of 10,000 or more). These major universities will have a mix of dorms and student housing for upperclassmen, graduate students, or even law or medical students. In college sports terms (assuming you are a fan), Division I schools are a good place to start.

So there are opportunities in student housing. And it can be perfect for a first-time rental property that you can invest in. We'll outline some of the pros and cons with student housing right now:

Pros of Student Housing

- **It's fully managed:** Not only will you have someone managing the property, but there will always be someone on site who can be able to check on the property regularly for any repairs, maintenance, and the like. Plus, there will likely be a maintenance crew on site (employed by the University or a similar entity).

- **The demand is always strong:** Think about it. There are students who come and go from schools. One class graduates and a new one enters. So the demand for student housing will remain strong so long as people are going to school. Of course, there will be options that students will have in terms of housing. The dorms may be good, but there's always the option for larger space if a dorm room isn't enough.

- **Amenities are usually available:** Even if you purchase the property, odds are there will be nearby amenities. So you don't have to provide them for yourself (unless there is a demand for them). Students won't mind the regular commute from their apartments to a place nearby.

- **Long-term tenants:** With student housing, you'll usually have tenants that will stick around for the long-term (i.e -- the duration of their schooling). Of course, one tenant will leave and another will soon fulfill the vacancy. So you won't have to worry about vacancies staying empty for long.

- **Multiple income streams:** Depending on how much per unit is, you'll have more streams of income for each apartment. Some may be the same price while some larger spaces will yield a higher rent. The more units that are occupied, the better.

Cons of Student Housing

- **No year-round tenants:** While there are long-term tenants, the caveat is that they won't be in these apartments year-round. Some of them will be returning home during the summer break. However, one way to remedy that situation is to offer summer housing for those who are taking short-term summer classes (or those who may be taking on internships in the local area).

- **Competition is solid:** Certainly, there is solid competition in the student housing market. While private developers are building their own complexes, the universities themselves might be doing the same.

- **There may be additional 'hoops':** There are some extra hoops that you may need to jump through depending on your jurisdiction. This may include extra licenses and regulations. This may be considered a necessary evil rather than something that discourages you from investing in student housing.

- **The lack of credit history:** Students may come into college with little to no credit history whatsoever. For landlords and property managers, they rely on credit history to determine whether or not a potential tenant has the financial stability. Couple that with the potential of what limited income they may have and it may be a risk that you may be willing to take.

- **Repairs and maintenance is likely:** We're not saying that all students love to get rowdy and make noise. However, there will usually be some parties going on. And people might just have a good time and forget about the surroundings. So things might get broken to the point where it might be a busy week for the repair crew. Consider setting off a percentage of money for repair and maintenance expenses.

Student housing presents you with some pretty good upsides. Yet, the downsides still exist. It's not as complicated of a property to invest in because you already have the management team already on staff (most of them will be employed and paid for by the school). Plus, there may be nearby amenities that are a quick skip and a hop away.

Finally, there's a steady stream of tenants who may be looking for off-campus housing. Dorm life may not be something that some students would want anyhow. So they'll need a place to live that is close to the campus, but doesn't include a ton of noise at 2AM.

Town Homes

Town homes (or known by alternative names like townhouses or a row house) is a multistory property that will share one wall with a property that is adjacent to them. Townhouses have their own private entrance, driveway, garage, basement, and backyard. One thing to keep in mind is that in neighborhoods where there are town homes, there is usually an HOA attached to it.

So what are the pros and cons of town homes as a rental property? Let's have a look:

Pros of town homes:

- **You have your own tenants**: Whether it's one or more town homes that you are renting out, there's a tenant for each one. It's not like you are renting out apartment units. So it's similar to renting out a single-family home (except it's a little different with town homes). With one town home, you own the exterior and the interior of the property.

- **Maintenance is fairly easy**: If there is an HOA on the property, they will take care of the maintenance on their end. So long as you pay the maintenance fees every month, that is. A majority of the maintenance will be covered, but sometimes you may need to cover it yourself. Regardless, consider saving up on repair and maintenance reserves just in case.

- **Lower costs**: The cost of investing in a town home is actually lower than you think. They are even lower in price compared to single-family homes. If you are someone who is looking to invest in rental property, but might be looking for a cost-effective option, chances are you can consider town homes as the best investment to start out with.

- **Modern design:** Townhomes mostly have modern designs compared to single-family homes. Designs that are modern and look brand new will more than likely attract more tenants compared to something that's been built decades ago. An attractive design and a great price might just be the two best things that your tenants may be looking for.

- **Excellent rental income:** Of course, rental income potential is what you're looking for. Town homes provide you with a great opportunity to snag a good amount of it. Town homes are usually popular with families that want a good amount of space. Not to mention, they are quite affordable in terms of rent (when compared to apartments, condos, etc.)

- **Extra fees:** Town homes will usually be attached to an HOA. This means that HOA fees will probably be an expense that you need to account for every month. Also, there are maintenance fees that will also get factored in (even though a majority of the maintenance is handled by the HOA).

- **Limited use:** In town home neighborhoods, the uses may be limited. The reason why is that there may be rules and regulations in place by the HOA. While there are town homes in one area that can be rented out, you may not have them rented out in the way you intended. So it's better to consult with the HOA first before making an investment in town homes.

- **Acquiring an investment loan can be difficult:** In terms of financing for town homes, it may be a challenge to acquire a loan. The banks have the final say on whether or not you'll get a loan. Usually this is due to the fact that compared to single-family homes, town homes are much more modern. And banks are hesitant on whether or not they should issue loans.

- **Privacy issues with tenants may arise:** Since town homes will likely share a wall with an adjacent town home, this can put off potential tenants. Especially the ones who place a high standard on privacy. You can come and go as you please, but don't count on not being watched by your neighbors.

- **Noise issues:** Since you are sharing a wall with the people next door, there's a good chance that you'll be hearing noises from their end (and vice versa). Potential tenants may be turned off by that considering that they need their peace and quiet for a good chunk of the day.

- **Space may be limited:** The space for town homes may be limited. Specifically, we're talking about storage space. Sure, you'll have a garage and a basement for all of that. But how much storage would you need for all the Christmas decorations and the like? Also, the living space may be a little cramped (or even a bit too cramped for anyone's liking)

Other Rental Properties To Consider

Now that we have covered some of the most common rental properties that you can invest in, we're not finished yet. There are other rental properties to invest in if you are not too keen on the idea of investing in one of the property types above. So what else is there to consider?

We'll be looking at three different types of property to invest: properties known as ' fixer-uppers', foreclosures, and of course commercial real estate. There are a set of pros and cons for each (which will take a look at so you know what to expect). In the meantime, let's start with fixer-uppers:

To simply put it into plain English, fixer uppers are properties that are not in the best of conditions. They are in need of repairs that may very well be major repairs at best. This could include replacing entire systems such as plumbing and renovating the entire home from the ground up.

If you got the extra cash to make repairs even after purchasing the property itself, then you might find a fixer-upper to be something that will be worth your while. After putting in the work by way of repairs and renovations, you'll see your hard work pay off in the form of your ROI. Certainly, it will take time to see an ROI because you will be spending time fixing the place up (hence the name).

What are the pros and cons? Let's have a look:

Pros of Fixer-Uppers:

- **Purchase prices are lower:** With properties that are in need of repair, the purchase prices will be much lower than those that are in good shape. No two houses are priced equally. The good news is that the house will have a low barrier for entry if it needs a lot of repairing. Fixer-uppers tend to go for prices under the average market value. Expect prices to be at least 8 to 10 percent below the average as a good starting point.

- **You control where the money goes:** Clearly, you'll be investing in plenty of money towards repairs. So you get to make the decision of where that money will go. Do you want to put money towards fixing the entire HVAC system? Go for it. Does it need any kind of renovations in the kitchen or bathroom? That's for you to decide. After purchasing the property, take a look around and make a list of repairs and renovations that you feel are worth the investment. The most urgent or highly prioritized repairs and renovations should be the first thing you focus on before anything else. For example, if the foundation or the structure is showing signs of wear and deterioration, focus on that first.

- **Competition is lesser:** If you are looking for investment property where there is less competition, then fixer-uppers are your best bet. That's because your competitors may not even bother with the idea of putting in an additional investment that goes towards repairs and renovations. The mindset for most of your competitors will be 'quick and fast gains' with as little work as possible. So they hate putting in more risk than they think is necessary.

- **An opportunity to increase value:** Think about it for a moment. If you put in plenty of work, then odds are you will increase the value of your property over time. So what are you waiting for? A single-family home that looked horrendous from the inside and out will gain plenty of value so long as you put in the work (no matter how long it takes). How much of an increase are you willing to aim for? That's up to you.

- **Forced appreciation:** When it comes to the overall value of your home, the only direction for a fixer-upper to go is up. Simple as that. It won't depreciate in value farther than it has to. Even if you add plenty of value to it, you can be able to sell the property at a higher price if you want to (or flip it). However, you intend on generating passive income out of the whole thing. So perhaps setting the rent price will be more sufficient.

- **Additional money is needed:** Even though you purchase the home below the average market value, that's just one of the lower hurdles to jump through. Now, the real challenge begins with needing additional money for the repairs and renovations needed. Once again, it's a necessary evil that is required for adding more overall value to the home. Not only that, you could be looking at hidden expenses based on unexpected repairs that may seem to pop up as the process moves along.

- **You may go over your budget:** You might already have a set budget in mind for renovating and repairing your fixer-upper. Yet, there's a good chance that you may go over that budget. 40 percent of rental property investors stay within the budget (but still, there's a chance that you may go over for some reason or another). Again, this can be connected to expenses that are unplanned or suddenly appear. You may discover some no so pleasant things like asbestos or even rotting beams.

- **An uncertain future:** The timeline for turning a fixer-upper into a home that looks great for someone to move into will usually be inconclusive. That's because you'll be dealing with some surprise discoveries, the repair process, and so on. So it would be wise not to make an estimate on how long it can take. Just focus on the repairs and know that the end result will be in sight sooner rather than never.

Foreclosures

Another investment property that has a low barrier of entry is foreclosure properties. The prices are below the market value like fixer-uppers. But still, there are risks that do exist.

Structural wise, they should be fine (unless there are some repairs needed). The problems that may lay ahead include the financial side of the property. We're talking liens, unpaid taxes, and similar issues.

While foreclosures are a good investment, you may want to do a little deep diving on the target property before making a splash. It's a good thing we have a set of pros and cons to help you out. So let's have a look at what to expect (including the common downsides):

Pros of Foreclosures

- **Discounted value:** The good news about foreclosures is that they will come at a discounted value. So if you want a lower barrier of entry on the financial front, this kind of property will be perfect for you. The even better news, there are low to no down payments (depending on the financial institution that you are going through).

- **A great ROI opportunity:** If you are looking for a great ROI opportunity, chances are a foreclosure property may be just what you're looking for. Granted, it won't take a long time to get a positive ROI because of the lesser need to make repairs. You can be able to get a tenant into the home quickly after the home is inspected and passes.

- **Closing process is fast:** If you want to snag the property and waste as little time as possible, then foreclosures will be your best property to focus on. The closing process is much quicker compared to purchasing the home going through the regular process. On average, it takes 30 days to close on a foreclosure. The length of time if it was just any regular house? Almost double the time (60 days).

- **You may not see or inspect the home:** There's a good chance that you as a property investor may not be able to see or inspect the home before making a decision. Almost every foreclosure on the market will be sold on an 'as-is' basis. So you'll mostly get what you get no matter what.

- **They may be fixer-uppers:** Nobody likes surprises. When purchasing a foreclosure and you see it for the first time, you'll notice it's more of a fixer-upper than anything. So think of purchasing foreclosures like a wrapped gift. You'll never know what's inside (or outside) until you tear off the paper. So the likelihood of putting in an additional amount for repairs and renovations is good. You might as well set off some extra money to the side in case such an obligation should be fulfilled.

- **Slightly more competitive than fixer-uppers:** Because of the mystery surrounding foreclosures, there are investors that want to get in on the action. They want to know what they are working with. For this reason, you'll be seeing some additional eyes (other than yours) watching the property and have their intent to purchase. Inventory can go quicker than it can be fulfilled. So stay one step ahead of your competitors and pay attention to auctions that focus on foreclosures.

Commercial Properties

Early on, we mentioned commercial properties as one other investment property to consider. However, this might be something that a beginner should refrain from focusing on until they have a bit of experience under their belt. But, if you do have plenty of money aside to invest in commercial properties, then it may be wise to know what to expect.

Here are the pros and cons that you'll need to be aware of regarding commercial properties:

- **Higher ROI:** Yes, the rents will be higher than residential investment properties. So right off the bat, you get a much higher return on investment. If you are looking to get a substantial gain, then a commercial property could be what you're looking for.

- **Leases are longer:** While long-term residential leases are basically 12 months or longer, the commercial leases are even lengthier. On average, a long-term commercial lease will range from three to five years. This will at least help you secure some long-term tenants. Who may be considered reliable in the long-term? Consider larger companies and corporations, well-known brands, or even the government (or a specific department).

- **Great for diversification:** As mentioned earlier on, investing is great when you are diversifying your assets. So if you have residential properties, you may feel inclined to invest in a commercial property. Residential properties here and commercial properties there? No problem. As long as you're getting a solid ROI on it, what harm can it do?

- **Vacancies can be lengthy:** When it comes to vacancies, it may be quite lengthy for a commercial property compared to residential properties. While you can be able to fulfill the residential properties much faster, it can take as little as six months to find the right tenant for your commercial vacancies. For this reason, it's important to set aside some cash just in case that happens.

- **Lease terms are complex:** With commercial leases, there are some complexities that exist. This may include some legal help on your end to help draw up a lease of some kind.

- **Upfront capital needed:** When purchasing commercial property, there is upfront money that will be needed to acquire the property. And that amount of money might be a lot. The amount of money needed will depend on the type of commercial property that you intend to purchase.

How Do You Choose?

Now, the million dollar question is this: Of the properties that we have listed above, how will you choose between one or the other. It's important to consider a number of factors before making a final decision.

At this point, you may have a good idea of which property you may be investing in. But what if you are still undecided? Let's take a look at some considerations that you'll want to mull over before making what could be the most important decision of your life (so far):

How much money will you have on hand?

The financial end of any deal should always be taken into consideration before anything else. How much money do you think you'll need? No one knows for sure until they do some research and come up with some estimates.

If you don't want to spend a ridiculous amount of money on properties, then you could settle for something like a fixer-upper or a foreclosure property. So long as you know what you're getting into or don't mind paying a low price for the initial property (and adding more money for repairs and such), these are the properties that you can spend money and time on.

If you are looking to acquire other properties, the base number you'll want to start with is the amount you're willing to spend on a certain rental property. So if there's a single-family home that you want to purchase that has a $100,000 price tag, then that's the base number to start off with.

How much work are you willing to put in?

If you are looking for rental property that will require less to no work, then you may look at different investments such as single-family homes, apartments, or even student housing (among others). These are the properties that you want to focus on if you are simply looking for a quick gain in ROI. Remember, these types of properties will be competitive, so you better come in with a solid strategy in mind.

However, if you don't mind putting in the extra work for the purpose of increasing the properties value and getting a much greater ROI in the process, once again focus on the properties that will give you less of a headache in terms of entry (i.e -- foreclosures or fixer-uppers). If competition is something that you don't want to deal with, fixer-uppers may be your best option in the long run.

What kind of ROI are you looking for?

For most rental property investors, they are looking for something quick, easy, and large in terms of ROI. While it might sound like a tempting thing to do, there are some downsides that you will need to contend with. For example, commercial properties will more than likely yield the greatest ROI compared to residential properties.

However, as a beginner you want to start off small and build from the ground up. Unless you have the cash to buy a commercial property (and cover initial expenses), any kind of residential property would be a good starting point in terms of a modest ROI. You can rent out a single-family residence or a townhome.

To start out with a base ROI and moving your way up would be a smart thing to do. That's because you'll deal with less hurdles and headaches like expenses and having to put in all kinds of work trying to find the right tenant.

Aside from a solid ROI, one major goal a property owner must fulfill is finding a tenant who can stay on for the long-term (12 months or more). On paper, commercial properties will likely be the best option since the leases tend to be lengthier than residential ones. However, if you want to stay within the residential side of things, your best options are single-family homes, multi-family properties and townhomes.

Student housing will yield some long-term tenants, but with some caveats. They won't be around for at least a total of three months out of the year. So if you are looking for long-term, year-round tenants then the aforementioned properties in this section will be what you need to focus on.

Simpler lease terms

Easy choice in this regard would be residential properties. The lease terms won't be that complicated. All you have to do is lay them out with little to no legal consultation as possible (only needed when there may be an issue).

The terms will be more complex when dealing with commercial properties. If you don't want to deal with all kinds of legal headaches throughout the process, residential properties might be right up your alley.

Final Thoughts

Now that you know that there are plenty of options for rental properties, you know that opportunities are pretty much everywhere. The choices may seem a bit overwhelming at first. However, you'll be able to make a process of elimination based on your needs and what you don't want to deal with in terms of obstacles.

That's why you should spend as much time as possible making the determination of which property will work best in your favor. Yes, it can take some time. But you'll feel that once you've made the right decision, it was worth the investment in time to look at the right kind of property that will give you a better ROI.

The world of rental properties is looking better than ever. While there are many options to look at, you'll want to pay attention to the barriers of entry and even the competition that exists within each type of property. Our advice is to take the road less traveled if you are a complete beginner.

In other words, find a property that will give you less competition (like fixer-uppers). Bear in mind though, you might want to be aware of the other obstacles that stand in the way (like repair costs and the like). Rental properties are great whenever you want a good overall ROI. Sometimes, it may take some work to get there.

But nevertheless, you have an opportunity to start building your rental property portfolio. With time and more money in your pocket, you will still be able to build your portfolio with a mix of properties that you might like. You may have a lot of residential properties with some commercial buildings mixed in.
It pays to find the right kind of property. So determine what benefits you want out of the whole thing and consider which obstacles and barriers that you want to avoid.

Chapter 3 - Meet Your Team Members

One thing you need to understand is that investing in rental properties will be hard to do when it's one person running the show. This is going to take quite a bit of work to do. Not to mention, you'll want as many eyes and ears on the ground as you can.

That's why it is important to have team members in your corner helping you find the best property that will give you an excellent ROI. In this chapter, we'll discuss why forming a team is important. You will learn the kind of roles that each team member will play and why they are essential to your success.

We may be tempted to go at things alone. However, there are some things that will take quite a bit of time. So doing a lot of time-consuming stuff by yourself will definitely take a lot out of your day. You may feel discouraged at first thinking that finding a rental property is easy.

However, the process is a bit more complicated than you think. But as long as you surround yourself with the right kind of people, you might be in a good position to snag the property you want to rent out and get a nice slice of the pie.

Now, let's dive right in and discuss why it will take more than one person to help you succeed at investing in real estate and the kind of people you want to find so you can leverage their expertise and strengths.

Let's get right to it:

There's No 'I' in Rental Property

It would be a mistake to tackle the great big world of real estate all by yourself. Especially when there are a lot of financial and legal things that are usually involved. Not to mention, you'll be working with people who want to be your tenants. And it would be your responsibility to keep them happy so they can stay on your property for the long-term.

Instead of saying 'I' in terms of rental property, adopt the following as your mantra: 'Team work makes the dream work'. Repeat it over and over again either in your head or aloud. This group of people should be people you trust and rely on for their expertise.

When it comes to success, it is always important to surround yourself with the right kind of people. Early on, we discussed that you should connect with local real estate groups on social media. These are people who know their stuff and will probably be happy to lend you a hand as a new investor.

If you haven't made the connections yet, now would be a good time to do so. You'll want a base network to help you build your team from the ground up. People know people who have a certain skill or talent that you are looking for.

Important People That You Should Include In Your Team

So who should be on your team? What kind of tasks are you looking to fulfill? This section will help you find the kind of people that you want to hire for a certain task and why.

Remember, there are some moving parts to the whole process of acquiring a rental property. And you certainly don't want to do everything. Let's take a look at the kind of people you'll need and why they are essential to your team:

Seekers

These are your realtors and 'property scouts'. These people are your eyes on the ground whenever you are in the hunt for rental property that has excellent ROI potential. You want people that know the local market like the back of their hand.

These are the people who have vital information about the local housing market. They know which areas are valuable and which ones that may be on the up and up. If you are looking for someone who has access to a list of properties that you can acquire and rent out, you want a seeker on your team.

As a reward, they can become one of your investing partners (and they too can have a slice of the pie). At the same time, they may be looking to build out their own rental portfolio as well. With their success in helping you find a property, they can be paid a finder's fee (which can be a percentage of your total ROI).

Lenders

Odds are that you may need to take out a loan that can be used for acquiring target properties. So it's good to have someone who is a lender on your team. These are the people who will loan you cash so you can be able to acquire the property you want.

On top of that, a lender that you can trust can also be someone who can open the door of new opportunities for you. One thing to look for is whether or not if a lender will provide you with some flexibility. You'll also be introduced to the wide variety of loans that are available.

These include but are not limited to fixed portfolio loans (available in 5-year or 10-year terms), 30-year fixed single asset loans, or acquisition lines of credit for those looking to fix and flip homes. The loans you'll want will depend on what your plans are for the property that you acquire.

Tax professionals

When it comes to taxes, you'll want a couple of important people on your team. This includes a certified public accountant or CPA. The other is a tax attorney.

A CPA will be someone who will keep track of your finances. Meanwhile, your tax attorney will be there to help you through the legal process in terms of paying taxes (and even giving you assistance whenever you want to challenge your tax bill or the like). An experienced attorney will know plenty about the tax code and will assist you in establishing a plan that can be executed in the event of something such as incapacitation or death.

Property managers

If you want people to manage properties for you (because you can't be everywhere at once), find someone who can do it. This can be one person or a management company. Self-managing might be something that you can try your hand at.

But unless you want calls at 3AM about something being broken or the toilet not flushing properly, a property manager will definitely be a worthy addition to your team. A property manager will also play a role in who will be able to occupy vacancies as a tenant and who may be denied due to policies that are in place.

Insurance agent

Let's face it: things happen. Disaster can occur at any point in time whether it's rain or shine. So it would make a lot of sense knowing that you have an insurance agent in your corner.

Especially someone who can give you an excellent insurance policy that will cover things such as severe property damage and the like. You'll want things like business liability, property protection, and some other essentials so that you are covered for the unexpected (whenever those things occur).

Not only that, but having an insurance agent in your corner may also give you the opportunity to snag a good policy at a reasonable price. When looking for insurance agents, see if you are able to find out how much each policy is worth. Remember, you don't want to start out with a large amount of expenses (nor do you want to skimp on some kind of coverage just for the sake of saving money).

Title company

Need someone in your corner to help you close the deal much faster? That's where title companies come in. They will help you determine the final evaluation of the property you want to acquire.

A title company will give you access to people who can do research on what you are actually looking to acquire. You might get a glance at the repair history so you know the kind of condition it's in. And you'll also learn about the kind of insurance coverage it has received in the past.

They will help gather the right data and information that will help make closing the deal a lot easier (or if you feel that you may be walking into a bad deal that could cost you).

Contractors

Having the right contractors on speed dial will put you a step ahead of so many rental property owners. There will come a time when repairs and renovations may be necessary. So you'll want to find the right team that will focus on any vital repairs needed such as the structural integrity, what systems can be installed like plumbing and HVAC, and even those who are experts at installing kitchen sets and the like.

Appraisers

Lastly, you want someone who has a good eye and knowledge of what valuable property looks like. You want someone who can give you an estimated value of the property before setting rent prices or even selling the property altogether when the time comes. Appraisers will give you the most accurate assessment possible.

Find an appraiser who has experience working with investors. Especially when it's someone who can give you a good estimate while the property is vacant. From there, you can either do one of three things: fulfill the vacancy with a new tenant, make some repairs to increase the value, or sell it outright.

Where to find your dream team

Though we mentioned it a bit earlier, finding your dream team may be closer than you think. For one, you should find out what real estate groups are in your local area. The ability to network with people who know a thing or two about real estate (and work with other investors) will help you get your foot in the door.

It's always important to leverage your network. The power of who you know will help you in the long run. Someone may know someone who is a mortgage broker.

Another person may know a CPA and a tax attorney that you can work with. There are real estate professionals out there that can help a new investor like yourself connect with the right kind of people. So where can you find these networks of people?

Here are a few ideas to keep in mind:

- **Social media groups:** You'd be surprised how many real estate experts you can find on social media these days. Especially in places like Facebook or LinkedIn groups. It wouldn't hurt to find a real estate group that focuses on your local area. Add yourself to these groups (if they are available). Find the right people who you think are worth connecting with. Also, don't be afraid to ask questions for the purpose of just picking their brains or getting a feel of the local market.

- **Networking events:** There has to be a lot of industries that put on networking events throughout the year. If there is a networking event that is focused on real estate and close to your local area, why not attend it? Meeting real estate experts face to face may be a little better than say meeting them online. Especially when it's hard to read a person on social media. You can attend seminars and learn of a few ideas of what may be going on in the world of real estate.

- **Check the real estate database:** Somewhere on the Interwebs (and beyond), there's a list of real estate experts that you can connect with. And it can be as simple as a Google search to gather the information on who the realtors are in your area. These are people who may work with investors in helping you buy your first property. And while they're at it, they may also recommend people who will become a part of your team along the way. Once again, don't be afraid to ask around so you can assemble the right kind of people.

- **Home and trade shows:** In-person events are great (as we have mentioned before). What better way to connect with those who know a thing or two about real estate than home and trade shows. You can strike up a conversation with people who do residential contracting and get a good idea of what their expertise is. You may also run into real estate agents who may have some property to take off their hands (so you can rent them out for your tenants).

There are so many opportunities at your disposal. Especially when you want to build your team from scratch. When you're starting out, you can choose one person as a point of contact and build out your network from there. Remember, this takes time and effort among all things.

The important thing for you to do is to not overwhelm yourself and focus on one thing at a time. Keep it as simple as you can get it. Plus, you can always refer to this book as a reference whenever you get stuck with something.

Final Thoughts

When you are building your rental properties empire, you should never go at this alone. There are plenty of things that need to be done in order to achieve the success you want. It's great to have extra sets of eyes and hands on the ground.

More important, you want to connect yourself with people who you can trust. These are people who will help you succeed in any way possible. Whoever you choose as part of your team must be knowledgeable, competent, and professional.

You know where to find them. And you can reach out to them at any time (or during business hours). However, you'll want to be respectful of their time.

Therefore, if you are planning on asking some questions or do some fact-finding about investing in rental properties, you can reach out to your people of interest. Ask them to speak to them for about 10 or 15 minutes at best. That way, they can give you enough time before moving forward with the rest of the day.

Keep in mind that aside from time and effort, you'll need good communication skills, a willingness to give something back in return, and nurturing your network for the long run. Don't expect a lot if you are not giving anything back in return or communicating with your team members once in a while.

When fielding through a list of people for certain roles, it's important to ask yourself some questions. Are they professional? Have they been helpful in one way or another?

Remember, these are the people who you will be dealing with for the long-term. So you better have a team that is professional, helpful, and willing to communicate with you regularly. When the team cultivates a relationship with each other, success can be closer than ever.

With the right kind of property manager, insurance agents, tax advisors, and other team members at your side, you can be able to build your rental property empire from the ground up. It takes a dream to make the dream. And be sure to give credit to those who have helped you along the way.

Chapter 4: Are You Willing To Take The Risk?

The one word that you will always hear no matter what you invest in is risk. It doesn't matter if it's property, stocks, bonds, or even cryptocurrency. There are risks that are usually taken when there is money involved.

You can lose it or make gains. The percentages will vary depending on various factors. But at its core, investing is putting a risk into something and possibly getting a return out of it.

Do not confuse investing with gambling (although carelessly spending or investing money in something without the due diligence may very well be gambling itself). It's important to know what you are getting into before you put any kind of money down. In this chapter, we'll be talking about risk (and whether or not you'll be willing to take them).

Investing isn't an easy thing to do. You can win some, but you will lose some. That's the nature of the business.

But don't let the idea of risk or potential loss discourage you. We'll talk about the common reasons why rental property owners fail (and thus risk losing their initial investment in the process). After the end of this chapter, you'll realize that taking risks in investing rental properties may not be all that bad.

Let's get right to it:

Risks Are Everywhere

Just like investment opportunities, risks are everywhere. Sure, you'll want to be aware of the returns that you get from putting down the initial amount of money. But you have to understand the risks that are involved as well.

There are some obvious risks that you'll need to look for before you decide to spend your hard earned money. That's why doing your due diligence is so important. Risks can depend on the performance of some factors like the economy.

What else could also be affected? Let's take a look:

- **Political change:** It doesn't matter your beliefs or if you care for politics or not. But political change can affect your real estate investment as a whole. Specifically, one such issue to pay close attention to is property taxes. Will they go up or down? Will there be any regulations that may hurt your investment in the long run?

- **Technology changes:** As you're reading this, we are living in an age where technology changes can have some kind of effect on a person's property. For example, the way we consume energy. People may be switching to solar panels to save up on energy costs. New technology can phase out the old and make way for the new. Thus, it creates uncertainty for your investment.

- **Consumer confidence:** If there is one barometer to determine whether or not investing in something is worth the risk, it's the market itself. The consumer confidence in a product, service, or even property will yield some kind of positive or negative feedback. And that feedback can generate more business or slow it down (to the point where almost no one wants to spend their money on it anymore). This is one more reason why you should keep your tenants happy while they are renting from you.

- **Company risk:** You may be part of a group and someone who holds a major stake in the partnership decides to cash out and call it good. This may happen unexpectedly and without prior knowledge given to the rest of the group. Their financial position might be even greater than their initial investment and they decide that cashing out and moving on would be a good move on their part. As for the rest of the group, what could that mean for the investment itself?

Unearthing hidden risks

While there are risks that appear on the surface, there are those that are located beneath it. So what exactly are they? Here's a brief list of those risks so you know what they are and why they can affect your investment:

- **Inflation:** Yes, inflation happens. And it can cause profits to go down as prices rise. For this reason, you'll see interest rates tumble (which can cause your overall investment to take a hit). The purchasing power that you may have once had may weaken.

- **Interest rates:** As mentioned before, interest rates are a hidden risk within themselves. These rates will rise as bond prices do in a downward trajectory. In a time when the economy is going strong, there will be a higher demand for money. And for that reason, you'll see interest rates go up. Could a good economy equal a better return on your investment? It's possible.

- **Liquidity or illiquidity:** So what's the difference between these two? Liquidity is the ability to convert something into cash without hurting the overall value of the investment. Meanwhile, illiquidity will force you to sell any investments even at a low price (so your return may not be the best). Also, you may not see your investment reach full maturity.

- **Currency fluctuation:** What kind of role does currency fluctuation play a role in? Are we talking about the valuation of the dollar? Or are we talking about the exchange rates between the US dollar vs other currencies (such as the Canadian Dollar, Euro, etc.)?

What Are The Risks?

Already, we've taken a look at some of the risks of general investing on the surface (and what's underneath it). So what are the risks of property investment? We'll be taking a look at them here shortly.

As someone who is fairly new to the idea of investing in rental property, you may need to know the specific risks that happen. So you'll want to know what they are so you can be more successful at choosing the right kind of property. Let's take a look at the risks that pertain to rental properties:

Vacancies

Vacancies occur for various reasons. One can happen when a tenant finds a better place to live (or purchases a home of their own). Another would be because of how poorly managed the property may be.

So it's important to reduce the number of vacancies on your property as much as possible. As we've stated before, vacancies equal a reduced income to no income at all (depending on the type of property you invest or own). Beyond the vacancy itself, there's usually the repairs and maintenance that can happen if the outgoing tenant left the place in worse shape than it was before.

This means having to dip into your cash reserves and the like to cover the repair and maintenance costs. Depending on the severity of the damage and how long the repairs take, that vacancy may not be filled for quite awhile. Otherwise, you'll want to find a new tenant as soon as possible.

Decrease in rent

One of the times when rent rates decrease would be when the economy is going in a downward direction. Clearly, a lot of people may not afford the rent because of lost wages and the like. And this means you may need to reduce the rent itself. When people lose money, so might you.

Not only that, you won't be the only rental property investor or owner dealing with this. You'll also have other investors lower their rental prices to stoke the flames of competition. And this can lead you to lowering the rent on your own terms.
So in an economic downturn, you could expect price wars brewing between rental property investors. And you might be in the thick of it all. And that is why it's more of a risk rather than a good move.

There's a difference between being forced to reduce the rent compared to reducing it to where you can get a tenant to fulfill the vacancy. The former will pose an even greater risk. So pay close attention to how things are going economically if you want to stay ahead of the curve.

Decrease in property value

Like the decrease in rent, the property value can decrease and thus present the possibility of losing a bit of money from your initial investment. When the property value decreases, that means selling at a lower price when the time comes.

What causes property value to decrease? There are a handful of factors. For one, the property itself may be in need of repair or renovation.

So it would be your responsibility to make those repairs or renovations when needed. However, the property value may decrease due to things that are beyond your control. This can be due to environmental factors or something that may affect property values throughout the entire area to drop altogether.

It can take a single 'eyesore' that is adjacent to your property to affect your value as it is. You can do something about it in a few ways. It could mean consulting with your local government or banks (assuming they may have control over any abandoned buildings that may be near your property).

Bad tenants

If you are just allowing people to become tenants without screening them properly, this can cause a ton of problems. For example, you could have tenants that will be lax in payment. You may also have people who can get rowdy and break things (which means more money going out the window due to repair expenses).

This is one huge reason why you'll want a property manager to handle all the tenant-related matters (including who gets to move in and who doesn't). There needs to be certain policies in place to ensure that you get the right kind of tenants (while warding off the low quality ones).

Bad credit scores, history of missed payments, or even a criminal record could be some strikes against tenants looking to move into a place located on your property. A bad tenant or two can trigger so many headaches. So choose wisely.

Operating at a loss (or negative cash flow)

If you are operating at a loss or have a negative cash flow, this can cause your investment to lose its value. That's why you want to operate at a positive cash flow so you have a positive return on investment. Operating at a loss on a temporary basis may be fine, just as long as you find a long-term solution in the process.

For example, let's say that one of your expenses increases. A property management company decides to increase their rates and it puts your cash flow slightly in the red. At that point, you can do one of two things: one, you can increase fees or the rent. Two, you can find a cost effective solution by finding a property management company that can get the job done at a lesser price.

In this situation, you may be faced with a decision that could impact the tenants. If you do have some vacancies, consider upping the rent before it's filled. The rent of your existing tenants should remain the same to ensure that they stay happy and are not surprised by any hikes.

Conditions of the market economy

The market economy is one of the major things that every real estate investor must pay attention to. Especially if you are going to focus on building your portfolio of rental properties. The market economy will play a role in the rental property's future value.

This is what affects your rental income, the resale value, and the like. So if you are contemplating the idea of purchasing property (or cashing out), see what the state of the market economy is like. If it's in good shape, by all means have at it.

The deeper you understand the market, the more you'll be able to make a few moves ahead of your competition. You'll be playing chess while the others may be playing checkers. And that alone could put you on top compared to those who have been in the game for quite some time.

What Makes Rental Property Investment Challenging

As a rental property investor, you may be aware of the challenges that lie ahead. But what are those specific challenges? This section will lay that all out for you.

Those who are willing to take on the risks and challenges of rental property investing can find success for the long-term once they stick with the plan and be able to conquer the challenges that are set before them. If you don't know how to overcome the challenges, you'll learn how right here.
These are the challenges that entail with investing in rental properties (and how to rise above them):

Financing

The first major challenge that you'll face as a rental property investor will always be the financial side of things. You may have a handful of cash to spend on a property that you've had your eye on. But the issue here is that it may not be enough to cover the purchase itself.

So it seems that the best route for most investors is applying for a loan. You may have $50,000 on hand, but need an extra $50,000 to purchase a $100,000 property. There may be a few lenders that can get you the cash you need.

You want to take a look at some of the terms, conditions, and policies that will ensure your approval. If you don't meet them, you will be denied (even right off the bat). As a property owner, one of your expenses will be the mortgage (or repaying that loan back to the lender).

The one thing that will help you rise above financial challenges is making sure that you have a positive cash flow. Yes, it can be solved with rent income (but let's not forget the expenses that go along with it). Speaking of which, let's move on to the next challenge.

Fulfilling the vacancy

Once you have purchased the property you want, the question that you must ask is: who will fulfill the vacancies? This means searching for the right kind of tenants that will stick around for the long-term. Who will be willing to sign a 12 month lease for an apartment or a single-family home?
A good tenant is usually hard to find (as strange as it sounds). You'll have some that will miss payments. You'll have one or two of them who can get rowdy and make noise.

The truth is, you'll need to set some policies and guidelines as to who will be able to become tenants of your property (and who can't). Before you even fulfill such vacancies, determine whether or not you want to do this yourself or have a property manager do it for you.

Knowing whether to renovate or not

Renovations can and will happen at some point. The question is: how long will it be until it finally happens? Whether it's small-scale improvements or something greater, you may consider renovations to be something of a positive rather than a negative.
One such thing that a renovation may yield is a higher return on investment (and even higher rents). Finding the right time to renovate may seem like a difficult task. The no-brainer option would be when there is a vacancy.

What if there are renovations needed when there are tenants currently occupying the unit? This is for you and the tenant to discuss. You can talk about what needs to be done and perhaps work out some kind of deal with them.
If it means the tenant possibly paying more, consider what they would be willing to have in order to justify paying a higher rent. You want both you and the tenant to come out of the deal with the two of you on the winning side.

Unreliable tenants

Of course, you'll have tenants that won't pay. Or they won't keep the place in good condition. The place may be damaged to the point where the handyman is there every day (and might as well be an additional tenant).

Before laying out your battle plan on how to deal with unreliable tenants such as evicting them, it's good to brush up on the tenancy laws in your jurisdiction. Also, you'll want to review the terms of the lease. Your tenant has rights and obligations and you want to honor them as such (and avoid legal headaches).

This is where a professional property manager will come in handy. When you are assembling your team, this property management (or management company) can handle all the heavy lifting regarding unreliable tenants so you don't have to.

This is a challenge that will likely happen in the beginning. And it may happen in situations where there are more vacancies than there are occupants. This is one of the largest challenges that a rental property investor faces regularly.

The two options to handle this challenge can't be simple enough: one, you cut down expenses or you increase the rent. With vacancies, increasing the rent may be easy to do. But what if you have existing tenants?

You may have tenants that will not be happy with the rent increase. And that could mean a turnover. So it would be wise to speak with them and let them know about your consideration before making a major move.

Is it possible to raise the rent while retaining the tenant? The short answer is yes. However, the tenant may not be the only person you'll want to consult with.

This is something that you'll want to discuss with your property manager. You want to raise the rent, but how much would be a reasonable hike? On top of that, are there any legal things of note to look into before making the move?

This could be a challenge that you will face if not enough money is being made. But thankfully, you have options to ensure that your cash flow stays in the green.

Top 3 Reasons Why Rental Property Owners Fail

When it comes to investing in rental properties, there is the possibility that someone will fail. We'll be taking a look at the top three reasons why. You want to learn which mistakes to avoid so you can be able to have a more prosperous future as a property investor instead of a bleak one.

These are the reasons:

1. Risking too much

As the old saying goes, big risk equals big reward. And for some investors, their greed can kill their chances of getting a good return on investment. They can do that by betting on a huge risk.

Overleveraging or obtaining deals that may be considered 'low-down' deals (or those that never have materialized) are just prime examples of taking risks. The more risks you are taking, the more than likely you'll be hearing the words 'bankruptcy' sooner rather than later.

No matter how hard you try to avoid it, there will be some risks. And no investment is considered 'too safe'. But if you are able to navigate it with ease, you'll stand to lose less as opposed to more.

2. Lack of education

If you know too little about investing, you'll lose quite a lot of money on 'this investment or that investment'. One of the reasons why you are reading this book is because you want to learn how to invest in a specific asset. Needless to say, you're in the right direction.

Even after you finish reading this book, the education continues. So it's important to learn the right things in order to achieve success with investing in rental properties. You'll want to build an educational foundation that will support your future success.

The best ways to acquire this education is by doing your research. And it also means connecting with people who have been dealing with real estate for quite some time. It also never hurts to have people who have rental properties In their portfolio as well.

Oh...and steer clear from those sleazy late night infomercials that promise that you'll get rich quick with real estate. Those are not real educational materials (and really not worth the money).

3. You are not doing any due diligence or analysis

With every investment, there's one thing that you absolutely must do. And that is do your due diligence and analysis. When you first start out, you might think you know what you're doing.

But the reality is, you might be doing something wrong and not know it until it's too late. In your analysis, you must be careful. You must study the numbers and see if there is a trend going in the right or wrong direction.

No, you cannot predict the future. But you can use your best judgement while analyzing things and determine whether or not it's worth the investment. And best of all, you better make sure that the math is right and on point.

You can simply avoid failure by not making the mistakes listed above. Be sure that you're not taking too much of a risk. And you'll want to learn a good amount about what you can regarding rental properties.

And as always, for the love of everything that is right in this world, look before you leap. In other words, do your research and analyze any available data. If the math appears to be off, then that might be a hidden signal to hold off on making an investment (or move on to a property that will yield a better return).

It is Not as Scary as it Seems

Even though there are risks, that should not discourage you in the slightest. Remember, it should be fun and exciting to get into the world of investing in rental properties. But you have to know your limits.

All it takes is good planning, relying on the right information, and being able to analyze and relevant data that will help get you on the path towards prosperity. It may also be a challenge to distinguish which information is considered the real deal from the stuff that may be false and full of empty promises.

Remember, finding success will take trial and error. Do you have what it takes to take the risks while making sure you stay within your limits? We hope so.

Final Thoughts

Indeed there are risks that take place whenever you are investing in rental property. It's about making sure that you understand the risks and finding ways to rise to the challenge so you don't end up losing your shirt. It's all about looking at the bigger picture and the long-term rather than look at investing as an opportunity to 'get rich quick'.

It's important that you find the right people and the right information so you know what you're getting into. If you make one bad investment due to some misinformation, that's one thing. But doing it repeatedly for one purpose or another may be asking for trouble.

Investing in rental property isn't for everyone. Those who are not willing to take some risks should refrain from it. Those who cannot embrace failure should consider something else.

And those who don't feel like putting in a lot of work and analysis should consider investing in rental properties. It may not be easy to do, but the rewards certainly are sweet.

Chapter 5 - Knowing What A Good Rental Property Is

There is a rental property that is waiting to be bought by someone who is willing to take good care of it. Not to mention, it's an opportunity that just might be hidden in plain sight. It might take a good set of eyes to spot it when everyone else is overlooking it.

For the investor that has spent a good deal of time generating rental income, they seem to miss opportunities that are considered to be hidden gems. In this chapter, you'll learn some of the ins and outs of knowing what qualifies as good rental property. Sure, you may find something that will be appealing enough to purchase (but there's always something better).

We'll also dive deep and discuss how you can find a good rental property with the help of a few different resources (including one that a lot of people don't seem to utilize all that much). You'll also learn about things like the price to rent ratio so it will help you generate a good amount of income in the long run.

Let's move on and talk about the choices that you might face when selecting your first rental property:

There's A Good Choice and a Better One

There will come a time when you'll come across a rental property that has some good quality features. You might be in a good neighborhood and the property itself is in good shape. You have the money to snag it today if you wanted to.

However, one of your 'eyes on the ground' spots something that might be a little better. And yet, there are some qualities about the property that might just make it more valuable in the future.

Good neighborhood? Check.

Commute-friendly? Check.

Close to the city center? Double check.

Location is one of the most important aspects of acquiring a good piece of property. However, you'll want to take into account the numbers. That's why analysis is so important.

Being able to crunch the numbers and examine them after words will help you make a choice on which property is the best. Sometimes, no matter how good it looks or how close it is to points of interest, the numbers will usually tell you otherwise.

What are some of the calculations to keep in mind while taking a look at the properties that interest you? Let's take a look at the following:

Return on investment (ROI)

Obviously, you want a good ROI. At the end of the day, the property that tends to have the highest overall ROI will win out. Remember, the overall ROI will be calculated by the following formula:

(Net profit/Cost of the investment) x 100

The percentage or ratio should be in the positive. After crunching and calculating the numbers, if it is positive, that's when you know that you'll be making a profit. Obviously, a negative percentage or ratio will equate to a loss (sounds simple enough, right?).

Net Operating Income

The net operating income is the amount of profit that is generated on an annual basis from an investment. You calculate this using the following formula:

Net income - net operating costs
Remember, the operating costs include your expenses such as taxes, maintenance, supplies, insurance, and so on. You might already have a few set expenses in mind. So be sure to calculate those whenever you are putting together the numbers.

Also, keep in mind that the expenses on one property will be manageable while it may not be the case on another property for some reason or another. Also, know that the older the investment, the more the operating costs will be.

Cash on cash return

This is defined as how much the cash ratio will be for the investor. The calculation for this will be useful for investors that want to finance their property investment with long-term debt. For this reason, investors won't be too focused on the operation costs.
The return itself will give them an indicator of how good the property is performing.

Capitalization rate

The cap rate is calculated as follows:

(Net operating income/Property value in the current market) x 100

Before you even snag the property that you're interested in, you must always look at the property value in the current market. Remember, there's a good chance that the market can change for the better or the worse (depending on economy and other factors). If the current market is looking solid, then the property values shouldn't be too shabby.

Bear in mind that if you invest in the property and get the same amount of money from it while the market gets better, the cap rate will drop. Obviously, you'll see the opposite happen if the market drops (albeit sharply).

The cap rate should be something you'll want to calculate with each property you are looking at. It does change from one property of interest to the next. The lower the rate, the better.

Rent Ratio

The rent ratio is the monthly income to the cost of the property. This is how you calculate it:

[Total annual rent/total cost of the property]

The ratio you want to aim for is higher than one percent. If the ratio is lower, then the investor will need more time to recover the total cost of the property itself. For example, let's say the rent per month was $1500 a month and the total cost of the property was $150,000.

Take the total amount of rent you pay annually (so in this case, $1,500 x 12 is $18,000). Now, let's calculate the rest of it to get the rent ratio:

[$18,000/$200,000 = 1.2]

So the ratio is just above a percent. But you get the idea. Sometimes, it may take a bit more time to recover the total cost of the property based on the rent you are charging per month because of a low ratio.

The Demand Is High But The Vacancy Is Low

Aside from the analysis of data, you'll also want to take into consideration the following things: the demand and the vacancy rate. The vacancy rate is determined as follows:

[Number of days vacant / number of rentable days]

For example, if there was a property that was vacant for 30 days, the rate would be the following:

30 / 365 = 8.2 percent

If you have a portfolio property of say 3 homes, here's how you calculate it:
Total Vacant days/Total rentable days (365 x # of properties) = Rate

Let's say for vacant days, Home #1 has 30, Home #2 has 21, and Home #3 has 14. In total, you have 65 vacant days. You multiple 365 by the number of properties you own. So in this case, you multiple 365 by three.

Let's finish up the formula:

65 / 1095 (365 x 3) = 5.9 percent

Then you have the occupancy rate that is calculated like using the following formula:

[Rentable days - vacant days]

So, in this case you have 30 vacant days. Minus that by 365 and you get 335 days that the property was occupied. Now, let's calculate that number to get the occupancy rate:

335/365 = 91.7

So the occupancy rate for this example is 91.7 percent.

Why are all these numbers relevant? For one, a low vacancy rate will equal a high demand. If the rate is below 2 percent, the rental demand will be high. If the rate is higher than 4 percent, the market will signify that there is plenty of supply to go around.

If there is a low vacancy rate on your property, your property manager will have plenty of applicants to field through. Many will apply, but not everyone will be approved as a tenant. Not to mention, with the demand being high and a low vacancy it's prime for the potential of upping the rent before the vacancy itself is fulfilled.

On top of that, the low vacancy data means that the competition will be a little less cluttered. There will be a pool of available tenants but you might have a good chunk of them applying to fulfill the leftover vacancies you may have.

One takeaway from this: if the vacancy rate is low, you and the property manager have to be selective when it comes to who will move into your rental property. So that may come down to a few tough decisions. Use your gut instinct if you need to.

Employment Opportunities Matter

Job growth and the housing market go hand in hand. Not only that, the latter is one of the biggest components of the US economy. Remember when the housing market crashed in the late 2000s?

Yep, for that reason the economy took a major hit from it. This further supports the statement that you want to check for how the rest of the economy is doing before diving in. That's why doing your due diligence is so important.

Naturally, the housing market will fare well when the job growth is positive. When the job growth goes in the opposite direction, the housing market will take a hit (and a lot of people may not be so keen with buying a house at that moment). Also, the likelihood of fulfilling rental vacancies may not be as good.

There is an issue where there is high unemployment rates and high vacancy rates. This puts property investors in a precarious position.

The job market and the unemployment rate will play a huge factor in your investments. Let's take a look at a few things that you'll want to be aware of:

- When the unemployment rate is high, your property value will take a hit. Likewise, the number of tenants will be lower since they may not desire looking to fulfill a vacancy somewhere

- If the unemployment situation is worse enough, the likelihood of property foreclosure will be even greater. If your property is located near other properties that are foreclosed (or in the process of doing so), that will drag down the value of your own property.

- If the employment rate is high and people are working, the demand will be steady. However, if the vacancy rate is high, you may want to consider reducing the rental rate so the vacancies get fulfilled.

When you are looking at vacancies to fulfill, the job growth is a key indicator. If the unemployment rate is at a low level, consider reducing rent to a point where it can be a reasonable amount for your ideal tenant. If the unemployment rate is high, be prepared to make some financially tough decisions.

If you have enough money lying around, you could consider acquiring some of the adjacent properties that have been foreclosed. However, you might risk putting yourself in a position that you'll have more unfilled supply with low demand. So it might be best just to bite the bullet and deal with a lower property value.

One thing to keep in mind is that job growth forecasts can play a role in rental prices. If there is future job growth predicted, that could give you enough time to choose which properties you want to up the rent for. Be sure to take a look at how the wages and total household income numbers are moving.

The Neighborhood is a Key Player

If there is one indicator that will help you make the determination of whether or not you are making the right choice in terms of property investment, the neighborhood is your best friend. You could ask people living in the neighborhood about certain types of information like the nearest schools, average commute time, safety, and so on.

Using that intel will help you get an inside track on whether or not the target property is actually worth investing in. Think about it for a moment: a family of four would want to rent a single-family home. However, they have some wishes and needs in where they want to live.

For example, they want to be near a school. They also want to be in a neighborhood that is safe and has a low crime rate. And they want to at least have a short commute to work at best.

Can you blame someone who wants all those things? No. And that's why you'll want some neighborhood information from the people that know it best: those who live there.

On top of all of this, you'll want to do some number crunching. While scouting the neighborhood, take a look at the number of houses that are currently up for sale. You'll want to get the exact addresses of these homes so you can get data on them (such as the asking price).

Also, the number of owner-occupied homes will help you determine whether or not if the houses up for sale are worth renting or if it's just for purchasing only.

Lastly, the vacancy and occupancy rate is key. Ask people living in the neighborhood how long they've lived there. The higher the occupancy rate, the lower the vacancy rate.

Average Rents and Average Property Value

One more number to focus on when looking for property to invest in is the price to rent ratio. This is calculated with the following formula:

[Median Home Price/Median Annual Rent]

If the median home price in one neighborhood of interest is $200,000 and if you plan on renting out a place at $1,000 a month, this is what you need to calculate:

$200,000 / $12,000 ($1,000 x 12 months) = 16.6

The price to rent ratio can be used to determine the potential demand for rental property in the area. The higher the price to rent ratio, the higher the demand.

Final Thoughts

At this point, you may be thinking about choosing a rental property that will be perfect for your portfolio. However, this will require you to do plenty of number crunching and analysis. Using the simple formulas we've listed above, the number crunching won't be too difficult.

However, it's better to get an understanding of how the numbers operate. They will be used to determine demand and whether or not the property you are looking at may actually be worth it. Some other property may come along and end up being better (not because of the location, but the numbers will tell you otherwise).

The vacancy ratio will determine a demand for rental properties (as will the price to rent ratio). Also, keep in mind that the economy and the job market will play a role in your decision. A good time to jump on an opportunity is when the job market is doing good. If the employment rate is high but the vacancy rate is high as well, then you've got plenty of supply that can be fulfilled.

It also doesn't hurt to get some information by going straight to the source, the people who live in the neighborhood you are interested in. The more you know about the neighborhood in general, the more likely you can consider snagging a rental property there.

Chapter 6 - Rental Properties and Where To Find Them

Now, here comes the fun part. Now it's time to find some rental properties that you might like. In this chapter, we're going to be taking a look at multiple approaches.

One thing you need to understand is that you shouldn't be stressed out too much about looking for a rental property. You may be asking yourself, 'where can I find a property'. Rest assured, this chapter will serve as a good starting point and help put your mind at ease.

There are plenty of valuable tools to use that will help you find the right kind of properties. Not to mention, you'll be able to determine whether or not if there is a good solid demand for such properties or if there is a supply just waiting to be fulfilled. Even in today's technology driven world, you'll find some prospective acquisitions to look at and put together a list of multiple properties by the end of the day.

You'll be learning about how to use a heatmap (and how they work). You'll also learn about the MLS (or multiple list services) along with an old-fashioned tool that has helped rental property investors like you in the past and still works today.

With that said, let's jump right in. This is one chapter that you really shouldn't skip for obvious reasons.

Finding Properties Are Easier Than You Think

We're in the 21st century. So it comes as no surprise that our current technology can be harnessed for a greater good. In this case, you'll be using it for the purpose of finding your rental properties. As mentioned earlier, we'll be taking a look at some tools of interest that will work to your advantage.

With the help of modern day technology, it takes off a lot of pressure and stress that happens when trying to find the right kind of property. We encourage you to use these tools often so you can be able to determine whether or not the property you are eyeing is actually worth it. Let's move forward and talk about heatmaps.

Heatmap Is A Great Tool To Start With

A heatmap might just be one of the coolest tools for any rental property investor to use. It is an analysis tool that can also serve as an investment tool as well. A heatmap uses color codes to determine hot and cold spots.

The hot spots will usually be darker in color ranging from yellow to red. Meanwhile, the cool spots will be yellowish-green to about green or blue (depending on what the indicator lists). You'll be using this tool to find out which areas have excellent property values, demand for such property, or even any kind of data that may be relevant to a target area.

You can find a real estate heat map anywhere online. There are plenty of different websites that have their own heat maps. So it's important to choose a couple of them and test them out for accuracy purposes.

The last thing you want is to acquire property and find out that the data that you've relied on was incorrect all along. The more accurate the data, the better. So if there is an area of interest, check it out on various heat maps online.

So how can a heat map help you find income properties? It analyzes your location of interest based on certain filters. These filters include but are not limited to the following:

- Rental income

- Listing price

- Return on investment (ROI)

- Occupancy rate (AirBnB)

Rental income

The heat map filter for rental income will help you determine which areas have the potential to generate the best rental income. Obviously, you want a high rental income (or something reasonable enough to give you a positive cash flow). You may be tempted to find a property that is high on the heat map.

However, it's important to determine your 'cut off number' in terms of how much rental income you want per property. Sometimes, you might just have to settle with a decent number. But rest assured, it may not be the only rental property that you'll invest in.

Numbers add up over time. $1,000 a month becomes $2,000. $2,000 can become $4,000.

You get the idea. So even if you don't land a rental property that's high on the heat map, no need to worry.

Listing price

The listing price filter is based on the price of homes that are currently for sale in the area. The lower the price, the 'warmer' the heat map will indicate. The listing price may be one element of importance to the rental investor.

So it would make sense to go after the properties that have a lower listing price (especially when you are starting out). The heat map will acquire the data based on the prices of houses currently for sale in that area. If you see any properties at a reasonable price, check it out and see if it might be worth using for rental property.

Return on Investment (ROI)

The overall ROI is another great filter worth paying attention to. And for some heat maps, they will do all the number crunching for you so you don't always have to. The heat map will give you a good idea of which properties will give you a good return on investment (and may tell you why).

Occupancy rate for AirBNB

Depending on your area, you may have people looking for a place to crash while they're visiting. However, they might not have enough money to cough up for a hotel room. Enter AirBNB.

With income properties that are for purchase, you could use it for the purpose of fulfilling the vacancies by way of the AirBNB route. There's a heat map that will determine the occupancy rate of these properties that are ripe for AirBNB. The higher the vacancy rate, that part of the neighborhood will be the perfect spot for people to go to for a place to stay.

And that alone can be a good opportunity to get some extra cash in your pocket. Because people are traveling and want to pay for something that is the fraction of a hotel room. And if your property is in a prime location, what have you got to lose?

Have You Heard Of Multiple Listing Services?

Believe it or not, internet listings are still a thing. And it's all thanks to Multiple Listing Services or MLS. What exactly is an MLS?

It's where properties that are available for purchase or rent are posted throughout various listings on the Internet. Name a real estate search engine like Zillow or even on a real estate website like ReMax and that property will be on there. The listing of the property is bound to be somewhere on the interwebs.

Under an MLS, the listing and selling broker will benefit by putting together the pertinent information and sharing it throughout these listings. MLS listings can be based on a local area or even a much larger region. For example, there could be an MLS strictly for New York City.

If you want to go a step further and go farther out of a metro area, check out a regional listing. So in this case, if you want something outside of New York City proper, you can search through a list that includes properties in New Jersey, Long Island, Southwestern Connecticut, and so on. Not only will you get a much larger list of properties that are available, it gives you the opportunity to open some doors for more options.

Multiple listing services take the guesswork out of which properties are for sale and which ones are not. You can browse through so many real estate websites and you'll see pretty much the same listings if you were to go to another site and search for the same area. As for the MLS itself, the brokers (both representing the buyer and seller) will get a nice commission for every sale that goes through.

One of the best benefits of an MLS is that you get more exposure. Since it's spread out across various listing sites, it will provide you with more traffic (and potentially interested buyers). Compare that to just one broker where the visibility is lesser.

Properties on an MLS must meet certain requirements in order to be on a list. They must be entered within a specific time period. Failure to do so may be grounds for a 'fine' (as will omitting any data that needs to be required for the listing).

The MLS needs to have accurate data, so if you list a rental property that you plan on selling in the future, take note of this. This means getting a specific measurement of the property, how many bedrooms and bathrooms there are, and so on. Also, be sure that the property has high quality photos so interested buyers get a good look at the property from the inside and out.

Opportunities in Direct Mail Marketing

Direct mail marketing may be the oldest and widely practiced thing to do in real estate. Especially when it comes to finding the right kind of rental property. It's worked for many years and still does today (even with modern technology being dominating in almost every industry).

Even though digital marketing reigns supreme, it means that the marketing channel itself will generate a ton of noise. And it will make things a bit more overwhelming. Since almost everyone in real estate is doing digital marketing, the competition is fierce.

And let's not forget, ad blockers are still a thing. So the digital ads may not be within reach of people who want to get rid of those distractions. Those who have been in the business for long know that the roads less traveled often lead to success.

That's where direct mail marketing comes in. Yes, it's a tried and true method that's been around for years. And yet, people look at it and write it off as a bygone thing.

What they fail to realize that the true value of direct mail marketing has never depreciated. A lot of people love getting things in the mail that are not usually considered bills or the like. So you'll want to use this opportunity to stand out.

If you are a rental property owner, you can use this later on when the time comes to sell your property. But what if you are looking to invest in rental property? You can use direct mail as a way to get seller leads better than any digital approach.

There are a few reasons why direct mail will work to your advantage. Let's cut to the chase and talk about them:

- **It's less crowded:** As mentioned, a lot of people will rely on digital marketing methods. However, you can take the road less traveled and since a postcard or something similar to someone who may be selling their homes or property. You can leave contact information for them in case they are interested in talking to you more.

- **It can be memorable:** No need to make it snazzy or over the top. When people receive cards or letters in the mail, it can trigger some kind of nostalgia. The feeling of excitement that you got something important in the mail. Direct mail will give it that personalized touch.

- **Wider reach:** Even though the digital approach can provide a laser focused reach, direct mail can reach the people you are interested in contacting as well. However, with direct mail there is a much wider reach. This can pick up the slack where electronic ads tend to miss the mark.

- **Lesser competition:** Where there are less people doing it, the competitive presence is slim. So you can generate success just by doing something that has little to no competitors. It's a hidden gem that people seem to mark off as 'dead' because of modern technology.

A few things to keep in mind while doing mailers. In your mailer, be sure to have a call to action (like a number that they can call or an email to send you a message). You should also define your audience before sending out a piece of mail.

And you should send test batches to ensure that your market is accurately defined. From there, you can measure the amount of engagement as well. The more responsive your audience is, the better.

Also, make sure that your mailers are grammatically correct. Misspellings and grammatical errors will hurt your credibility. Be sure to double check or even triple check before sending things out (even test mailers). And last but not least, don't forget to follow up with the people that you sent your mailers to.

Does direct mail mean neglecting anything that has to do with an online presence? Not at all. In fact, you still want to have a digital presence in order to keep your bases covered.

Considering Wholesale Deals

Wholesale deals are where you can find properties for a lower price. In other words, the wholesale market is 'buy low, sell low'. Wholesaling in real estate is where the property goes under contract and is later assigned to another buyer (who has plans on using the property).

In wholesale deals, there are three people: the buyer, the seller, and wholesaler. The wholesaler acts as the middle man of the deal. When a seller wants to get their property off the market but does not have the essential means to do so, that's when they will connect with a wholesaler.

From there, the wholesaler will find a buyer who will agree to purchase the home at a value that is greater than the seller's asking price. Once the buyer signs the contract, the property is sold. And the wholesaler makes money on the difference.

For example, the seller's asking price would be $250,000. However, the wholesaler finds a buyer who can take it off the seller's hands for about $400,000. The wholesaler in return will get $150,000 for that successful sale (and the seller gets the amount they want).

If you are someone who is looking to buy property at wholesale prices, you may want to see which properties are being sold and for how much. Remember, you will be paying more than what the seller wants. So be sure you have enough cash on hand to purchase the property.

After you purchase the property, you can do what you want with it. You can get some necessary repairs and renovations in. And then you can rent it out to someone who may be looking for a place to live for the long-term.

Smartphone Applications Are Powerful Tools

If you are on the go or in a neighborhood of interest, you can definitely rely on smartphone applications to help find the right property for you. You could be in an area in real time and be close to something that might be your first ever rental property.

What kind of apps are you looking for? It may depend on the kind of property you are going after. For example, if you are looking for an app that will help you find the best residential properties, Zillow or Realtor.com will have mobile apps that you can use. Trulia may also be a good app to have on hand if you are searching for single-family homes.

There are also different apps that will be perfect for when you need to go paperless for signing documents and the like. For this, we recommend an app like DocuSign. You can e-sign contracts, agreements, tenant disclosures, and more. Less paperwork and more convenience right at your fingertips.

Using Online Databases To Find Properties

Online databases are perhaps one of your best alternatives. You can access them both on a mobile or desktop device. Here are a list of online databases that you should consider checking out:

- LoopNet (Note: this is perfect for commercial properties if you are interested in purchasing one as a rental property)

- Auctions.com (great for acquiring foreclosures or even luxury rental properties)

- CraigsList (if you want to look within your local area and beyond)

- Trulia (great for single-family properties and foreclosures)

These are just a sample of online websites and databases that you can check out if you are scouting out potential rental properties. When you spot a property of interest, see if you can get an address so you or your 'scout' can check out the property and see if it's worth looking at further and eventually worth buying.

Final Thoughts

Finding a rental property isn't easy. But it doesn't have to be too complicated. You have a lot of handy apps and websites at your disposal.

Spend time looking through various websites and real estate listings in your local area. Also, take a look at the heatmaps in your area and even miles beyond that. You never know where you'll find your perfect property.

Multiple listings of properties will definitely help you find the right place. And you can even rely on good old-fashioned direct mail marketing to help point you in the right direction. You can send a postcard to home sellers, real estate agents, and other relevant people who can help find your first ever rental property.

Chapter 7 - Dealing With The Numbers

No matter what you invest in, you're going to be dealing with numbers. And that's all part of the process whenever you are planning on getting an excellent return on investment. You don't have to be a math whiz to crunch all the numbers.

And we promise you that we won't throw so many equations that only a genius would figure out. Yes, you'll be dealing with numbers (but we'll do our best to make it as simple as possible). This chapter will be dedicated to how you can run the numbers properly, putting that analysis to good use, and allow yourself to increase your cash flow.

At the same time, we'll show you how you can make an offer and ensure that it will get accepted sooner rather than never. We are approaching what could be one of the most exciting moments of your time as an investor. You are aware of the risks that you're about to take and the rewards that go along with it.

Let's get started and start talking about the numbers:

Do I Really Have To Do An Analysis?

The short answer: yes. The reason why you need to do this is simple. You want to reduce the risk of losing so much in an investment.

Without doing an analysis, you are basically flying blind into the unknown. Nine times out of ten, you'll end up on the losing end rather than the winning one. An analysis of the numbers including the data that will help you figure out whether or not the property you want to rent out is important.

Let us remind you that you'll need to know some numbers including the total return on investment. Aside from that, you want to know about how much the expenses will be and the kind of income that you want to generate to ensure a positive cash flow. Putting those numbers together will help you determine whether or not the property you want to acquire is worth it.

In a previous chapter, we said that there could be one rental property you'll like, but you may come across something better. And by better, we mean a better return on investment. Two separate rental properties in different locations that have the same amenities and the like and one of them could be better than the other.

Remember, the location is usually a huge factor when choosing the right kind of rental property. But keep in mind that you'll need plenty of reliable data to ensure that you are getting the right return on investment rather than some fake numbers. If you need to double check your analysis, you can reach out to members of your team that can confirm whether the numbers are accurate or not.

Running The Number Properly

Now, we get to the good stuff. Running the numbers is not as difficult as you think. It's a necessary task that needs to be done before making the most crucial decisions.

We'll discuss what cash flow is and how you can properly analyze it (along with some other numbers). There are also some things that you'll need to take into consideration as well. When you run the numbers carefully and make sure that everything is accurate and up to date, that will make the deal making process a lot easier.

Now, let's show you how to run the numbers like cash flow and the like:

Calculating your cash flow

As mentioned before, cash flow is what you will be collecting for profit every month after expenses. The goal here is making sure that your cash flow is more than what you spend for expenses every month. That's the key to financial independence.

In case you may have forgotten the formula for calculating your cash flow, here's a quick refresher:

Income - Expenses = Cash flow

See, we told you we weren't going to throw complex equations at you. Your income is your rent that is collected from your tenants. Your expenses include but are not limited to the following:

- Repairs and maintenance

- Mortgage payments

- Property taxes

- Insurance

- Utilities

- Property management

- Vacancies

- Closing costs/filing fees (if applicable)

This is just a sample list of the expenses that you'll want to look at. It's important that you take a look at how much money you plan on spending per month on such things like insurance policies, the mortgage, and the property taxes (since they could change over time). Remember, some of the additional expenses like utilities and services like garbage pickup can be covered by the tenant's rent (which will usually mean the tenant will pay more by default).

Calculating the cap rate

Before you even close the deal, you'll want to consider the cap rate as your best indicator. This will help you determine whether or not the purchase price itself is a good deal on your end or not. With that in mind, let's show you the formula for calculating the cap rate:

Net Annual Income / Purchase Price = Cap Rate

The cap rate will depend on two factors: the area of the property and the state of the market. You'll want to shoot for a cap rate that is 6 percent or above. If the rate is on or above that, you'll have a good deal on your hands.

Now, let's run some numbers in this example:

Let's say you are charging $1,500 a month for rent. The net annual income is the monthly rent multiplied by 12. Therefore: **$1,500 x 12 = $18,000.**

So, you take $18,000 and divide it by the purchase price of the property in question. So let's say this property you want to acquire is $250,000. Is it a good deal if your ideal net annual income?

Let's find out:

$18,000/$250,000 = 7.2

So that rounds to about 7.2 percent. So the cap rate is above the ideal 6 percent. So there you go, that's a deal that you want to put together.

Don't forget the Cash on Cash return

The cash on cash return is the amount of money you'll get for your return on investment. This will depend on how much money you'll put in. Like the cap rate formula, you will be using the net annual income as a way to crunch the numbers.

The formula for calculating the cash on cash return is:

Net Annual Income / Total Cash invested = Cash on Cash Return

Oh...one more thing, the cash on cash return is very similar to the cap rate. So if you purchase the property using cash, you'll get a 7.2 percent return on investment. So remember that the cap rate and the cash on cash return will be the same.

So can you purchase the property outright? The short answer is yes. When you purchase the property outright with cash, there is no need to include the mortgage as an expense.

If you want to save a little extra and have a bit more cash flow, then your best bet will be to always purchase the property outright. No mortgage plus interest to deal with. Pretty cool, huh?

But if you are purchasing with the plan to pay a mortgage per month, you should consider consolidating that expense with the interest plus insurance. Sometimes, you may not have all the cash you need to buy property outright (and that's OK).

One thing to keep in mind is that you want to avoid your cash flow going into the negative. The last thing you want is to pay additional expenses out of your pockets. You'll want to put yourself in a situation where the rents are reasonable enough for your tenants (rather than hike them up because you are bleeding cash).

Putting Your Analysis In Action

Now, it's time to put those numbers into action. In this section, we'll show you an extensive example on how to run the numbers so you know that you'll have a positive cash flow for your property. Let's start with the income and expenses using an apartment building as an example:

Income

Number of Units: 10

Average monthly rent per unit: $550

Total monthly income: $5,500

Total annual income: $66,000

Monthly Operating Expenses

Property management: $550 (10 percent of your total monthly income)

Repairs and maintenance: $500

Property Taxes: $350 (per month)

Utilities: $550

Mortgage/Interest/Insurance: $900

Vacancies: $550 (10 percent max of monthly income)

Total monthly operating expenses: $3,400

Net operating income (annual)

Total annual net operating income: $66,000

Total annual net operating expenses: $40,800

Annual net operating income: $25,200

Cap Rate

Note: With the net operating income being $25,200 in this example. Let's say the purchasing price for the apartment building was $400,000.

$25,200 (Annual net income)/ $400,000 (purchase price) = 6.3%

Keep in mind that there is a desired capitalization rate and an actual capitalization rate. This number will depend on how much the actual purchase price of the property is. The offer price will usually differ from the actual purchase price.

Loan expenses

If you have purchased a property using a loan, there are some things to take into consideration when analysing your data. This include the down payment, the loan amount after the down payment itself, acquisition costs and loan fees, and the annual interest rate. Also, the length of the mortgage in terms of years will also be something to take into account.

Cash on Cash Return (ROI)

Remember, the cash on cash return may be the same as the cap rate. However, if you are paying a mortgage or paying off a loan, the number will differ. In one example, let's say that your total annual debt service (or the loan expenses) is $10,000.

So you take the annual operating income and subtract it by the total annual debt service like so:

$25,200 - $10,000 = $15,200

So your annual cash flow will be $15,200. So what about the cash on cash return? It's the net income and your initial investment.

So if you put a $75,000 down payment on the apartment building, you've invested that amount of money up to this point. Therefore:

$25,200 / 75,000 = 33.6

If our calculations are correct, that's a 33.6 percent return on investment from the initial one itself.

Six Ways To Increase Your Cash Flow

Let's say the numbers are not working into your favor. That doesn't mean the end of the world. It should indicate that you'll need to increase your cash flow.

Somehow and some way, you'll get there. With that said, let's take a look at six ways to help you bump up that cash flow so you stay out of the red:

1. Increase the rent

You can increase the rent as you so choose. But as we've stated before, it's better to increase the rent with available vacancies. Yet, if the need is even greater, it may be time to swallow your pride and let your current tenants know what's up.

Depending on where you live, there may be rent control laws that may prevent you from increasing the rent while you have current tenants occupying your units. Before considering the idea of upping the rent, check to see if there are any rent control laws where you are.

2. Consider income from other sources

If increasing rent is out of the question, you could consider the idea of implementing fees for additional services. This may include an on-site laundromat (if you have an apartment building) which will allow people to pay for using the washer and dryer. You could also consider the idea of charging for parking or storage (if your apartment building has these features available).

Depending on the location and what's included on the property, you may need to get creative. If you own a regular apartment building with no parking garage, there is no sense in charging tenants extra for parking.

3. Consider reducing expenses

This can't be said clearly enough. When considering the idea of reducing expenses, you'll need to take into account what you're spending on per month for specific expenses. For example, if you are paying for trash service per month, see if there is another service that offers something for less (which would mean fewer pickups).

Or, let's say you have a property management company that deals with mowing the lawn every month (while charging you for extra monthly services). You can find another property management company that can only charge you for just mowing services and nothing more for less.

4. A larger down payment

At the outset, you may want to put down more money for a down payment when acquiring the property. For example, if your plan to put down $50,000 on a property is hurting the cash flow, consider upping the down payment to perhaps $55,000 or even $60,000.

The more of a down payment you put down, the less likely you'll deal with expenses eating away at your cash flow every month or year.

5. Allow pets

This might be a good time to consider whether or not you want to include pets on the property. If you own an apartment building, including pets may be a good opportunity to generate additional income. That's because you'll be able to charge tenants an extra fee for allowing a pet.

Also, you can decide which pets are allowable and which ones are prohibited. You can even charge a fee based on the size of a dog. A tenant with a chihuahua may pay less than a tenant who owns a husky.

That's all up to you. But think carefully if you want to include pets on your property. Also, keep in mind that there could be potential repair and maintenance. Although we love our pets dearly, they may have accidents or just have a little bit of fun tearing up a place.

6. Make improvements to the building

If you want to increase your cash flow, then why not make some kind of improvements to the property. Something that will increase the overall value of the property such as offering amenities or making widespread renovations. Increasing the overall value may even increase your ROI in return.

Not to mention, you may use these upgrades as an opportunity to provide additional streams of income. As mentioned before, there's a laundromat you can build (if there is enough space), charge for parking, and so on.

Now It's Time To Make An Offer

At this point, you've already run the numbers once or even twice. You've come to the realization that the property you want to purchase will give you a positive income. Now, it's time to make an offer.

So now, you're about to purchase your first ever property. There might be some excitement with a hint of nervousness (which is usually the norm). In this section, we'll discuss how you can make an offer and be able to come out on top.

Will your offer be the right one on the first try? Don't expect it. But once you are able to make an offer that is reasonable, the property will be yours.

Let's take a step-by-step approach on how you can make the best possible offer:

1. Know what you want in a deal

Before entering a deal with someone willing to sell a property to you, you'll want to know what you want. What exactly are you trying to get out of the deal? What are some features of your ideal property that you are looking for?

There are many questions that will come into play such as the location you're aiming for, the type of property that you want to acquire, and so on. You can even whittle it down to when the property was built, how many bedrooms and bathrooms it has, and so on.

It's important to have a criteria for the kind of property you want to acquire. Now that you have spent time putting something together, let's move on to the next step.

2. Compare property already sold in your area to your criteria

If you have an agent, contact then and have them send you information on every property that has been sold in the last six months. From there, you can compare each piece of property against the criteria that you're using for your own acquisition. There are a couple reasons as to why you want to do this.

One, you may look for a similar deal based on some properties that have been sold with the same criteria over that time period. Two, there may be no properties sold at all. In the event of the latter, this might mean making some changes in your criteria such as the area change or the kind of property you want to look for.

3. Make your decision before your next acquisition hits the market

What do we mean by this? You don't need to make an instant decision. You've decided to purchase a property.

Long before the rest of the market knows about it, you can snag the property for yourself without everyone else knowing about it (until after the fact). The sooner you jump on it, the better. You might be lucky enough to get a property that will match your criteria and interest.

The sooner, the better. You can make an offer now as in immediately. You want to pre-prepare and be comfortable with the offer you want to give.

Before doing so, you must be pre-approved by your lender for a loan that is worth the purchase price. Also, you'll want to maintain any liquidity that will allow you breathing room to buy more properties (should you consider expanding your portfolio in the future).

Pick a starting price with the help of your agent. The price may not be the final decision. But your agent will be there to help you acquire the property at a deal that is reasonable and fair for both you and the seller.

Once all is said and done, decide how much money you want to put in escrow. In other words, how much money are you willing to put down as a down payment? These money deposits are usually one to three percent of the purchase price.

Four Tips To Get Your Offer Accepted

To wrap it up, we'll provide you with four tips that will help you get the offer you want. Pay close attention to these if you want the process to be as quick and painless as possible. Check out these tips below:

- **Be 100 percent prepared:** Make sure all of your bases are covered. Get pre-approved for a loan. Analyze the numbers of your target property. And make sure that it's the property you want.

- **Personalize the offer:** If you want to stand out among the crowd, then make the offer more personalized than the generic offers the seller is fielding through. If there is no competition, offer for less than the asking price. If there is competition, come up with an offer that will best the competition. A little negotiating never killed anyone.

- **Protect your acquisition:** After the offer is made, you want to protect yourself from anything that may go sideways. For example, if the seller accepts the offer and later backs out, that can be very painful for you. Instead, consider sending a seller a small deposit. This will give you and the seller a win-win.

- **Never ask the seller to pay the closing costs:** The closing costs should not fall on the seller. As the buyer, you should consider ponying up the extra money to cover it. And it will give the seller a chance to walk away with more cash in their pocket.

Final Thoughts

Now that you know how to analyze the numbers, you can use the formulas listed above to help you find out whether or not you are getting a good deal. Analysis is an absolute must when it comes to investing. You can crunch the numbers and make the determination of whether or not the rent price is just right or if you need to make a few tweaks until you get it right.

Remember, you can also consider a few ideas that will help you increase cash flow as well. If there is no laundromat located at an apartment building that you want to acquire, build one. Not only does that fulfill a need, but it also gives you an additional amount of cash to add onto your income.

Before making an offer, make sure that you know what you want and be prepared to negotiate what should be a fair deal for both you and the seller. Your first offer may go down in flames. So be sure to make your decision before the property you want hits the market.

Not all offers have to be perfect. And they don't have to be ridiculous either.

Chapter 8 - Financing Your Rental Property Investment

Like any other investment, it takes money to get there. However, we're dealing with real estate. So there's a good chance that there will be some financing involved.

You could buy it outright with enough cash. Or maybe you need a loan to put a down payment on it. Either way, you have financing options that are available to you.

In this chapter, we'll talk about financing your rental property and what you'll need to do in order to finance the investment. We'll discuss some of the risks and benefits of doing so. If you are worried about how your loan application will look, this chapter will show you how to get it approved (and we guarantee that it will).

At the same time, we're going to show you how to keep your finances above water. You do not want to make enough mistakes to the point where you'll feel it squeezing your wallet. Too many people have made mistakes while investing in rental property.

But now is your chance to get a deeper understanding of how financing your property works. This is something where many people mess up. But if you follow the steps and tips in this chapter, you'll be ahead of the game.

Let's dive right in:

Do I Need Truckloads Of Cash?

It's easy for us to think that we need a lot of money for a rental property. We often ask: how can we afford this? Indeed, there are expenses that come with the territory of investing in property.

However, we can say that the amount of cash you need will depend on the kind of property you want to acquire. Taking out a loan doesn't always have to be a bad thing. In fact, it might be your best option going forward.

What you need to understand is that it's not a truckload of cash that you need before getting started. It's the ability to get your financial structure in order. Here's what we mean by this:

- **Do you have high-interest debt:** If you have debt that is high in interest, you want to make sure that you get that paid off first. This might be the biggest blemish on your loan application when the time comes to acquire property and something hits a snag. If you have a high-interest credit card that you have yet to pay off, you can do so outright or at least get it to where you have a 0% APR balance transfer.

- **Set up an emergency fund:** An emergency fund will put you a step ahead of a lot of people. We're not joking when we say that there are a lot of people who are unprepared for the unexpected. This emergency fund is basically a general fund that you want to set up just in case the investment itself fails. This 'insurance policy' will protect you against unexpected expenses and financial hardships. How do you set up an emergency fund? Consider setting aside enough money that will cover no less than six months worth of expenses. Keep it in a bank account that you can easily access.

Having enough money to buy a rental property again will depend on the property. Clearly, it takes more money to purchase a $400,000 apartment building than a $150,000 single-family house. But what about the down payment?

The down payment is something you need. But it's not the only thing that you will need money for. You'll also need money to pay for any closing costs (since you don't want to place that burden on the seller).

But let's not stop there. You also need enough money set off to the side for repairs and maintenance. And lastly, there's also money you need for reserves.

The reserves are basically enough to hold you over due to vacancies and the like. To get an idea of how much money you need to put in a reserve account, consider putting in six to 12 months worth of mortgage payments inside a reserve account.

Simply put, you can afford a rental property if you have the financial discipline to do so. We can't define what consists of a 'truckload of cash'. But we will say that you need enough for a down payment and enough to help cover any of the necessary expenses like mortgage payments and repairs.

Ways To Finance Your Investment

There are so many ways to finance your rental property. Yet, it circles back to one word: loans. What kind of loans are out there for rental properties and the like?

Which loan will you need for your property? These questions we'll answer shortly. But after you read this section, you'll get a good understanding of the types of loans that are available.

You may take out one for your first property and take out a different type of loan for any of your subsequent acquisitions. It all depends on what you want to include in your real estate portfolio. Let's take a look at the types of loans that are available to you and why they are important:

Conventional mortgage loans

The first loan will be taking a look at the conventional mortgage loans. These are the most common investment property financing options that are usually issued to real estate investors. Especially if they are focusing on residential properties like apartments or single-family homes.

If you own your own home, chances are you took one out when you purchased it. A conventional mortgage loan is usually offered by a bank or a mortgage broker. Obtaining a mortgage will depend on the state you reside in (assuming you live in the United States).

If you are a property investor, you'll want to put down as much as 20 percent of the property's purchase price as a down payment. For example, let's say the property you want to purchase has a price tag of $300,000. The down payment itself will be $60,000 at minimum.

Don't forget that your credit score and your history will either make or break your chances for getting approved for a conventional mortgage loan. That's why we mentioned paying off any high interest debt you may have before considering a purchase of a property.

If you have a credit score of 620 or higher, then you will likely obtain a conventional mortgage loan. However, if you are aiming for a good interest rate, a credit score of 740 will probably help you. Also, having six months of cash reserves will also give you a leg up in making sure you qualify for a loan.

Hard money loans

Hard money loans are given to investors by individuals or companies that lend you money specifically for the purpose of investing in properties. The good news about these loans is that they are much faster to acquire. Not only that, these lenders don't look at your credit score.

So if you find that acquiring a conventional mortgage loan may not be in the cards, consider getting a hard money loan. However, there is one caveat to keep in mind. These loans are short-term loans.

Specifically, the life of these loans will be up to 36 months. On top of that, these loans command high-interest rates. For this reason, this kind of loan may not be suitable for any rental property. These may be used if you plan on snagging properties that have a low price tag (or if you want to buy the property and flip it after making improvements).

If you are planning on acquiring a long-term investment property, then a hard money loan may not be the route to take.

Private Money Loans

Unlike hard money loans, private money loans are not provided by those who are hard money lenders. This is one other alternative route should you be rejected for a conventional mortgage loan by a bank.

This loan is for individuals who have a good amount of money set off to the side and aim for a good return on their investment property.

These private money lenders may even be in your existing network. This network can include friends, family members, or even real estate investors you have managed to connect with along the way. These loans are secured by way of a promissory note or an existing mortgage on the property.

Keep in mind that the private money lender can have the power to foreclose the property if the loan payment isn't paid off by a specific deadline. So be sure to honor your promise to pay back the loan in the best arrangement possible.

Fix-and-Flip Loans

Fix and flip loans are aimed towards property investors that want to purchase a property, fix it up to increase the overall value, and then sell it for a profit (or flip it). These are short-term loans, so the interest rates will likely be higher compared to other loans.

That's why flippers will need a short amount of time to renovate the house and sell it. And they can do so in the quickest way possible. They'll have the money to pay off the loan and keep the rest if they wish.

Like hard money loans, it's easy for them to get approved. Lenders can look at your credit score, but will not use it as part of their decision making process. They want to make sure that the property you are acquiring has potential profitability.

These loans will usually take a year or less to pay off. So if you are a flipper, you don't need to worry about lenders tracking you down unless you have a reason to worry.

Home equity loan

Home equity loans are another common loan that will be used by investment property owners. If you plan on purchasing a single-family rental property, this might be one worth considering (since it may be considered a loan for getting a second home). The loan will be based on the difference between the homeowner's equity and the current market value of the property itself.

The lender will run a credit check and will appraise your home to ensure that you have the right creditworthiness to secure a loan. This kind of loan is easy to obtain and will provide you with a good source of cash when you need it. The interest paid on these loans are tax-deductible, so that will come in handy when it comes time to file.

If you are a property investor that plans on being responsible when it comes to handling the finances, this kind of loan will work to your advantage. You'll know how much you'll need to borrow (while the investment itself will be a reliable source of income so you can repay it).

Suppose you want to go down the road of commercial investing. No problem. Just apply for a loan that focuses on commercial real estate.

Like the residential loans, you'll have loans such as hard money loans (from lenders that specialize in commercial real estate) and conventional loans as well. The only differences are the down payments, the length of the loan, and the interest rates. Let's take a look at the numbers for these kinds of loans.

For one, the down payment will range anywhere between 15 to 35 percent of the purchase price. Second, the financing options will range anywhere from 12 to 36 months. And lastly, the interest rates will run between 8 to 13 percent.

Depending on your current financial situation and the type of property that you want to acquire, there's a good chance that one of these loans will be a big help to you. As you start your career as a real estate investor, you'll understand how each of these loans work and what you need in order to qualify for them.

Be sure to take a look at your credit score and set aside money for your cash reserves. Before you even apply, look over any of the requirements. They may vary from one lender to the next, but you need to double check to see if you have things in order before being approved.

What are the Risks and Benefits?

Like all kinds of investing, there are risks and benefits. And you need to be aware of them when you are beginning your journey as a real estate investor. Knowing the risks and benefits will keep you a step ahead of the others.

This will usually pertain to loans and the like. While there are benefits, people tend to forget about the risks that are a part of them. Let's take a look at the risks first:

- **Short-term loans equal higher interest:** You may have noticed a pattern over the course of the previous section. A short-term loan will usually yield a higher interest. Therefore, you should consider your options carefully about the types of loans you quality for. Higher interest rates could mean a higher amount of money that you'll need to pay if you miss a loan payment (or continuously fail to pay it on time).

- **You may get rejected repeatedly due to credit score:** It happens. And all you lose is time. So be sure to check out what requirements you meet (and which ones you fall short of) prior to applying for a loan.

Now, let's take a look at the benefits:

- **Loans are temporary:** Yes, these bank loans are temporary. Which means they won't last as long as you live. Once you pay off the loan, you own the investment property outright (which means less expenses).

- **Interest is tax deductible:** As mentioned earlier, the interest that you pay on the loan is tax deductible. Which is perfect for when you want to reduce the tax bill that you get every year from Uncle Sam. The less taxes you pay because of these deducibles, the better.

- **You maintain control of your investment:** The bank doesn't control the investment. Nor do they take any ownership position in your business. This means you make the decisions on what you can do with the property. The bank cannot say 'hey, let's build a laundry facility on the property'. Nor can they have a say in which tenants can move in and who can't rent a place.

The Guaranteed Way To Get A Loan Approved

If you want to get your loan approved, then pay close attention to this section. While loans may be hard to attain for the average real estate investor, it might not be hard for you. You need to put yourself at an advantage to where lenders see you as someone who is responsible and ahead of the curve.

In order to be guaranteed approval for a loan, you'll need to consider the following:

- **Make sure your credit is good:** Your credit score will be the difference between getting approved for a loan or getting rejected. Your credit score will be impacted by the following factors: payment history, outstanding balances, length of credit history, the types of accounts you have, and the credit inquiries. Sometimes, a credit score may not outright deny you. But the size of the loan may be smaller than what you want. Also, consider a credit audit as well as dispute any inaccurate information, late charges, and the like that may have caused your credit to take a nosedive.

- **Pay off any debt:** This can't be stressed enough. Any debt that you may have will carry on you like a weight. Obtaining a property loan will be based on the debt-to-income ratio. Lenders will take a look at how much you make and compare it to how much you can spend. If the debt is 35 percent or more of your total income, you will be rejected. Reduce the debt as far off as possible before you even consider applying.

- **Make a determination of what you can afford:** Consider an accurate number of what you can afford in terms of the properties you want to acquire. Depending on the lender, there will be guidelines in place of how much money you can borrow (minimum or maximum). Also, you'll want to consider your current and future finances as you are starting out.

- **Compile your work history:** Your work history will be looked at by your lenders. Ideally, they'll give a plus to anyone who has worked two or more years in a single job. The work history will verify that you have a reliable source of income. This may also determine the level of risk you may be eligible for.

- **Gather other income information:** Aside from work history, you may want to consider gathering any information where income is generated. This includes any bank statements, tax returns, pay stubs, statements from brokers, and more.

- **Down payment:** The down payment is the amount of money you'll want to put down. As mentioned before, it can take up to 20 percent of the purchase price. At the lowest, it can be 3 percent.

- **Compare lenders:** As mentioned before, the guidelines and requirements can vary from one lender to the next. Pay close attention to what they are so you can determine which lender will approve you and which ones may reject you due to not meeting one or multiple requirements.

- **Get pre-approved:** When you are pre-approved for a loan, this places you at an even greater advantage. Not only will you be viewed favorably by the seller, it will also make the process a lot easier.

Tips To Keep Your Finances Afloat

If you want to keep your finances above water, these tips will help you out. It's important to know about these so you are able to keep your head in the game and not run into any issues. These are the following tips:

- **Put down at least 20 percent:** Yes, we mentioned the down payment can be as low as 3 percent. But you're better off putting down 20 percent of the purchasing price anyways. Because the sooner you pay it off, the better.

- **Don't expect getting the same rate:** Mortgage rates may differ when compared between primary home mortgages and what you could borrow for rental properties.

- **Keep your credit score clean:** 640 is good. But if you keep it in between 670 to 739, then you have an even better shot at landing a loan.

- **Know that not every lender is alike:** Again, the requirements are different. One lender can give you $100,000 while another can give you $75,000 at max. Remember to determine how much you can actually afford.

- **Your finances do get a little tricky:** The banks will consider your debt-to-income ratio and the cash reserves you may have. So it's important to keep your debts low and make sure you have enough cash in your reserves to cover expenses should things don't go as planned.

Final Thoughts

Being able to finance your rental property investment is easier than you think. However, if you have unpaid debts and the like, it might be difficult to get approved. But do not despair, because you have more than one option.

The type of loan you want to get will depend on the type of property you are willing to acquire. You may qualify for one loan, but not for another. Choose the loan that will work best for you based on your current financial situation.

Once you've acquired the property and have managed to generate a good amount of income, you can then refinance it and pay off the loan if you so choose (and we'll show you a cool way to do that in the next chapter). In the meantime, pay off whatever debts that you may have and clear up any credit issues.

When you finally get that squared away, that should give you a good chance at getting approved for a loan.

Chapter 9 - The BRRRR Strategy: No It is Not A Cold

BRRRR. Is it cold in here? No, it's not.

But the one cold thing that we'll be talking about is the cold hard cash you might be getting every month from your rental properties. Before you do, we're going to talk about a strategy known as the 'BRRRR' strategy. This is a method that is making its rounds amongst the real estate world.

In this chapter, we'll explain what it is and how to use it step-by-step. We'll also discuss the main risks that are involved with this strategy. And lastly, we'll discuss how to use it as one of the investing methods that you can use every time you have your eye on a rental property.

At this point, you're unsure of what kind of strategy you want to use in order to snag the property you want. However, this is one in particular that you might like since it's simple, detailed, and easy to follow. The last thing you want to do is find a strategy that is complicated and will cause you to lose one deal after another.

We encourage you to follow along in this chapter so you have a good idea of what to do and how to get the deals you want using this strategy every single time you do it. Let's get right to it:

The Famous BRRRR Method

The BRRRR Method stands for the following: buy, rehab, rent, refinance, repeat. Read that over again as many times as you need too. This is the strategy and framework that rental investors typically use when they want to generate passive income using properties.

It sounds simple enough, right? And the strategy is basically the words in the order that they appear. You can't mix them up nor switch one 'r' with another.

This method just might be your go-to strategy whenever you want to invest in properties more than once. And it's a sure fire way to help increase your cash flow while solidifying your portfolio over time. If you are looking for a roadmap towards financial independence with no shortcuts, this is exactly what you want on hand (and you can repeat the process as many times as you need to).

Examining BRRRR: Buy, Rehab, Rent, Refinance, & Repeat

In this section, we are going to break down every bit of BRRRR so you understand what to do in the process. This is something that you can do repeatedly over and over again until you feel like you've acquired enough property for your portfolio. As mentioned before, this is a straightforward roadmap that takes you from point A to point E (ABCDE not ACDEB or any ridiculous combo).

It's important to follow this strategy from the beginning so you have all your bases covered before moving on to the next stage. Once you get the hang of it, you'll be able to repeat the process over and over again. Let's break it all down:

Buy

This part is obviously self-explanatory. You buy the property outright with cash or with a financing method like a loan (which we've outlined in the previous chapter). Ideally, the buy strategy here requires a specific kind of property.

It's a property that is in need of some repairs or renovations. In plain English, you're looking for a fixer-upper. So you'll want to purchase a property that you can be able to acquire at a below market price.

As mentioned, you can purchase it with enough cash on hand. However, should you go the financing route, there are some loans that are perfect for this kind of property. Specifically, go for the hard money, private money, or even the fix and flip loans.

The reason why you want to consider these loans is because you'll be able to acquire the money fairly quickly without a credit check. On top of that, the loans are short-term. But that will give you plenty of time to repair the property and pay off the loan in time.

We'll show you exactly how to go about doing that plus more when we talk about the 'refinancing' part of this strategy.

Repair

After you've acquired the property, that's when you can be able to repair it, rehabilitate it, or renovate it (depending on the needs). That's when you'll need to be investing in quite a bit of money. Before the repairs begin, you want to thoroughly examine the house from top to bottom.

What are some things that are urgently in need of repair? Are there some hidden issues that exist (such as structural damage)? You'll want to inspect the property yourself or have a professional do it before repairs or renovations are made.
Ideally, you should at least take a look at the property before you even buy it. That way, you'll know ahead of time how much money you can put in for repairs and renovations. Once you have a good ballpark estimate, you can go from there.

Remember, repairs and renovations will increase the property value. So if you put in a good amount of work into it, you'll be able to make it attractive enough for the appraiser to put a high value price tag on it.

It will certainly work to your advantage when the time comes to rent it out or even sell it outright. Don't forget, with increased value you can also better your chances of refinancing the property. Before you do that, let's talk about how you can get there.

Rent

The repairs and renovations have been made and the place looks like it's in good shape. So now, you need to fulfill the vacancy with a reliable and trustworthy tenant. The process can take a bit of time (or it can take awhile).

This can also depend on the property you have acquired. If the property is a single-family home, then it shouldn't be a lot of trouble to find a tenant. However, if it's an apartment building that has been renovated, that could take some time (and a bit of screening to find the right tenants).

In the event if you are fulfilling multiple vacancies, you'll need a property manager to help field through the pool of applicants to help you decide which tenants are reliable and which ones may be rejected due to the policy requirements that they don't meet.

Without tenants that pay, you get no income from the rental property. That can't be simple enough to say.

Refinance

Now this is one of the fun parts about the BRRRR strategy. This is where all the hard work pays off. Because you now have a source of steady, consistent income in a rental property. This will allow you to let the lenders know that you have equity in the property and you can do a cash-out refinance.

The cash-out refinance will be used to pay off the hard money loan (or other loan) that you used to acquire the property in the first place. At that point, you can be able to reduce the expenses and have an increased cash flow.

So, what are you going to do at this point? Is one property enough? Do you want to snag another rental property and increase your portfolio?

There's only one simple answer to those questions.

Repeat

Yup. You repeat the process. And the best way to go about doing that is using whatever leftover profit from the cash-out refinance to do the whole thing over and over again.

This includes putting a new down payment on your next rental property. And as a result, you get increased cash flow and enough money to balance out all of your expenses. This seems pretty easy to do, right?

However, there are some caveats and snags that you may run into with this strategy (which will discuss in a little bit).

The 4 Main Things To Consider

Before you even go through with the strategy, it is important to consider the four main things about this strategy. This will make the approach a lot easier rather than miss a step (and not even realize it). The BRRRR strategy can work to your advantage if done properly.

With that in mind, let's take a look at the four main things you'll want to consider before you even buy the property:

1. How much money will you actually need

This can't be said better than it already is. You'll want to know how much money you will need for the initial purchase of the property. Not to mention, you'll need to consider how much you'll need for the repair (or renovation/rehabilitation) of the property.

You may already have some money set off to the side for the purpose of repairing or rehabilitating it. And all you need now is a loan for a down payment. So get a good idea of how much money in total you need for your first property and how much of a budget you'll need to repair or rehab the property.

Also, one more reason why you should inspect the property before even buying it is to determine how much money you need for the repairs themselves. Get a good estimation from your perspective (and perhaps get a second opinion from a home inspector who might just catch what you've missed).

2. How long will it take to repair or renovate

The time it takes to repair or renovate will also be another thing to consider. Not only will you be aware of what needs to be fixed, but you'll also need to be prepared for any unexpected surprises. Once you assess the initial repairs and renovation plans, you'll get a good idea of how long the entire project will take.

The scope of the project will depend on the size of the property. It will possibly take less time for a single-family property to be repaired or renovated compared to a small apartment building. So keep this in mind whenever you are searching for a property.

3. What will be the right rental amount

Obviously, you'll come to a point where you'll need to set the rate of rent. How much will the tenant pay per month to ensure it will be enough to cover expenses on your end (while maintaining a positive cash flow)? Remember to use the formulas in the previous chapter to determine that the rent rate you desire will meet your cash flow needs.

There may be rental rates that are too low and others that are too high. So you really want to find the sweet spot. One caveat would be to find a tenant who would be willing to pay that amount of rent every month.

It takes the right tenant to fulfill the vacancy. They pay on time, have a solid source or income, and will cause you no headaches at all at three in the morning (unless there is an urgent repair or if something is actually happening like a fire).

4. What will be the appraisal after the fact

After you've put in the money for repairs, found a tenant, and get a good stream of income as a result, now the appraisal process begins. This will play a role in how you will be able to refinance the property (and eventually pay off the loan).

What if the appraisal comes up short? What may be the cause of it? There are some things that could play a role in getting an appraisal that might be not what you expect.

Look no further than the current market itself. In a strong market, you'll probably get an appraisal that is exactly what you want in terms of value (or more). The market could take a downturn while you are in the process of renovating the property.

When you're in the early stages of the BRRRR method, it's important to watch the market and see how it holds up. Because a change in the market can make or break your chances of getting a better return on investment. As you move from one stage to the next, take a look at how the market is doing.

You may not get the appraisal that you want. But be outcome dependent and have options in case you get an appraisal that you want (or didn't expect).

Using BRRRR as an Investing Method

Before using the BRRRR as a method for building your portfolio, we'll be discussing the advantages and disadvantages. This is the one approach that we highly recommend for newbies starting out. You'll want to acquire your first rental property (and subsequent properties after that) using this method if you so choose.

Let's start with the following advantages:

- **Your ROI is scalable:** You can easily scale up your return on investment. The best way to do that is to acquire additional properties. You can even acquire properties with as little investment as possible. Heck, depending on how much extra cash you have lying around you could acquire your next properties with cash.

- **A proven formula:** Indeed, the BRRRR method is a tried and true formula that can be repeated over and over again. There is no tweaking or major changes needed. It's even proven to work over and over again regardless of the economic and market conditions.

- **Excellent rewards and benefits:** A lot of money in your pocket, more chances and opportunities to get more properties, and the ability to get people to manage the properties for you while you step away from the day to day operations. The BRRRR method could be exactly what you need to follow in order to achieve financial freedom and freedom from the heavy lifting that occurs with day-to-day operations.

Disadvantages

- **Repair/renovations may go over budget:** You might already have a set budget for renovations and repairs. However, you may come across some new things to fix. And that could mean more added time and money. That's why you want to do a thorough inspection (or get a second opinion from a home inspector) before deciding how much you'll want to spend on repairs and renovation.

- **Repairs/renovations could take longer:** Tying to the previous point, new needs for repair can take a bit of time. And it could extend the schedule. So the time you estimate for these repairs and renovations can be a little off.

- **Vacancies may take longer to fulfill:** This may depend on the property. And it also may depend on the rent you've set it to. Either way, you won't be able to fulfill it immediately. It takes time to find the right tenant. So be patient and you will eventually find one.

Final Thoughts

The BRRRR Strategy will be your roadmap to building your rental property empire. As easy as it is to follow along, there are some disadvantages that you'll run into. Not only that, you'll need to follow the strategy to a tee and not make any shortcuts in the process.

You now have a proven formula that will help you easily acquire a property and be able to find the right kind of financing options. At first, you'll likely need a loan like a hard money loan. After putting in the money for repairs and renovations, you can get a tenant and earn income for the property.

At that point, you can refinance, pay off the loan, and repeat the process all over again. It's the simplest way to build your portfolio and increase your cash flow in the process. But you'll want to follow the steps carefully as you go.

So through the motions when you are in the buying process. Be thorough and know exactly what needs repairing. And finally, get a tenant that will be able to pay the rent on time every month.

There is no strategy quite like this. And it's even the perfect formula for beginners.

Chapter 10 - Going With A Long Distance Investment

Sure, it might be nice to find a property in your local area. But there will come a time when the pickings will be quite slim. It might be to the point where you'll need to go outside of your localized area (even way out of it).

Is it a good idea to go with a real estate investment that might be a longer distance from you? That's for you to decide. But we'll talk about that in more detail in this chapter (and why a long distance investment might benefit you).

There are experienced real estate investors that not only have local rental properties, but they do have some out of the state as well. But you will still have the money coming from tenants that you can easily access. And you will also have someone who is overseeing the property when you are not in the area.

So a long distance investment may not be a bad thing at all. And you don't even have to be in the area often. If you are looking for a great way to find rental properties, it's better to find something that is actually out of the way.

Let's go long distance and talk about why finding an investment outside of your local area might just be what you need to do to get started:

Not Everything Is In Your Backyard

As mentioned earlier, you may have tough luck finding the property you want in your local area. And it can get to the point where the selections are so slim that you'll need to go farther. It's OK to have a property that may be hundreds of miles away or a few states over.

One of the reasons why a long distance investment is so important is that you can get more bang for your buck elsewhere. Sure, you can get a rental property in larger cities (where the rents are high). But the expenses of acquiring the property may be even higher.

Instead of purchasing a rental property inside the city limits, your next step up is the suburbs. However, if there is nothing doing out that way, going much farther would be sufficient. Think about it, a 100 unit apartment building in New York City may cost you more than one that is located somewhere in Pennsylvania.

Yes, you can find the same kind of apartment building and pay less just by switching up the location. At some point, you may have just enough money to purchase properties in the city. Then again, even if you do have the money those properties could be hard to come by.

Long distance rental property investing is great because you can purchase a property from an area that's far away from you. And you don't have to be there all the time to manage it. On top of that, the farther you go, the more opportunities you'll have.

This will allow you to open the door to possibly starting your rental property empire sooner rather than later. You'll be able to build out a portfolio and at least get the attention of local sellers at some point. Rather than wait for a local property, you can build a reputation of being a good landlord sooner with a long-distance property investment.

You'll have a few good references as well such as the property manager you hire to take care of the property itself. You'll also have others that will go to bat for you. These are people who you build a professional relationship with and they trust you with everything in terms of property management.

There's also passive income too

No matter where the property is, you can still earn passive income. It's not like you cannot access your fund outside of where the property is. But it's going to take some careful planning to adopt a financial model that is reasonable and realistic.

You still need to determine the rent price, the expenses, and everything in between to ensure that you get positive cash flow. At the same time, you'll want to find someone who is responsible and is able to handle everything from tenant requests to setting up a relationship with contractors, landscaping businesses, and more. You and your property manager can talk on the phone or even use video chat to make decisions regarding the property itself.

Yes, having a long-distance property does have it's own challenges. But believe us when we say that it's not as bad as some people think. As long as you have the right kind of people dealing with your property on a regular basis, you don't have to worry.

It Isn't As Risky As You Think

One of the biggest concerns about investing long-distance is that you might be taking a huge risk. Some will even go so far to say that you might be getting scammed. Sure, there may be some truth, but there is a difference between playing it smart and just handing over money to someone without thinking twice (or seeing the property first hand).

There are a few reasons why long-distance investments are no longer as risky as they used to be. You'll be able to make determinations of whether or not the property is worth the investment just by looking at the data. Not to mention, you have reliable sites like Trulia and Zillow to help you find the property of your dreams.

Obviously, the number one key when it comes to all investments is doing your due diligence. This task will help you determine whether or not the property is the real deal or if it's a property that might be a scam. Doing your due diligence will reduce all kinds of risks that could lead you to getting screwed over.

Also, you can get video confirmation of the property and get a good idea of what it looks like from the inside. It's a lot better than having to travel a lengthy distance to see it for yourself. You can even talk about the property with the seller over the phone or via Skype (or Zoom).

Another thing that you'll want to pay attention to is the online reviews. Look through them thoroughly. Although some of the positive reviews are short, it's hard to take them at face value. If the positive reviews are detailed and slightly longer, take those a little bit seriously.

The negative reviews is something you'll want to pay attention to as well. Again, the detailed reviews will give you an explanation as to why someone would leave negative reviews. That will give you a good idea to find a different property.

As long as you do your research and your due diligence, you'll find the property you want. From there, you can go through the motions using the BRRRR method as outlined in the previous chapter. But what if there needs to be repairs?

That's when you'll need a property manager to handle all of that. Have someone local onsite oversee the repairs while the contractors work on it. They can handle the expenses after you send them money (or you can yourself once they bill you).

Important Steps To Take When Investing in Other Places

If you plan on investing in a long-distance property, it's always a good idea to consider taking as many important steps as possible. Not only will you do your best to cover your bases, but you'll make sure that everything is done properly. Even if you won't be physically on the property, you still want to play it smart as far as investing and managing your properties are concerned.

We'll be taking a look at seven tips that you'll want to follow. These will help you in the long run if you are starting out with your rental property career by choosing a property outside of where you live. These are some of the things to take into consideration:

1. Find a property manager you can trust

A property manager will handle everything from which tenants can move in to overseeing maintenance and repairs while you are not in the area. This is someone who will perform the day-to-day operations. They will keep you in the loop on what's been going on regularly.

Both you and the property manager will discuss the policies on what kind of tenants are allowed and what could deny them from moving in. The property manager will also relay any information regarding repairs, unexpected expenses, and so on.

2. Build your network with people located in that area

You might already have a local network of real estate investors, property managers, and so on. However, since you have property in a long-distance area, you'll need to repeat the same process. This time, you can network with those in the local area who handle repairs and maintenance and other important tasks that pertain to the property.

When you are in the area where the property is located, you'll know people in the area rather than nobody at all. If something happens on your property, you'll know who to call. It's nice to have connections in every place where you have a rental property.

3. Consider automation where appropriate

We live in a time where automation is possible for mundane, repetitive tasks. One such thing that can be automated is the rent payments from the tenant. You can make arrangements where a tenant will pay their rent every month using methods like wire transfer.

This way, you won't need to worry about tracking people down and receiving physical checks from them on a regular basis. Post-dated checkers are still an option as well. You can receive those checks from tenants and be able to cash them every first of the month.

If there is a task that is menial and is usually repetitive, chances are it can be automated.

4. Communicate often

This can't be stressed well enough. Communicate with your property managers, the tenants, and the people that are working to keep your property in ship shape. A phone or video call goes a long way.

Also, if you plan on traveling to the area, let your tenants and other personnel know ahead of time. The same way when it's the other way around. That way, you will all know where everyone is so you can be able to get in contact with them face to face should the opportunity to do so arrives.

5. Do a regular inspection

You can do a regular inspection without having to travel. That's when your property manager can be your extra set of eyes in terms of finding possible issues with the property (and assigning a contractor to make said repairs). You as a landlord should reserve the right to do inspections on a regular basis.

Even when you have an on-site property owner to do it for you, you'll know about the condition of the property every single time. When repairs are needed, either you or the property manager will make the call to get the right people over to take care of the issue.

6. Always get insurance coverage

Insurance is a must-have for any property whether it's local or long-distance. You may be able to cover every property you'll invest in under the same policy (depending on who insures you). That's because disaster can strike anywhere.

Yes, it can also happen on properties that are far away from where you live. Find an insurance company that can be able to assist you in terms of covering your properties no matter where they are located. Having it all under one policy rather than have multiple policies at the same time can be easy when handling all of your expenses.

7. Set the terms and the policies

The terms and policies must always be set. This is to ensure that the tenants follow them. You will have a property manager that must be willing to enforce them.

It's your property, and it's your rules. You want these to be as clear as possible before any tenant moves in. This includes whether or not smoking is allowed on the property or if you can allow pets in the units (assuming it's an apartment building).

Final Thoughts

A long distance property might be one of your best options when you're starting out. You may have the worst luck finding property in your local area. You will come to the realization that sometimes, starting out local won't be a reality.

Not to worry, you will invest in local properties at some point. But if you want to start building your rental property empire sooner rather than later, you'll want to get out of your local area and see how far you can go. The perfect property is out there, even if it's hundreds of miles away (or in the next state over).

Investing in real estate properties from a long-distance away isn't as risky as it once was. Thanks to technology, you'll be able to know what you're getting into. And you'll be able to do the due diligence to ensure whether or not it's a worthy investment.

Follow the seven tips that we've outlined above and you'll find that investing and managing a rental property from afar isn't all that bad. You'll still get a good amount of money to help your cash flow. As long as you have the right kind of people handling your property, you'll be in good shape.

Chapter 11 - A Choice In Management

One of the biggest tasks for having a rental property is managing it. While you have the option to manage it yourself, you also have another choice to have someone else do it. Let's face it, you're not going to be on all of your properties at the same time.

So now, it comes down to whether or not you should manage it yourself or rely on a property manager that you can trust to do it for you. In this chapter, we'll discuss when is a good time to choose either option. At this point, you might have already made your choice.

We'll be taking a look at whether or not if you can self-manage your properties (while weighing the pros and cons). We'll also discuss the same in terms of when you want to get someone else to do the job for you. Either way, one choice will be easier than the other.

When you invest in multiple properties, the choice is pretty much a no brainer 90 percent of the time. This chapter will alleviate any concerns you may have in regards to property management. Let's get right to it:

Choosing Between Self-Management and Property Management

As a property investor, you'll be faced with the choice of managing the property yourself or having someone else do it. When you already have multiple properties under your belt, the choice will lean towards more property managers compared to managing them yourself.

It doesn't matter if you are the greatest multi-tasker in the world. You can't always be on all of your properties at the same time. And you may find running around from one property to the next to be quite stressful.

This might work to your advantage if you don't mind running around from one end of town to the other. That is if your properties are all located in the same town. However, you could have properties spread out by five miles from each other.

As mentioned before, you may also have long distance properties. Obviously, you cannot make the trip that will be hundreds of miles away. If it's a long distance property, you have no choice but to have a property manager oversee the day-to-day operations (unless you intend to move to that location in the future).

We'll be taking a look at the pros and cons of self-management as well as having someone else do it for you. After this, you'll be able to make a decision with ease. You could manage one property by yourself and have the rest of them managed by other people.

Or you can have the properties all managed by one company and you can just sit back and collect the passive income once a month. It's all up to you. Let's move on and discuss the idea of self-managing your properties.

Can You Self-Manage Your Properties?

Self-managing is defined as maintaining the properties yourself. This means you are responsible for approving or rejecting tenant applications. You will also perform the day to day operations as a property manager.

This may be one of your best options if you are planning on focusing on one property from the start. If the property is in your local area, it will be a lot easier to manage it yourself. Especially when you have plenty of time throughout the day.

Take a look at the pros and cons below so you'll make a decision on whether or not self-managing is right for you. Let's start with the pros:

Pros of self-management

- **You have more control:** Of course, you have even greater control over your property if you manage it yourself. Just because you decide that you let someone else manage it, doesn't mean you lose your 'final say' on what happens to the property. This is more apt towards the day to day operations.

- **Closer relationships with tenants:** When you manage the property yourself, you'll be mostly in contact with the tenants. You'll see them on a daily basis. However, you may be dealing with tenant issues that could hurt the relationship. Do your best to make it healthy and productive on your end.

- **You'll save money:** You'll save yourself money on an expense that would otherwise go towards your property manager. Ten percent of what you earn per month will usually go towards property management.

- **You gain knowledge and experience:** You will learn about your property both inside and out. Plus, you'll get experience and know-how in terms of managing a property. That way, you can train the right person whenever you want to rely on someone else to manage your additional properties.

Cons of self-management

- **It can be stressful:** Yes, handling the day-to-day tasks of managing a property can be stressful. Especially if you are handling multiple properties at once. Imagine getting a call at 2AM from a tenant regarding a broken pipe. Then, you'll need to figure out how to take care of it as soon as possible. Other stressors include unreliable tenants and the like.

- **It requires time:** Yes, it will require time out of your day to manage the property. Even one managing one property will require a good amount of time out of your day. If you manage multiple properties, the responsibilities will multiple.

- **Rent may be too low or too high:** You may set the rent price and it may be too low for the average market or too high for your ideal tenant to pay. If you know a good reasonable price when you see it, that's when you can set it and go from there.

Taking The Steps Toward A Successful Management

Successful management isn't easy. But it can be done. It's important to follow these tips below so you can be able to manage your properties with ease (whether it's by yourself or via a manager).

If you are doing self-management, follow these tips and be able to train your property manager so the both of you can be on the same page in terms of how the business is run. Let's take a look at the following:

1. Automate the process

Automation is possible whenever you or someone else is managing the property. There are different tools that you can use to automate tenant payments, issue order tickets for repairs, and tedious administrative tasks that a property manager does quickly and repeatedly.

Find the tasks that are automated and find the appropriate apps and software that will allow the automation process to work like it's supposed to.

2. Pick the right rental rate

You'll be dealing with the numbers on a regular basis. This is because you want to keep your cash flow above water. So finding the right rental rate that is fair for both you and your tenant is essential.

Consider the market averages in your area and start from there. The right rental rate could draw in tenants quicker compared to units or properties that command a higher rent.

3. Screen your tenants with diligence

You want to screen your tenants for a few things. This includes reliability of payment, whether they are known for respecting the property, and other requirements that you'll want for an ideal tenant. The last thing you want to be is lax in who you want in a tenant since there are some bad apples out there.

You want your properties to be a safe place. So you might not be apt to allow career criminals to become tenants on your property. Think about the kind of tenants you want on your property and the ones you want to steer clear from.

4. Brush up on landlord-tenant laws

Just so you are on the same page with your tenant, you'll want to learn about landlord-tenant laws. This way, you want to make the right moves rather than make a wrong one that can get you into legal trouble. One other way to go about doing this is adding an attorney to your network.

This should be an attorney who is familiar with landlord-tenant laws. This is someone who you should consult in case you need to make hard decisions such as evictions, raising the rent, and anything that may be grounds for legal action if one wrong move is made.

There are local, state, and federal landlord-tenant laws that you'll need to familiarize yourself with. You should know enough to know what is right and what is wrong.

5. Make sure the property is maintained regularly

This cannot be stressed enough. A well-maintained property will keep the tenants happy. And it will make it more attractive for those who want to fulfill a vacancy.

When there are repairs that need to be done, they need to be done promptly. The tenant and the property manager (be that you or someone else) need to be in communication when the need arises (yes, even at 2 in the morning).

6. Perform regular inspections

Of course, having regular inspections done will keep you ahead of the curve. Especially when you want to avoid disasters from happening. During an inspection, you may find something that may be a minor issue that cannot be ignored.

The sooner you address the issue with some minor maintenance, the better. If they go ignored, then it becomes an even greater problem. At the same time, you want to inspect the properties to ensure that the tenants are following the rules and policies.

7. Prep for tax season

As a property manager, you'll want to prepare for tax season and at least be ahead of the curve. When you have a number of properties, you'll have property managers send you the pertinent documents that you will need to use for tax purposes (when the time comes to file). If you have multiple property managers, the tax prep is a lot easier.

With a network of rental investors that you can easily access, you can be able to get ideas from them in terms of managing their properties. What's been working for them? What hasn't been working?

These investors aren't your competition to the point where you want to put them out of business. These are the kind of people who will help you out whenever you are stuck with something or have a question.

Opting For Property Management

Truth be told, self-managing your property isn't always for everyone. Therefore, you might find that property management is the best option. Even if it's just for one property, having someone else handle the day-to-day operations just might be the best course of action.

Now, let's take a look at the pros and cons of property management so you can make the decision as far as whether or not it becomes the best option:

Pros of property management

- **They have more experience:** Obviously, those who are in property management whether they are an individual or part of a company have the experience. They have the know-how to handle the day-to-day tasks of property management. This includes selecting tenants, handling requests from said tenants, and also coordinating with contractors should any kind of repairs and renovation needs arise.

- **More time on your hands:** Since you will be removing yourself from the day-to-day operations, you'll have more free time on your hands. What you do with it is all up to you. You can still collect the money from all of your properties and be able to use it as you please. The stress will be even less. And you will only be needed in case of emergencies.

- **The response times are quicker:** Yes, the response times will be quicker when you have a property manager on site. When a tenant has an issue with the property such as a broken pipe or the like, the repairman will be there in a jiffy.

- **Vacancies are shorter:** If there is a vacancy, then it won't be long until it's fulfilled. That's because property managers always have a pool of tenants that are available to move into a new place. So they'll screen the applicants and be able to choose the right tenants quickly. On top of that, property management will also have the know-how to retain tenants for the long-term.

- **It's an additional expense:** Sure, having someone else manage the property will require you to set some money off to the side. Typically, it'll be 10 percent of your monthly income. For example, if your total monthly income for one property is $2000, then $200 will go towards property management. The property management company will earn 10 percent per property that they manage. So if you own five rental properties and the same management company does the day to day operations, that's $1000 a month in total.

- **Communication is needed:** Yes, it's a necessary evil. But you have to be in contact with your property managers on a regular basis. That's because the property you own is still your baby. And you want to know if it's still in good shape. The more you communicate with your property management team, the more peace of mind you'll be knowing that the property is in good hands.

What Should You Ask When Hiring People For Property Management

No smart rental investor will be flying blind when it comes to choosing a property management company to do the day-to-day operations. They need to ask questions that will screen the quality property managers from those who may not do such a good job.

However, there may come a time when they need to make a tough decision because the candidates are highly qualified and bring a lot to the table. So what are the questions you should ask when hiring people for property management? Let's take a look at the following:

Do they hold a license for property management?

Depending on the state you live in, there usually is a license that is required for property management. If they hold a license or have some kind of certification, then there's a good chance you'll place a good amount of trust in them.

What services do you offer?

When it comes to property management, they will usually offer a wide variety of services. Some will usually do leasing and managing. While others go a little further than that.

They may have a wide variety of services such as their own in-house groundskeepers and maintenance crew. If they have that available, that just might be a major plus rather than having to find separate people to handle such tasks. However, that could mean that they'll command higher fees just for the extra services.

How many properties do you currently manage?

This is a key indicator to see how small or large the management business is. This will also give you a look at their current workload. If the property manager is responsible for more than 100 properties, be careful.

If they are handling that many properties, that may mean that they could be paying less attention to some of the properties they are already managing themselves. As a supplemental question, consider asking what kind of properties they normally manage. That way, you'll be more aware of the experience they have.

What are the management fees?

The management fees will be based on the services offered. If the fees exceed 12 to 14 percent of your monthly revenues, then you may want to consider other options. Higher than average fees are fine if they include services that are needed like repairs and maintenance.

Keep in mind that not every management company will offer a fixed monthly fee. Some have different packages at different price points.

How do you decide on rent?

The rent amount may come down to what the property manager thinks is best. They will analyze the market analysis while comparing your property to others. So they may suggest a higher rental rate compared to what you desire. Or it might be lower than what you're gunning for because it might be too high on your end.

How do you screen prospective tenants?

Screening prospective tenants is definitely something that needs to be addressed. So how will a property management go about screening them? Will they look for criminal records?

What about work history? Or perhaps run a background check? This will depend on the kind of tenants you want on your property.

You have a criteria and you want to make sure that it's being followed to a T.

What's the cancellation policy?

If you are looking to sign a contract for a property manager, it's important to know the details. This includes the cancellation policy. Sometimes, things may not work out between you and the property management company.

So it would be incumbent upon you to make the final decision in terms of the contract. You want to cancel at some point if you are not happy with the service. If the terms and conditions are created to keep you tied to each other forever, then that should be a disqualifier (no exceptions).

Do they have references and sample documents?

If the prospective property manager has been doing this for a while, then you want to check with their references. You'll get a good idea of how well they treat their clients. Also, sample documents such as rental leases, applications, financial reports, and even communication between the tenants are highly recommended.

Final Thoughts

Choosing a property manager can be a tough task. But so will managing the property yourself. So it's up to you to make the decision on who will manage the property.

Be sure to carefully weigh the pros and cons. What are you willing to do in terms of property management? What will work best for you?

You may have the time to manage one property and that alone. However, the rest of the properties you own can be managed by a company. In short, make it easier on yourself.

If you are investing in properties and want to sit back and collect some cold hard cash, then a property manager is the way to go. Sure, there is the additional expense. But it's less stress on your part.

Chapter 12 - Agreement: What Should You Include Here?

Now comes the part where you and the tenant will be working out an agreement on the lease. The question that is always asked is what kind of terms must be included? We'll discuss this in more detail as we move farther along in the chapter.

The agreement that you want to put together must be fair and reasonable. It should benefit both you and the tenant. There are important terms that you want to include (and you never want to leave them out either). Once the tenant signs on the dotted line, it's a done deal.

But you want to make sure that all the wrinkles are ironed out first. And the agreement has to be in writing. There are things that you can and cannot do (and the same goes for the tenant). Ensuring that it's all on paper will be one of the most important steps you take as a rental property investor.

If you are ready to go in-depth about how rental agreements would and how you can hammer one out right from the start, keep reading. Let's discuss about protections for yourself and your tenants:

Protecting Yourself And Your Tenant

A written agreement between you and a tenant is obviously one of the most important documents between the two of you. Things can go sideways and it may cause headaches for you or even the tenant themselves. That's why having a binding, written agreement is pretty much required when you are renting out properties.

That's because the tenant may do something that may be prohibited from the agreement. Or you may be doing something that goes beyond the boundaries. Either way, the agreement is designed to keep you both in check.

As far as other types of agreements go, a verbal agreement or even a handshake will never hold up in a court of law. You want physical, written proof just in case the agreement does get contested in a legal setting. You have a document with both yours and the tenant's signature.

If you seem to have any issues with putting together a lease agreement, you may want to consider talking over such terms and conditions with an attorney (assuming you plan on self-managing). If you are handing over the reigns of property management to a property management company, chances are they'll already have a pre-written agreement drawn up.

One of the most important things you'll want to consider when meeting with a property management company before signing them is getting a look at their agreements. You want to find a property manager that can provide a lease agreement that is both fair and balanced for you and the tenant.

What kind of terms should be included? We'll discuss that in a later section. But the point is that the lease agreement must be balanced rather than lop-sided to favor one party or the other.

Two Types Of Agreements

Rental and lease agreements are two types of separate agreements. So it's important to know the difference between the two. We will explain what differs between these two agreements so you are able to draw up the right one for you and your tenant.

There are various items that you want to be aware of in any type of agreement. Before you have a tenant provide you with their signature, here's what you need to know:

Rental agreements

A rental agreement does have similarities to a lease. The most distinguishable difference is the length. The rental agreement will be perfect for shorter periods of time.

If the renter is planning on staying for at least 30 days max, then a rental agreement will be used. Rental agreements will usually be considered on a month-to-month basis. However, the tenant or the landlord can consider making changes if the need arises.

As for the agreement itself, the landlord and the tenant can change the terms of the agreement when the time comes to renew. However, advanced notice should be issued before a new agreement is drawn up.

The pros of a rental agreement will allow more flexibility for the tenant. And the terms can be changed once the old agreement expires and prior to a new one taking place. This will give you and your tenant time to discuss some potential changes.

The downsides of this will basically be on your end. You may deal with a frequent turnover rate. Furthermore, it can also make your rental income stream very unpredictable.

Lease agreements

So as you've figured out by now, the lease agreements pertain to the long-term. Most lease agreements will last anywhere between 6 to 12 months. This will allow the tenant to live on the property for a fixed period of time.

The lease is drawn up using clear and thorough terms that both the landlord and the tenant must understand. The agreement must also include a set of rules, the duration of the agreement, the rental rate, and other terms and conditions. It is important for you to have your prospective tenants look over the lease agreement before it is signed.

You want to give them a chance to solidify their decision and at least allow them to ask questions or address concerns regarding the lease agreement itself. This lease agreement must be organized, well thought-out, and well-written so that both parties have a clear understanding and be aware that they are both protected.

The agreement cannot be altered or changed for the duration of the lease. So the lease must be honored by both parties. Any breach or violation can lead to a legal situation that neither you nor your tenant want to get into.

The pros of a lease include a structured long-term agreement. The occupancy will be stable at best. For these reasons, you will also get a predictable stream of income.

The cons of this are that the rental costs will stay the same for the life of the lease. This means you won't be able to raise the rent rate while the space is being occupied. Lastly, you could lose out on incremental gains of income should the market value increase.

10 Important Terms To Include

Now, it's time to consider what kind of terms that you want to include in the agreement. You don't have to be a legal expert to know what to put in one. However, you'd be smart to have it reviewed by an attorney before it is even signed by both you and the tenant.

But for the time being, let's focus on the important terms that you want to put in. These are items that you also don't want to omit from any agreement. Once these terms are included, you can make some changes (but not get rid of the terms altogether).

Here are the ten key terms you want to include in your agreements:

1. The names of all tenants and occupants

Who is going to reside on the property? This should include members of couples who are married or unmarried. Any adults living on the property even as roommates must be included in the agreement.

The reason why all adults must be included is due to the fact that it provides you with additional insurance. Each tenant must be responsible for paying the monthly rent in full and follow all terms of the agreement itself. Also, it puts you in a position where you can seek out rent from the other occupants if one tenant fails to pay it.

Also, if one tenant violates an agreement, you can terminate the tenancy of that tenant or all of them. That decision is entirely up to you. But you'd be more apt to remove the violator rather than the rest of the tenants who may be among the innocent party.

An occupancy clause should also be included so that you can put in writing that only tenants or any of their dependents (i.e -- minor children) can live in the rental. You can also include a clause regarding how long guests can stay. You also can include in the clause regarding sublets or new tenants.

Any new tenants or persons subletting must be notified by you in advance. Failure to do so can provide you with enough power to terminate the tenancy and evict the offending resident (or all residents).

2. Description of the property

The information of the property must include the physical address. If it is an apartment building, it should also include the building and the unit number. Also, take into account the number of parking spaces and storage areas it has.

If there is an assigned parking space for an apartment unit, be sure to have that mentioned in the agreement itself. For example, if the tenant is living in Building 1, Apartment A then the parking space marked as 'B1A' or the like should be provided. The same will go for any storage space.

Meanwhile, you should also include in the agreement any areas of the property that the tenant can or cannot have access to. If you have a locked shed in the backyard of one of the apartment buildings, you'll have to include in the agreement whether or not that can be accessed by the tenant.

If the shed cannot be accessible by the tenants, make sure you have a notice saying so on the shed itself. You'll want to cover as many bases as possible without it looking like overkill.

3. Time Period Of Tenancy

Pretty self-explanatory. If it's a rental agreement, usually it's a 30 day agreement. If it's a lease, then it can be anywhere between six months to a year. Month-to-month or one fixed date (i.e January 1, 2021 to January 1, 2022), it should be addressed in this part of the agreement.

Be sure to take note of the start date, how long the tenancy length will be, and when the lease will expire.

4. Rental rate

The rental rate will vary from one agreement to the next (assuming it's a rental agreement). A lease agreement will have one rental rate that will stay the same for the life of the lease. Meanwhile, don't stop with just a numerical figure.

The payment terms must include how a tenant can pay. Will cash be accepted? Will they be able to pay the rent via check, credit card, wire transfer, etc.?

Consider the payment acceptance options and get a good idea of how a tenant wants to pay you. Also, you should consider the idea of charging a late fee should a tenant miss a rent payment. You may want to consider a grace period (and the conditions that will allow a tenant to qualify).

You should consider additional charges if a rent check bounces. The state and local rent laws should be consulted upon while you are working on putting together this part of the agreement. There are laws that may allow or disallow how a tenant must pay the landlord (such as by mail).

5. Security Deposits and Fees

Typically, a security deposit and any additional fees must be included in the agreement. One thing to be sure of is to take a look at the security deposit limit laws in your state. Typically, a security deposit will usually equal out to the same amount of money compared to your rental rate. For example, if the rent is $1000 a month then the security deposit can be $1000.

It's also important to determine how the security deposit will be used. The purpose of the security deposit will usually cover any unpaid rent or any repairs stemming from damage caused by the tenants themselves. It may not be accepted in lieu of rent payment for the previous month.

You can also determine whether or not you want the tenant to replenish the security deposit should there be a mid-tenancy deduction. Also, you want to lay out the terms on how the security deposit will be returned once the tenant moves out.

Lastly, let's take a look at the fees. What kind of fees will be included in the agreement? For example, you could have a tenant that will move in with a pet.

The fees can vary on how you set it. It can be a flat fee or it can depend on the size of a pet. In the event of the latter, you could charge a lesser pet fee for someone who may have a chihuahua compared to a tenant who may have a larger breed. Also, if you are planning on implementing non-refundable fees, then consider taking a look at any state laws that allow such fees in the first place.

6. Policies for maintenance and repairs

When it comes to the stress that comes with rent-withholdings or security deposit disputes, a repair and maintenance policy will definitely come in handy. The policy should outline what the tenant should be responsible for. For example, the tenant must be responsible for keeping the property clean and in good condition.

It may also be the responsibility of the tenant to alert you of any conditions that are considered unsafe or unsanitary. You should also outline any procedures that the tenants must follow should such things arise.

Also, you may allow or disallow what a tenant can do in terms of any repairs or maintenance (i.e --
allowing them to paint one of the rooms or not).

7. The right to enter the rental property

Yes, it's your property. And it's clear that your tenant deserves the right to privacy. It's important to make
sure that the right to enter the rental property is included in every agreement. You do not want to be
accused of illegal entry or invading the privacy of the tenant.

Take a look at the access laws in your state before drawing up this agreement. You can implement a
policy for situations like repairs or showing the unit to a new tenant that will occupy it when the outgoing
one moves out. You'd be smart to inform the tenants with a 24 hour advance notice that you will be
entering the property in the event of repairs or maintenance (or showings). In case of emergency, you
may provide advance notice, but it may be less than a 24 hour time frame.

Either way, this is one good reason why communication between you and a tenant must be important.

8. Other rules and policies

What other rules and policies can be included? For example, is smoking allowed on the property? Will
you allow pets?

All of this is completely up to you. You should include what is allowed on the property and what is
prohibited. Illegal activities like drug use, drug dealing, violating noise ordinances and laws must also be
addressed here as well. This will ensure that your property will be safe for other tenants (especially when
young children are living on the property).

9. Contact information

Include information on how a tenant must contact you. At the same time, you'll want to keep records of
any conversations between you and the tenant. This can include text messages, instant messages,
phone calls, written communication, and so on.
In the event of some legal occurrences, you can use the communication made between you and the
tenant as evidence. This also includes any advanced notices such as entering the property for repairs,
maintenance, or showing the property to a new tenant. Make sure that you check your email regularly or
any kind of communication so you and your tenant are on the same page.

10. Required disclosures

This term must be in compliance with any federal, state, or local laws (if any). You will need to inform the
tenant of any potential issues such as lead paint, the unit's history of any invasive species such as bed

bugs, and more. Also, you'll want to make sure that your lease agreement is free of any violations that may be related to anti-discrimination laws, rent control laws, or any health and safety codes outlined by the government.

The Signing Process of the Agreement

So now, the ink will go to the paper. However, the question is: who signs first? Let's take a look at the step-by-step process of the agreement and the signing process:

1. Make sure all parties are involved

If there is one tenant and you, then get to signing it. If there are multiple tenants or adult occupants, make sure that all are present before the agreement is signed. You must have all signatures on the document before the agreement is finalized.

2. The tenants sign first

Tying it into the previous step, all tenants who are occupying the property must sign the agreement first. Once the tenant's signature is on the dotted line, you can advance to the following step.

3. You or the property manager can sign it

The agreement can be signed by you or the property manager that is deferred to handle the process. Once it is signed on yours or the manager's end, be sure to have copies prepared for both yourself, the property manager, and the tenants involved. It's important to have these copies kept in the records in the event of any misunderstandings or potential legal proceedings (should they arise).

Unfortunate Events and How To Deal With Them

On rental properties, the unfortunate things can and will happen. It's important to have a battle plan drawn up so you can make the right decision. Such events can result in a tenant getting evicted and the agreement being terminated in accordance to your terms.

Is it possible that a tenant can break a lease agreement before they even move in? What happens if they break the lease itself? What will be your decision going forward?

Things do happen to where it might send you scrambling for answers. For example, a tenant can change their mind at the last minute about moving into one of your rental properties. Or there may be various circumstances that can happen to where a move in cannot occur.

Let's take a look at the various situations:

When a tenant breaks a lease before moving in?

This can occur in events that a tenant may have no control over. They can include but are not limited to job transfers or family emergencies. However, a prospective tenant may also have cold feet over the idea of moving into the property.

This is where things can get really tricky. But it's up to you to make the right decision. However, there needs to be documentation present.

It is yours or the property manager's responsibility to document everything including any early termination letters. In the event if something goes to court, you'll have these to fall back on. The question that needs to be answered is whether or not there are legal obligations that need to be fulfilled should a tenant break a lease before moving in.

Consider the following:

Advanced Notice

If a tenant is breaking a lease before moving in, you want to request a written notice. This should be done at least 30 days before the tenant's scheduled move in. The tenant must notify you or the landlord that the lease will be broken.

Inform them of the next steps

From there, you can notify the tenant that they are legally liable for paying the rent for the duration of the agreement. However, you will inform the tenant that you will also re-rent the property in accordance with any good faith efforts that are required by state law (depending on the state).

Once the property is rented out again, the previous tenant can no longer pay rent on the property. But in the meantime, they must do so whether they occupy the property or not.

Find a new tenant

As part of the good faith efforts, you must find a new tenant. Start by marketing your vacancy as soon as possible and have the new tenant sign a lease agreement quickly. This way, the old tenant can no longer have the burden of paying rent on a property that they do not occupy.

What is the standard protocol?

The standard protocol in this situation includes the following:

- Requesting an early termination letter

- Explaining that the tenant is responsible for the rent while you search for a new tenant

- Collecting rent once the new tenant has agreed to a lease (or applied the security deposit)

Also, you have the option of retaining the security deposit if the lease is broken before a tenant moves in. This will cover any losses that may have been accrued due to this early termination. Remember to consult your state and local laws regarding security deposits before determining whether or not you should keep the security deposit.

When a tenant breaks a lease with advanced notice

In the event of this occurrence, use the same standard protocol above. On top of that, it's important to communicate with your tenant to get a good timeline of when that tenant will vacate the property. Be sure they give you as much advance notice as possible.

This will allow you enough time to find a new tenant so the outgoing tenant may not be stuck with paying the rent for the duration of the lease. Fill the vacancy as soon as possible. And go about fulfilling the screening process like you normally do when finding a new tenant.

When a lease is broken without notice

You may have a tenant that can vacate the property without giving you any notice whatsoever. Especially when they knowingly do so. People can be quite inconsiderate.

This kind of occurrence is not uncommon. And there's a good chance that this will happen to you more than once (usually on an occasional basis). While finding a new tenant, try to find the former tenant and explain to them the situation.

You may consider legal action if necessary. If you breach a rental agreement or lease, then that will allow the tenant to end the agreement itself before the expiration date. The tenant will not be subject to any penalties or legal trouble because the lease was already broken by you in the first place.

Keep in mind that if there are any violations to the agreement, you can invoke the right to terminate the tenancy and evict the tenant depending on the violation itself. For example, if the police have discovered that a tenant is dealing drugs on the property, they will notify you. From there, you can evict the tenant.

Final Thoughts

The agreement between you and the tenant must be a sacred document. Both of you must sign the agreement and pledge to honor it for as long as it's in effect. When the agreement expires, that's when you and the tenant(s) can renew it.

When the time comes to renew an agreement, you can consider exchanging ideas with the tenants on what could be included (and they can suggest some ideas as well). This could mean a possible bump up in rent (or even a reduction). Or the tenant may want something that the landlord may be willing to allow.

You should have a good idea of what to include in the agreement. That way, if something ever gets challenged to the point where it's a legal issue, that agreement will be a good piece of evidence. An ironclad agreement will help keep you and your tenant(s) in check.

Chapter 13 - Let's Talk About Your Tenants

Your tenants are the lifeblood to any rental property. Without them, the property doesn't generate income. And you don't get the return on investment that you want.

Sounds simple enough, doesn't it? With that said, we're going to talk about how you want to find the right kind of tenant. We'll even give you the definition of a good tenant and how you can find them.

We'll also walk you through the application process so you know what the tenant will need to fill out and how the application will be viewed by you or the property manager. We'll also be taking a look at five different kinds of tenants that you need to keep an eye on. Finally, we'll also discuss how you should deal with difficult tenants.

As a property manager, you want to work with tenants who are reasonable, easy to get along with, and are known to not cause all kinds of trouble. Not only that, you'll want to consider the health and safety of your other tenants. One bad tenant may cause trouble for your property (or even the neighborhood itself).

If you are serious about finding the right kind of tenants, this chapter will be your go-to guide on how to fulfill your vacancies with them. Let's dive right in:

Defining a Good Tenant

The question on every property owner's mind is what makes a great tenant? We'll be taking a look at some of the characteristics that makes one stand a head above shoulders over the rest. You'd be hard-pressed to find a good tenant that will have these attributes that we'll be listing below.

You want to keep this list handy especially if you are putting together a series of screening questions while looking through their application. The more they fit your criteria, the better off they will be. Here are the following things that define a great tenant:

Their credit history

A good credit history is a green flag. You know that they are in good financial standing. And they will be reliable when it comes time to pay the rent.

Granted, you will know for a fact that they will be financially responsible for as long as they are a tenant (be it for the short-term or long-term). If their credit is not the best, then that may be a cause for concern. For others, it might be automatic denial.

This decision to approve or deny a tenant based on their credit history should be all up to you.

Income

Proof of income is one more good indicator that you will find a tenant that is financially stable and able to pay monthly rent. A good steady income is what the ideal tenant will have in order to qualify to become a tenant. If their income is roughly three times the monthly rent (i.e -- if the rent is $1,000 a month, their income must be $3,000 a month) then that's a good sign.

Remember to factor in any debt that they may also have. If they have a high level of debt, that's typically a red flag that you want to pay attention to. Even if they have the income to pay monthly rent, the debt may be too great to bear yet another expense.

Criminal background

If you want an apartment building that is safe for all tenants, then a criminal background check is a must. This should go the same way for single-family properties. A lack of a criminal record is obviously a plus.

Criminal information is public record, so you can obtain it somewhere however you wish. Your property management company may also have access to resources where they can perform background checks including criminal records. But what about the crimes themselves?

Various misdemeanor crimes may not be grounds for automatic rejection. But there may be some violent crimes that will also not be tolerated as well. Also, you may be faced with the difficult task of dealing with a tenant who may be a registered sex offender.

The cleaner a tenant's criminal record, the better. But if there are any crimes that they are convicted of, sometimes you should consider asking them for an explanation. At the end of the day, who would you want to occupy your property?

Rental history

The tenant's rental history is usually a good indicator of what kind of a tenant that you are going to deal with. This will allow you to contact past landlords and ask them questions about the tenant who wants to move into your property.
If you hear nothing but positive things about them, then that's a good sign. And that should put the prospective tenant at the top of your list. You'll find out information about how good of a tenant they were, why they moved out, and if they honored tenant agreements.

Respect

A tenant that respects you is someone who will not take advantage of you. And they won't play games with you whenever they miss a payment or are about to. They also will take great care of the property itself.

Those who have damaged the property or play games with the landlords will usually be the ones that lack respect. They may not respect your time, nor will they care about the fact that you are trying to run a business. And they will always make excuses when things go wrong and they try to avoid fault from it.

Honesty

You want a tenant that is honest. You want a tenant that is transparent. And you want a tenant that will be upfront with you.

Therefore, it is important to find a tenant that is someone you can trust. A good honest tenant will protect the property and hold themselves accountable whenever they damage something. Trust goes a long way (and it's a two-way street).

You and your tenant should build a trusting relationship that lasts well beyond the time when the tenant leaves the property and relocates elsewhere. That in turn gives you the opportunity to put in a good word for them whenever they decide to rent another property or buy a home.

Cleanliness

You want a tenant that will keep the property in good condition. So cleanliness is a must. You might have heard plenty of horror stories about tenants leaving a property without warning.

And when the landlord comes to check on it, the floors are covered in trash and a place is an absolute mess. You can feel your skin crawl just thinking about it. To avoid that from ever happening, you'll want to refer to other landlords that rented from this tenant.

How was the property when the tenant moved out? Was it clean? Did it pass any inspections?

If you see the tenant in person, how do they look? If you walk them to their car, how does the inside look? There are some things you need to look for to determine whether or not they will keep the property clean or not.

Are they prepared for the worst?

Will they alert you if there is anything bad that is happening like a burst pipe or a fire? Will they purchase renter's insurance if things go wrong? These are questions that you might be considering to determine whether or not they are prepared for what may be the worst that can happen on a property.

How To Find Good Tenants

Now that you have a good idea on which characteristics to look for in a tenant, it's time to find them. It's not easy finding tenants that will pay on time, be respectful, and able to stick around for the long haul. Knowing where to find them will be key.

There are tenants that work in different industries, come from different walks of life, and so on. Are you looking for tenants who work in professional fields? Are the tenants you seek out students?

There are many tenants out there that have well-paying jobs. And some are usually working minimum wage jobs, but can afford an apartment or split the rent with a roommate or their significant other. Here are some ways to find a good tenant:

Know where to advertise

If you are in search of a new tenant, it's important to know where to advertise. What are the local newspapers in your area? What about groups on social media that are tailored to your local area?

Why not rely on digital advertising? What kind of tenants do you want to attract? Where do those ideal tenants like to 'hang out' all the time?

You can advertise using social media, print ads, or even print flyers on a bulletin board. Either way, you'll want to let people know that there is a vacancy on your property that has yet to be fulfilled. And it's available to any tenant who can be able to fulfill the requirements.

Be sure to include the location, how prospective tenants can contact you, and include the amenities and what's included (if applicable). You want to disclose as much information about the property as possible as it might be the perfect property for your tenant to live in.

Post good photographs of the property

Whether it's online or on the flyer, you want to take good photographs of the property. You want it to be attractive and appealing to the prospective tenant. Also, make sure that the property is clean and free of any damage.

Be transparent

When a prospective tenant wants to know more about you and your properties, they will usually do some research themselves. They will find out reviews about you as a landlord and the properties that you have rented out.

If the reviews are more positive than negative, then they may be convinced that you're the kind of landlord that they trust. If there are negative reviews, don't 'scrub' them or delete them just to make yourself look good.

Be honest and transparent as possible. Likewise, you will have tenants who will do the same.

The Application Process

The application process for you and your tenant should be straightforward. On their end, they fill out the specific information such as their name, current employment, proof of income, and references. On your end, you want to check to see if they gave you the right information so the background checks and the like are quick and easy to do.

Also, you want to avoid some kind of interview process. You may not have time to interview everyone and prospective tenants may be turned off by the idea of being interviewed for a place to live. So avoid that at all possible.

Here are some other tips to keep in mind of when you are going through the application process:

Check their credit history

Again, this will give you an indication of whether or not they are reliable for payments. The better their credit score, the more likely they will pay you on time without any issue.

Check their income

Same reason as above. You want their income to be stable and predictable. Remember, if it's three times the rent price, that's a good sign.

But don't forget, they also may have debts that are paying off. If the debts are manageable, then don't worry about it. If they seem to be piling up, then you may want to consider other tenant applications.

A criminal background check is a must

When it comes to your property, you want to make sure that your tenant is someone that is not a threat to themselves or anyone's safety. Conduct a background check and see if they have a clean criminal record. You may want to consider avoiding those who have been previously convicted for crimes like drug crimes, sexually based crimes like rape, sexual assault, etc., or even domestic violence.

However, this is based on your own discretion. Decide where you draw the line in terms of which crimes are not grounds for disqualification.

Eviction history

Has the prospective tenant been evicted before? And if so, how many times. The more times they have been evicted, the less likely that tenant will fulfill your vacancy.

It may seem like a no brainer just to reject their application.

Keep Watch Against These Five Tenants

The last thing you want is to deal with tenants who are going to be a headache. Lucky for you, we've been able to provide you a list of the types of tenants that should not even be on your property. During the screening process or even showing them the property, you'll want to get a good idea of whether or not these are one of the five types of tenants you want to avoid or not.

Enough talk, let's get to the good stuff and inform you on who to potentially avoid:

Those that don't pay on time

Let's face it, there are those who will miss a rental payment from time to time due to sudden expenses. And that's where a good grace period comes in handy. But what if they don't pay on time habitually?

That's going to become a problem. So it would make sense to reject a tenant who has a repeated history of paying rent late or never at all. You want predictable, reliable streams of income and this kind of tenant does not provide that.

To avoid this kind of tenant, a simple credit check will do the trick. That way, you'll know whether or not they are caught up on their payments or if they are drowning in debt.

Tenants that damage the property

You already have enough repairs and maintenance to deal with. So extra damage should be the last thing you want to deal with. Not to mention, it can cause an overrun in your repair expenses.

This is where a background check comes in handy. You can also check out their rental history. From there, you can ask landlords how that tenant took care of the property. If they say that they have damaged the place on a regular basis, then that's grounds for an automatic rejection.

The tenants that refuse to leave

Ah yes, they have broken the lease or have failed to pay. But when the time comes to evict them, they refuse to leave the property. In some cases, they may need to be forcibly removed by law enforcement.

To avoid this nightmare from happening, refer to the background checks. Also, see if there were any past landlords that had to deal with such an issue with the specific tenant you are looking at. If the residence history on their application is lacking information, then that may be a red flag (but that's where other references come into play).

These are the people who make a lot of noise, have strange odors coming from the unit, or they are just rude and obnoxious people that are being a nuisance to the other tenants. If they have a history of upsetting their neighbors, including them on your property could crank up the tenant turnover rate.

Again, this is the perfect reason why you should always ask past landlords or even references about any behavioral issues a tenant may have. If they are not bothersome in the slightest, that's a green light to move forward.

These tenants are going to be a problem. And there's a good reason why you want to consult with past landlords. These tenants will always find something to argue about with you and then try and find a way to drag you to court.

If this tenant has applied to occupy your vacancy and they tend to bring other landlords to court because of some odd reason, do not for a single second approve their application or look at it any further.

Difficult Tenants: How Should You Deal With Them?

Granted, the best time to deal with difficult tenants is before you even approve or reject their application. However, what if the background checks and everything else go well without a hitch? What if the nightmare begins well after the fact?

In this section, you will now have a proven battle plan on how to deal with tenants who will give you more stress than not. First and foremost, it's important to keep a level head and be able to control yourself emotionally.

Secondly, it's important to know your boundaries as a landlord and know the tenant's boundaries as well. Also, remember that the terms of the agreement are yours and you will exercise them as such. Here are some things to consider when dealing with difficult tenants:

If they don't pay on time

As mentioned before, if they miss a payment but are usually on time then you should consider giving them a grace period to catch up. As a courtesy, you can waive the late fee (if you have one implemented). Sometimes, emergency expenses can happen to a point where they have to postpone a rent payment.

However, the habitual offenders will need to be dealt with accordingly. If they make a late payment, you tack on an extra charge. If they don't pay at all, you have it within your right to evict them in accordance to the lease.

As it is, the tenant agreed to pay on time in accordance to the lease. Therefore, it's technically breaking it if they do not pay on time or refuse to do so.

If they damage the property

Again, things can happen. They can accidentally damage the property and hold themselves responsible. Be sure they have a written copy of a damage report (as should you). You can deduct it from their security deposit or waive the charge if it was a no-fault damage.

But if they continuously damage it to the point where the handyman is spending most of his time on the property, that will also give you the power to evict them. Once again, damaging the property frequently does breach the lease (especially the term to where they agreed to keep the property in good condition).

Those who sublet without prior notification

Subletting is perfectly fine. Unless the tenant notifies you ahead of time and you give them the go ahead. Depending on where you live, subleasing a property is against the law.

If that's the case, you want to make that clear in your agreement with the tenant. It's OK for them to have guests so long as they stay for a few days (but never beyond that). However, no one should have to live on your property without them paying their share of the rent.

The overindulgent pet owner

Pet owners can be a nightmare tenant for one reason or another. Oftentimes, they always respect the rules and boundaries. These are pet owners who allow them to do their business inside the property.

You'd be surprised by how much damage can be caused by pet urine. Not to mention, it can leave quite a smell. You can deal with these tenants by charging them extra for the pet fee.

To prevent this from happening from the beginning, then you'll want to establish a strict 'no pets' policy on your property. But evicting them from the property will be difficult since they may not have any other place to go with their pets.

And if you love your pets, it would be very hard to get rid of them. Or, you can persuade the tenant to have them rehomed with a member of their family or a friend.

The ones that won't leave

If they are being evicted and refuse to leave, then you contact law enforcement. However, you can't kick out a tenant while the lease is still valid either. An eviction can be done as a last resort or if the tenant has engaged in illegal activities.

However, you'll want to go through the proper legal channels to ensure you are not violating the lease or any kind of laws.

If a tenant is breaking the law on your property, the best move is to call the police. They will deal with the situation from there. Drug sales and violence will always need to be dealt with by law enforcement.

As such, you can prevent this from happening just by simply doing background checks. A criminal history could be the difference between a reliable tenant and a difficult one.

Final Thoughts

Finding the right tenant is all part of the process. That's why you need to screen each applicant (or have your property manager do the screening). You have an idea of what your perfect tenant should be.

For one, they are reliable when it comes to payments. Second, they are honest and transparent. And finally, they are willing to respect the rules and be a good tenant (and a good neighbor as well).

Also, it's better to catch on early to avoid dealing with one of the five types of tenants we've listed above. If one of them seems to 'fall through the cracks' after awhile, that's when you'll need to take matters into your own hands if needed.

Remember, you must also follow the laws to ensure that you are not taking an unjust action against a tenant. No matter how much of a pain they can be, you can find a way to deal with them. Even if you have to go through the legal channels, it can be done.

However, doing a thorough screening that includes a background check is something that you or a property manager should be doing all the time when reviewing tenant applications. It's a decision that can mean more cash flow or less.

Chapter 14 - Before, During, and After Renting Out Your Property

In this chapter, we'll be guiding you through the process on what you'll need to do before, during, and after renting out your property to a tenant. It's always a good idea to know that the property is in good shape and is ready for a tenant to occupy once everything looks good. The last thing you want is a tenant to move in one second and then call you the next after experiencing a myriad of issues.

We'll be discussing why preparing the property for tenants will be essential. And we'll also talk about how to go about doing a walk-through and inspection. This is where you really need to pay attention to detail here.

Also, it would be a good idea to consider the idea of insurance coverage and determine the kind of policy you want. We'll discuss insurance policies in depth and what can be covered by them. Finally, we'll discuss maintenance and repairs and everything you need to know about them.

As you are about to rent out your first ever rental property, it's good to know these things so you have happy tenants. Not only that, you want to keep your expenses to a minimum. The last thing you want is to be throwing money out the window due to constant costs with repairs and maintenance.

Let's keep going and talk about what to do before renting out the property:

Preparing The Rental Property For Tenants

Preparing the rental property will require you to make sure that everything is clean and in good condition. But that doesn't stop there. Here are some of the other things that you need to do when preparing for tenants:

- **Check for phone and Internet connections:** These days, many people rely on their smartphones. However, there are still those that rely on a landline. See if there are appropriate setups for phone and Internet. If WiFi is included in the rent, make sure that it's set up properly and the tenant is able to connect once they move in.

- **Test the HVAC and plumbing:** You want to make sure that things are in working order. Test the plumbing by running the sinks or even flushing the toilet. Also, see if the HVAC system is running properly. Is the place heating up good?

- **Are there curtains for privacy:** Privacy matters most to a tenant. So it's better to make sure there are curtains set up in appropriate places. Blinds and shades are acceptable as well.

- **Make sure there are smoke detectors:** There should be an unwritten rule that all of your rental properties must have working smoke detectors. Safety is paramount for your tenants. Have smoke detectors set up in the kitchen, bedrooms, or any place that is appropriate.

- **Are the locks working properly:** Security should be just as important as safety. Check the locks on entryway doors and ensure that they are working properly. A failing lock or a door that doesn't lock can be quite the goldmine for those who want to break in and steal valuables.

- **Make sure that everything is clean:** How are the rugs? Is everything mopped and swept? Did you wipe down the sinks? Everything must be clean or even spotless before the tenant even sets foot on the property.

- **Complete repairs and maintenance tasks if needed:** If there is something broken, fix it. If there is something that needs cleaning, clean it. You'll want to see if the appliances are in working order and are not faulty. Make sure everything else isn't faulty or in need of repairs.

- **Don't forget the outdoors:** Preparation isn't just for the indoors. Make sure that the front and back yards are clean, the lawn is mowed, and the property looks like it's in good condition. Clear the front entryway of any cobwebs. Make sure the driveway is nice and clean.

Doing A Walk-Through and Inspection

This is a task that you absolutely, positively gotta do. Especially when you are steps away from handing over the keys to a tenant. Because you want to make sure everything is running smoothly.

Not only that, you want to see if the structure of the property is in good enough shape rather than crumbling and falling apart. Inspections should occur not just before a tenant moves in, but during the time when a tenant is occupying the property and after they move out. In the event of the 'during', you want to give your tenants advanced notice (and make sure that the tenants themselves acknowledge it).

When you do a move out inspection, it will help you determine if there are any repair costs that may incur. The inspection could yield no need for repairs or just a few tweaks and adjustments, if necessary. If there are repairs needed, then it may be the responsibility of the tenant to get it fixed before they move out.

This will also determine whether or not if the tenant will get the full security deposit back or part of it. If there are some damages that need to be fixed, it can be taken out of the deposit itself before the rest is handed back to the outgoing tenant. At the same time, these inspections are important so they minimize the amount of disputes between the landlord and the outgoing tenant.

Both you and the tenant should each do an inspection of what's in good shape and what needs repairing. This includes inspecting every room. Check the floors, walls, ceilings, light fixtures, closest, and everything else. If there are repairs that need to be done, you or the tenant will need to get an estimation of how much it will cost (assuming one or the other decides to repair it).

If your tenant is in the process of moving in, consider doing a pre-move in walkthrough and inspection. Again, this will help you double check whether or not things are in working order. Things can happen between the last inspection and the pre-move in inspection, so you want to make sure your bases are covered.

As mentioned before, check every room. See if the plumbing system is running properly. Test the HVAC, smoke detectors, and locks to ensure if they are working properly. If things are working properly, that's an all-clear for the tenant to move in.

Also, you should have the tenant on site while the both of you are doing a walkthrough. That way, the both of you can confirm that things are in good working order. And it can give the tenant peace of mind knowing that they are moving into a place that isn't falling apart.

Damage can happen even before you and the tenant set foot on the property. So it's better to do the walk-through together. The tenant will most likely not be at fault for such damage, so it's better to take their word for it (especially when the damage is minor).

Insurance Coverage Needs Some Adjustments

Insurance coverage for your property is designed to protect your property from certain dangers, disasters, and damages. You'd be wise to have it on every piece of property you own. Having an ironclad insurance policy is key whether you own one rental property or several.

Also, it's important to remind your tenants that your insurance policy is different. If something happens to the property, it does not cover and damage that occurs to a tenant's possessions. Therefore, you'll want to let them know about renter's insurance.

Renter's insurance will cover the tenant in the event of things happening on the property. So while your property gets damaged due to the fire and your tenant loses everything, the both of you should have peace of mind knowing that you're both covered under property and renter's insurance respectively. You should also look for a rental insurance company that you can recommend to your tenants while the two of you are discussing things about the property itself.

One of your number one goals is to keep the tenants happy. So giving them valuable information like renter's insurance and how important it is to them is a good idea. Your tenants should be a priority to you and taking good care of them is all they ask for.

Remember, there are different insurance policies that cover specific properties. For example, if your property is a long-term rental, make sure that you find an insurance policy that covers them. Likewise, there are insurance plans that are aimed towards properties that are considered short-term rentals.

There may also be requirements that you need to fulfill prior to covering your property. For example, if it's a long-term rental, then you'll want to make sure there's a landlord or rental dwelling insurance policy that is available. This policy will cover about a quarter more than the usual homeowner's insurance.

These policies will usually cover physical damage to the property caused by fire, lightning, snow, ice, wind, and other natural dangers. Also, find a policy that allows coverage for personal property that is designed for maintenance purposes such as lawn mowers and snow blowers. The policy should also cover tenant appliances such as refrigerators, washers, dryers, and so on.

Everything You Should Know About Maintenance And Repairs

Maintenance and repairs keep the property in good condition. The last thing your tenant wants to do is live in a place that is falling apart completely. In other words, you don't want the place to be a 'death trap'.

As far as repairs and maintenance is concerned, there's often a lot of confusion of who would be responsible for them. The short answer: it depends. For simplicity sake, we can say that if something happens and damage occurs through no fault of the tenant, it shouldn't be their responsibility to repair the damage.

However, it is their responsibility to let you or the property manager know. That way, you or the property manager can contact the right person to deal with the issue at hand. But if the damage is incurred by the tenant (be it accidental or intentional), then there's a good chance that it will be their responsibility to get it repaired at their own expense.

At the same time, they must be aware that such damages and repair expenses can be taken out of their security deposit. That's just the basic structure of how it all should work. But what else should the landlord or the tenant be responsible for?

Let's take a look at the following:

What the landlord or property manager is responsible for:

- **Keeping up with health and building codes:** The best time to ensure that your property is following health and safety codes is before a tenant moves in. The second best time is when the property is occupied and you need to notify the tenant.

- **If there is pest and mold present:** Damage caused by pests or mold are of no fault of the tenant. These things can occur without the knowledge of the tenant. And usually these are discovered when it's later rather than early. Preventative maintenance is important to ensure that pests and mold do not make their presence known on the property.

- **Changing the locks:** It should be the responsibility of the landlord to change locks in between tenants. In fact, there are most states that require this by law. However, if you fail to change the locks, then the tenant will have the legal right to do so on their own accord.

- **Structural integrity and protection against weather:** The property should always be in good shape. You don't want it falling apart or being susceptible to damage when nature decides to unleash something nasty. Make sure that there are no major cracks or broken doors and windows. Any damage that may create an unsafe or uninhabitable condition must be addressed immediately.

- **HVAC and plumbing:** You want to make sure that the heat is available in the winter and air conditioning is present in the summer. You also want to make sure that the water can run cold or hot. Lastly, make sure that the property has power. There are things that can happen to them to where you need to repair them.

What the tenant is responsible for:

- **Trash disposal:** Clearly, the tenant must keep the place clean. Trash must be taken out on a regular basis for pickup. Failure to do so can draw in pests, molds, and odors. Trash service may be covered under the rental agreement as part of the rent or must be paid as a tenant expense.

- **Reporting issues for maintenance:** If something is broken that needs to be fixed (and it's under the landlord's responsibilities), then they must inform the landlord or property manager. The same goes for any damages that the tenant themselves occur. This way, they claim responsibility and will inform the landlord that they will be paid for the repairs and damage.

- **Issues that indicate misuse of property:** To define this, this means that a tenant may be doing something that goes against the lease agreement. For example, if a pet causes damage or if there is damage due to smoking on the property (when the agreement explicitly disallows it).

Final Thoughts

Your rental property is your baby. That can't be said enough. And when someone else is moving in as a tenant, you want to make sure that they are doing their part in keeping it in good shape.

Make sure that inspections are done before, during, and after the property is rented out. Your tenant and yourself (or the property owner) should be in regular communication to ensure that the property is in good condition. If there are issues, you or the property manager must be aware.

You have to make sure that everything is in working order. A pre move-in inspection is necessary so things are working properly and that the right safety precautions are taken (such as installing smoke alarms and properly working locks). Your tenant deserves safety and security in a place they want to call home.

Remember to lay out the boundaries in terms of repairs and maintenance. Have them understand what kind of repairs and maintenance they are responsible for. Meanwhile, let them know of the kind of maintenance and repairs that fall under your responsibilities when something happens.

Also, remind them that it is their responsibility to report and need for maintenance or damage on the property. And they also need renter's insurance to cover the damage or loss of possessions should something happen to the property. Simply put, you and your tenant should be able to have the confidence in knowing that when a problem arises, all of the bases will be covered.

Make this a win-win for both you and your tenants. They want a landlord that they can trust and you want the same out of your ideal tenant.

Now that we've got all of that out of the way, let's talk about your 'exit plan' should you have one.

Chapter 15 - Exit Strategies: What To Do When You Want To Sell Your Rental Properties

If you are planning on purchasing rental properties to generate income for a lifetime, then that's one thing. In fact, that's one of the strategies we'll talk about in this final chapter. But what if you decide that it's time to move on?

We'll be talking about some of the exit strategies that are available to use so that you can be able to cash out after a positive return on investment and then some. Having an exit strategy that is well-thought out and executed properly is your aim here.

When it comes time to sell a property, you do not want to be sloppy about it. You want things to be straightened out, well-organized, and walk away knowing that your now former property is in the right hands. We'll explain what an exit strategy is and what it will take to put one together.

While there are more than a few proven exit strategies out there, we'll be taking a look at the four most common types: the fix and flip, the buy and hold, wholesale options, and the 1031 exchange. We'll provide you with the pros and cons of each so you know which option may work for you.

Now, let's move forward and talk about exit strategies:

Exit Strategy, What's That?

An exit strategy is defined as a contingency plan that is put together by an investor. The purpose is to liquidate or sell an asset that belongs to them. This is a plan that must be outlined and executed properly.

As a property owner that is in the process of getting out of the real estate game, it's important to think of yourself as someone who is looking to get the best deal. In essence, you are pretty much doing something similar to what someone else is doing while selling their house. However, as a property owner it's slightly more complex.

Clearly, you need to have a buyer that will acquire your property. When this process happens, you want to give them a run through of the property itself. This includes how many tenants are occupying it, any history of repair and maintenance, how much money they'll be getting out of the property each month, and the expense that goes along with it.

An exit strategy shouldn't be something you rush into. This is something that will take time, effort, and preparation. Not to mention, it takes the right kind of buyer to help take the property off your hands so you can cash out and be on your merry way.

As for the exit strategies themselves, we'll be taking a look at four in total. As mentioned before, we'll be looking at the fix and flip, buy and hold, the wholesale strategy, and the 1031 exchange. Which one works best for you?

Let's find out starting with our first strategy:

The Fix-And-Flip Strategy

The 'fix-and-flip' strategy is defined as purchasing a property that's a fixer-upper. You put in the money that goes towards repairs and renovations. Once the repairs have been taken care of, then you have the option of selling it as a single-family home for someone who wants to live there permanently.

Or, you can also rent the place out to a tenant on a short-term or long-term agreement. Regardless, you can keep the property in your portfolio for as long as possible. There are a couple of types of flipping strategies: the rehab flip and the wholesale flip.

One difference is that with the wholesale flip, you'll probably have to pay a fee so the wholesale can find a buyer. Remember, the wholesaler gets the difference on the purchase price. Therefore, the buyer must purchase it at a price that is higher than the original listing (sound familiar?)

What exactly are the pros and cons of this strategy? Let's take a look:

Pros of Fix-And-Flip

Quick profit: This is pretty self-explanatory. With flipping, you can sell the property in as little time as possible. Whether it's selling it outright or increasing the value when it comes time to finally sell after a few years, you'll get a good amount of money out of it.

You'll have some construction know-how: Whether you do the repairs or not, you'll understand the ins and outs of construction work. You'll understand what kind of building permits are needed, what may cause delays, and be able to spot out even larger problems such as structural issues, mold growth, and so much more.

You'll be aware of the local market: With this strategy, you'll have your finger on the pulse in terms of the local market. You'll be aware of what's being bought and sold. You'll also get a good idea of what buyers are looking for. Especially those who are in search of a rental property that someone wants to invest in.

You'll increase your network: You'll have more people in your network than you know what to do with. This network includes contractors, building inspectors, insurance brokers, real estate agents, attorneys, and more.

Cons of a Fix-And-Flip

You may face potential losses: Losing money is the last thing you want to do. And flips can become flops. What could cause this to happen? You could be looking at expenses that pop out of nowhere. Property taxes could increase between the time you fix up the place and when you are in the process of selling it. Lastly, capital gains taxes could also eat up some of that money you've earned from selling a property.

Holding means less money: The longer you hold onto a property, the less money you'll stand to make. And that could also mean continuing to pay on the mortgage, taxes, and insurance until there is a buyer. Let's not forget the other expenses such as repair and maintenance.

Stress: Yes, stressful things can happen. There can be delays in the repair, no one biting on your offer, and so on. It takes patience when these things happen. So relax and come to the conclusion that a deal will be made at some point in the future.

The Buy-and-Hold Strategy

The buy-and-hold strategy is basically buying a property and holding it for the long-term. However, there are investors who are selective of what kind of property they want to hold onto and why. The goal of this strategy is long-term returns.

Your exit strategy would be to buy a property and hang onto it for as long as possible. Then, you find the right buyer who will use the property for whatever they see as fit. The longer you hold, the better your return on investment will be.

This strategy will work on properties that only have an upside in terms of value. So it would make logical sense for someone to purchase a fixer-upper, repair it, and generate income via rent. Over time, that property will increase in value.

When there is enough value to cash out and call it a career, that's when you begin to make your exit if you so choose. Other rental investors can just take it off your hands with little to no worry about repairing it (since you've done the inspections yourself).

Let's look at the pros and cons of the buy-and-hold strategy:

Pros of Buy-and-Hold

A proven strategy that works: Needless to say, it's a proven strategy that has worked to the advantage of many real estate investors. You'll know exactly when to get in and when to get out. It's kind of like investing in stocks. But you can get a predictable return on investment depending on the kind of property that you purchase.

You can hang on for the long-term: You can buy the property and hold onto it for as long as you like. This also means that you'll also be able to receive income from it and get a nice return on investment from it. The more money you get from rental income and the eventual sale, the better.

You are taxed less if held for a long time: Unlike short-term investments, if you buy and hold on to an asset you'll be able to pay less taxes on it. Yes, taxes are a necessary evil. But long-term assets that you hold onto will be viewed as more favorable. So the longer you hold on to a property, the better.

Cons of Buy-and-Hold

Markets changes: The market changes from time to time. It can go in a positive direction and it can go in a negative one. And when the market changes, so does the value. You cannot really predict the market. And for this reason, you won't know for sure about the overall value until it comes time to appraise it and perhaps sell it.

It may take awhile to get a good ROI: Let's face it, depending on your target ROI it may take time to get there. But that's where the 'hold' in buy and hold comes into play. Eventually with time and allowing the property to increase in value, you will see a long-term ROI that will work in your favor.

Looking Into Wholesale

If you are thinking about selling your property but want to quickly find a buyer, then there's a good chance the wholesale route will be best. However, what we should tell you is that the wholesaling method here is different from what we've outlined in chapter 6. Also, this shouldn't be confused with the wholesale flip method that we just discussed briefly early on.
This kind of wholesaling is coming from the seller's perspective. You'll need to find a buyer that is willing to acquire the property at a price that may be more than the listing price itself. So the price you set is usually below the average market value.

A wholesaler will usually purchase a home that is distressed and needs repair. Once the wholesaler gets the address and pertinent information, that's when they will contact the owner. From there, the wholesaler can get the owner to sell the property for a price that is below the market rate.

And of course, you know how it goes from there. What makes it different is that this time it's you that is the seller after you've rehabbed the place. Or, you can sell it at a price that is affordable even if the property is in good shape.

Wholesaling is a great way to build capital and experience over time. Yes, you may be sourcing the deal, you'll also need to find a buyer. Other than that, there's nothing else you can do.

But you want to make sure that the terms of the contract set forth by you, the wholesaler, and the buyer are honored. Also, you want to be upfront as the seller. So communication as always is key.

What also makes this different is that you are wholesaling the property before it even hits the market. Someone else will get wind of the property being for sale and then make an offer.

Now, here are the pros and cons should you take the wholesale route:

You'll understand how real estate works: As a property investor, you may have a basic understanding of how real estate works. However, you'll have an even deeper knowledge knowing that you get to see the process from start to finish. You'll even learn some new terminology as you go.

More money in a short amount of time: This is a great strategy for those who want a large sum of money in the quickest time possible. That's because you will have the ability to have more properties under contract. The short amount of time is a few months tops. So you can make off like a bandit with a ton of cash in a single year if you so choose.

Little capital needed on your end: As far as capital is concerned, there is little of it needed. At this point, you as an investor will have enough cash to handle things on your end. All you need to do is assign a contractor to the buyer and that's that.

Cons of wholesaling

No buyers: Self-explanatory. No buyers, no deal.

Unpredictable income: With wholesaling, the income may be unpredictable at best. It may be more than you expect or less than that. Or worst yet, this won't give you a stable, predictable income. If and when this happens, set some money off to the side so you can be able to cover any additional expenses that may arise before the sale occurs.

The 1031 Exchange

This is the fourth and final exchange that we'll be covering. What is the 1031 exchange all about? And how will it work to your advantage?

A 1031 Exchange is an exchange of real property that is used for investment or business purposes. The number 1031 comes from the IRS code section 1031. The only properties that quality are those that are considered real properties.

In this strategy, a 'like-kind' exchange takes place. When this happens, capital gains taxes are deferred should you reinvest the proceeds to a new property that you want to invest in. One of the things that will get you in good graces with the IRS is that you don't acquire 'dealer status'.

One thing to clear up: 'like-kind' exchange doesn't mean a property for a property. It means that the new investment has to be a rental property. That's it.

This means with this new property that you have acquired, you'll need to hold on it for at least two years or longer. After that, there is no limit to how often you can do a 1031 exchange. You can sell the property and reinvest in like-kind properties while being able to build your portfolio over time and never pay capital gains taxes.

Now, here are the pros and cons of the 1031 exchange:

Pros of the 1031 Exchange

Allows you to invest in a portfolio: You'll have the opportunity to build a portfolio of properties if you want to. So this kind of exit strategy isn't for those who want to get out of the game completely. But you will come out with a great deal most of the time.

You can reset depreciation: If you want to write off any depreciation of the asset, then you are more than welcome to do so. And for this reason, you can also be able to reduce your income taxes that you pay.

Easy to trade up: It's possible for you to trade up your current properties for something with a little more value. You can exchange your property and get something that will give you more income in return. Plus, you do not pay taxes unless you actually sell the property itself.

Cons of the 1031 Exchange

Timeline is strict: There is a timeline requirement of 45 days. This will allow you the time to look for the property that you'll want to buy. After you have found the property, you will have 180 days to close the deal. That's a timeframe that is short from the get go, so you need to act fast.

Like-kind properties are hard to find: Identifying like-kind properties can be tough. On top of that, you'll also need to find separate properties that you'll want to buy so the exchange happens. So you'll have to field through the subpar properties that may not fit your investment goals.

Choosing The Best Exit Strategy For You

The best exit strategy for you will depend on your personal needs and preferences. If you want to build your portfolio from the ground up with excellent rental properties, the 1031 exchange is where you'll fare best. Most of the time, you may choose the buy and hold strategy as your default.

You can buy a property, hang onto it for years, and sell it when the conditions seem right. Or you can be quick about it and purchase a fixer upper, repair it, and flip it for a profit. Either way, it all depends on your financial goals.

Please note that selling the property isn't always the only exit strategy to depend on. You can exchange 'like-kind' properties and trade up.

Final Thoughts

Having a well-structured exit strategy will be key. Especially if you are either getting out of the real estate business or if you want to build your portfolio. Using one of the four strategies listed above, you will be able to choose one that will allow you the best benefits possible.

One strategy may work for you and another may not be your favorite. Find one that you are comfortable with. And make sure it is in alignment with your financial goals.

Conclusion

There you have it. You are now armed with plenty of information on how to build a rental property empire. Everything you have learned must be applied in order to achieve success as a rental property investor.

One thing that we encourage you to do is use this book as a reference. If you happen to be stuck with something, there's always a chapter to refer to. For example, if you are having a hard time with the financing side of rental properties, go to chapter 8.

If you don't remember one of the formulas for calculating the cap rate, chapter 7 has all the necessary formulas you need. All the information is in your hands and very simple to apply. So keep this book handy just in case you need it for any information or if you're trying to figure out what you need to do next.

We may have said it once, twice, or many times before. Investing in rental properties is fun, but it will take work to get where you need to be. And it will take a team of trusted people that you can rely on to help you find the right property to invest in, someone to manage it if needed, and the right kind of people to handle all of your finances, legal stuff, and so on.

At this point, you may have performed some of the actions steps that you needed to do. You may have got in contact with some real estate agents, built your network, and even scouted out a few properties for yourself. Or maybe you're a little farther along.

Even if you haven't started yet, you now have a roadmap that will help you build your rental property empire from start to finish. You can use every chapter as a milestone to get you from one stage to the next. Obviously, one of the first things you must do is accept the mindset that this will take work, but you have it within you to get the job done.

You will take the time to build a team as outlined in Chapter 3. Don't be afraid to put yourself out there and contact people who know their stuff about real estate and rental properties. It takes one call, email, instant message, and so on to open more doors and build a network.

And from there, you can be able to build your rental property empire from there. You'll have trusted advisors, extra eyes on the ground scouting your prospective properties, and people who will keep the property itself in ship shape no matter if it's vacant or occupied. These are people that you will be sticking with for the long haul, so be sure to give them some kind of value and they will do the same in return.

Remember, you must do your due diligence and your analysis before deciding on a rental property. The last thing you want to deal with is loss after loss. You don't want to sink a lot of money into a rental property that ends up being a money suck.

The path towards a prosperous career in rental property investing is no easy path. There will be potholes, roadblocks, and obstacles to navigate along the way. You may know what the destination will be, but how long it will take will depend on how you take on each task.

Your rental property empire may start in your local area or a hundred miles away. It all starts with finding that one rental property that will help you get started. From there, you can be able to add more properties to your portfolio. With a proven strategy like the BRRRR method as outlined in chapter 9, you might be able to build that portfolio faster than you think.

However, it's better to take it one step at a time rather than rush things. If you rush into it, you'll be missing a few crucial steps. Take your time and always ask for help from your team if you feel stuck on something.

Before you know it, you'll be acquiring properties left and right because you have the cash to do it. You can purchase one property, fix it up, rent it out, refinance, and repeat the process all over again. How many properties you want to own are all up to you.

This can take months or even years to finally reach your financial goals by way of investing in rental properties. So long as you set aside your emotions, be aware that it takes patience and work to get there, you are definitely in the right line of work to generate some awesome income.

Some say you might be crazy for doing this. Some will say that you'll lose your money before anything comes to fruition. But don't let the doubters and naysayers get you down.

There are many people who will want to invest in rental properties. But most of them might give up after a short period of time without ever performing a task like acquiring properties or networking. You may be one of the few that decides to stick it out, put in the work, and reap the rewards that so many have given up.

Now what?

Depending on where you are in your journey, it's important to move onto the next step. Do you have a team of people set up? Great...find a property that you want to invest in.

Do you have a list of people that you want to talk to about rental properties? Contact them during business hours or shoot them an email to plan a time to chat. You'll probably have a real estate agent even refer you to people in their network.

Are you considering the idea of refinancing your property and paying off the loan? Great. Go forth and do just that (but not before double checking with chapter 8 to see what to do.

This book might represent the next year or decade in your life. Use it to your advantage and you will have a prosperous future in your sights before you know it.

Resources

5 Popular Types of Rental Properties. (2021). Best Rent. http://www.bestrent.vn/5-popular-types-of-rental-properties/

5 Things You Need to Know About Rental Property Loans. (2021). The Balance Small Business. https://www.thebalancesmb.com/5-things-you-need-to-know-about-rental-property-loans-4772292

5 Tips On Preparing Your House For Rental. (2020, February 25). The Spotahome Blog. https://www.spotahome.com/blog/5-tips-on-preparing-your-house-for-rental/

7 Basic Parts to Include in Your Rental Lease. (2021). The Balance Small Business. https://www.thebalancesmb.com/the-5-most-basic-parts-of-a-lease-agreement-2124974

9 Ways to Make Money in Real Estate. (2021). The Balance Small Business. https://www.thebalancesmb.com/types-of-investment-properties-2124869

A Href=/Author/Peter-Gianoli Title=Plg_Content_Authorlist_Title_View_Author>Peter Gianoli16 Jun Budget changes impact both buyers and sellers, says REIV. Which Investment Property. https://www.whichinvestmentproperty.com.au/blog/13900-are-townhouses-a-good-investment

Abulatif, N. (2018, January 17). *Why Are Rental Properties Among the Best Passive Income Investments?* Investment Property Tips | Mashvisor Real Estate Blog. https://www.mashvisor.com/blog/rental-properties-passive-income-investments/

Ainley, M. (2020, September 28). *Top 5 Mistakes When Using The BRRRR Strategy*. GC Realty Inc. https://www.gcrealtyinc.com/blog/top-5-mistakes-when-using-the-brrrr-strategy

Albaum, M. (2019, September 19). *What is The BRRRR Strategy and Should You Do It?* RoofStock. https://learn.roofstock.com/blog/brrrr-strategy

Andreevska, D. (2016, September 27). *How to Build and Maintain a Real Estate Investment Network*. Investment Property Tips | Mashvisor Real Estate Blog. https://www.mashvisor.com/blog/real-estate-investment-network/

Andreevska, D. (2020, March 26). *The Complete Guide to Price to Rent Ratio in Real Estate Investing*. Investment Property Tips | Mashvisor Real Estate Blog. https://www.mashvisor.com/blog/price-to-rent-ratio-complete-guide/

Aragon, A. (2021). *What is Direct Mail Marketing? Strategies, Examples & More*. Sendoso. https://sendoso.com/direct-mail-marketing/

Backman, M. (2021, February 4). *The Pros and Cons of Townhouses*. Millionacres. https://www.fool.com/millionacres/real-estate-market/homebuying/townhouse-pros-and-cons/

Baker, H. (2019, March 30). *Investing in Multifamily Properties: The Pros and Cons*. Investment Property Tips | Mashvisor Real Estate Blog. https://www.mashvisor.com/blog/investing-in-multifamily-properties-pros-cons/

Baker, L. (2018, August 6). *Loren Baker*. REWW. https://reww.com/investment-property-loans

Bhakta, H. (2017, August 23). *The 5 Success Principles Of Rental Property Investment*. Gold Path Real Estate. https://goldpathrealestate.com/5-keys-considerations-successful-rental-property-investment/

Bilen, A. (2018, June 21). *4 Advantages of Purchasing an Investment Property*. RoofStock. https://learn.roofstock.com/blog/advantages-of-investment-properties

Borrowing to invest – the risks and benefits. (2019, May 23). Wealth & Lifestyle Pty Ltd. https://wealthandlifestyle.com.au/latest-articles/borrowing-to-invest-the-risks-and-benefits

BRRRR Strategy – Advantages And Disadvantages | TurnkeyPropertyPro.com. (2021). Turnkey Property Pros. https://turnkeypropertypro.com/property-investment-blog/turnkey-property-investment-what-are-the-disadvantages-and-advantages-of-the-brrrr-strategy-2/

Buy-and-hold investing is a strategy Warren Buffett swears by for long-term financial growth — here's what you need to know. (2020, October 15). Business Insider. https://www.businessinsider.com/personal-finance/what-is-buy-and-hold-investing-strategy?international=true&r=US&IR=T

By Harvey Raybould Managing Director, Creative Property Group. (2021). *Revealed: the mindset and success principles of a property investor*. Property Investor Today. https://www.propertyinvestortoday.co.uk/breaking-news/2020/7/revealed-the-mindset-and-success-principles-of-a-successful-property-investor?source=newsticker

Can tenant break lease days after signing contract? (2006, September 28). Inman. https://www.inman.com/2006/09/28/can-tenant-break-lease-days-after-signing-contract/

Cohen, G. (2012, June 10). *Is Real Estate Investing a Job or a Hobby?* JWB Real Estate Capital. https://www.jwbrealestatecapital.com/is-real-estate-investing-a-job-or-a-hobby/

Cohen, G. (2014, January 6). *Investing in Single Family Homes: 4 Pros and Cons*. JWB Real Estate Capital. https://www.jwbrealestatecapital.com/investing-in-single-family-homes-4-pros-and-cons/

Colley, A. (2021). *8 Issues with Buying Rental Property and Becoming a Landlord*. Money Crashers. https://www.moneycrashers.com/five-issues-with-buying-rental-property-and-becoming-a-landlord/

Cormack, F. (2019, December 18). *How to get a home loan for your first investment property*. Lendi. https://www.lendi.com.au/inspire/property/home-loan-first-investment-property/

Coverage for renting out your home | III. (2021). III.Org. https://www.iii.org/article/coverage-for-renting-out-your-home

Esajian, J. D. (2021, February 19). *Multifamily Investment Properties.* FortuneBuilders. https://www.fortunebuilders.com/multifamily-investment-property/

F. (2020a, February 10). *Landlords Duties: Repairs, Maintenance, and Notice to Tenants for Entry.* Findlaw. https://www.findlaw.com/realestate/landlord-tenant-law/landlords-duties-regarding-repairs-maintenance-and-to-provide.html

Fairless, J. (2018, December 5). *5 Ways to Make Real Estate Your Business Instead of a Hobby.* Joe Fairless. https://joefairless.com/5-ways-make-real-estate-business-instead-hobby/

Finance, C. (2021, March 2). *Fantastic 4: Assembling the Perfect Real Estate Investing Team.* CoreVest Finance. https://www.corevestfinance.com/real-estate-investing-team/

Finch, C. (2017, July 24). *Exit Strategy: How to Choose Yours.* StartupNation. https://startupnation.com/manage-your-business/choosing-exit-strategy/

Frankel, M. C. (2020, December 11). *Buying an Investment Property: 3 Ways to Make Your Offer Stand Out.* Millionacres. https://www.fool.com/millionacres/real-estate-investing/articles/buying-an-investment-property-3-ways-to-make-your-offer-stand-out/

G. (2020b, November 28). *12 Pros and Cons of Investing in a Multifamily Home.* Green Residential. https://www.greenresidential.com/12-pros-cons-investing-multifamily-home/

Goodwin, K. (2017a, November 8). *Why Is Real Estate Market Analysis So Important?* Property Metrics. https://propertymetrics.com/blog/why-is-real-estate-market-analysis-so-important/

Goodwin, K. (2017b, November 8). *Why Is Real Estate Market Analysis So Important?* Property Metrics. https://propertymetrics.com/blog/why-is-real-estate-market-analysis-so-important/

Gray, R. (2020, July 24). *07/05/15: Putting Together Your Real Estate Investment Team.* The Real Estate Guys Radio Show. https://realestateguysradio.com/b070515-putting-together-your-real-estate-investment-team/

Greene, D. (2019, July 11). *7 Reasons Why Long Distance Investing Isn't As Risky As You Think.* Forbes. https://www.forbes.com/sites/davidgreene/2019/07/10/7-reasons-why-long-distance-investing-isnt-as-risky-as-you-think/?sh=7bf56813669e

H. (2019a, August 15). *How to Decide Which Exit Strategy for Real Estate Investments is Right for Your Business.* Homevestors Franchise. https://homevestorsfranchise.com/blog/nationwide/2019/08/how-to-decide-which-exit-strategy-for-real-estate-investments-is-right-for-your-business/

Hamed, E. (2018a, June 20). *6 Types of Loans for Investment Properties in Real Estate*. Investment Property Tips | Mashvisor Real Estate Blog. https://www.mashvisor.com/blog/6-types-loans-for-investment-properties/

Hamed, E. (2018b, September 13). *The Pros and Cons of Investing in a Fixer Upper*. Investment Property Tips | Mashvisor Real Estate Blog. https://www.mashvisor.com/blog/pros-cons-investing-fixer-upper/

Herriges, D. (2020, September 2). *What Vacancy Rates Tell You About a Housing Shortage (And What They Don't)*. Strong Towns. https://www.strongtowns.org/journal/2020/8/30/what-vacancy-rates-tell-you-about-a-housing-shortage

How Much does it Cost to Hire a Property Manager? | Mynd Management. (2021). MYND Management. https://www.mynd.co/knowledge-center/cost-to-hire-a-property-manager

How To Perform A Rental Property Inspection | SmartMove. (2021). My Smart Move. https://www.mysmartmove.com/SmartMove/blog/how-perform-rental-property-inspection.page

Insider, P. (2019, January 9). *The Pros & Cons, Investing In Student Property*. Property Insider. http://www.propertyinsider.info/the-pros-cons-of-investing-in-student-property/

Investment Real Estate. (2021). Investopedia. https://www.investopedia.com/terms/i/investmentrealestate.asp

Jahnke, T. (2019, August 26). *What is Real Estate Cash Flow and How Do You Maximize It?* RoofStock. https://learn.roofstock.com/blog/real-estate-cash-flow

Jason, A. (2020, October 24). *How to Negate the Risks of the BRRRR Strategy*. BRRRR Investing. https://brrrrinvest.com/how-to-negate-the-risks-of-brrrr-strategy/

L. (2020c, August 27). *10 Tips for the Long-Distance Landlord*. LawDepot Blog. https://www.lawdepot.com/blog/10-tips-for-the-long-distance-landlord/

L. (2020d, October 19). *How To Hire The Right Property Manager*. Affordable Property Managment. https://www.apm7.com/how-to-hire-the-right-property-manager/

Larson, M. (2018, November 8). *Pros and Cons of Investing in Commercial Real Estate*. Www.Nolo.Com. https://www.nolo.com/legal-encyclopedia/pros-cons-investing-commercial-real-estate.html

Lease Agreement Vs. Rental Agreement | LegalNature. (2021). Legal Nature. https://www.legalnature.com/guides/lease-agreement-vs-rental-agreement

Liu, S. (2021). *12 ways to attract quality tenants | PropertyMe*. Propertyme. https://www.propertyme.com.au/blog/property-management/12-ways-to-attract-quality-tenants

M. (2019b, November 24). *Best Property Search Tools for Investors in 2020 - Mashvisor*. Medium. https://medium.com/mashvisor/best-property-search-tools-for-investors-in-2020-68209f9bb972

Manassero, B. (2018, December 19). *The Pros and Cons of Investing in Foreclosures*. Copyright (c)2004-2021 BiggerPockets, LLC. https://www.biggerpockets.com/member-blogs/8266/80929-the-pros-and-cons-of-investing-in-foreclosures

Manolas, K. (2020, October 14). *6 Types of Nightmare Tenants and How to Avoid Them*. Avail. https://www.avail.co/education/articles/6-types-of-nightmare-tenants-and-how-to-avoid-them

Mansur, N. (2017, December 8). *5 Risks Associated with Owning a Rental Property*. Investment Property Tips | Mashvisor Real Estate Blog. https://www.mashvisor.com/blog/risks-owning-rental-property-2/

Mattson, C. R. B. R. (2013, September 7). *Advantages and Disadvantages of Flipping Houses*. Coldwell Banker Rizzo Mattson, Realtors. https://www.rizzomattson.com/blog/posts/2013/09/07/advantages-and-disadvantages-of-flipping-houses/

Mburugu, C. (2020, September 21). *Single Family Homes: Advantages & Disadvantages*. Investment Property Tips | Mashvisor Real Estate Blog. https://www.mashvisor.com/blog/single-family-homes-advantages-disadvantages/

McDonnell, M. (2021). *1031 Exchanges Provide Exit Strategy for Business Owners*. 1031 Corp. https://www.1031corp.com/exchanging-thoughts-blog/bid/87004/1031-exchanges-provide-exit-strategy-for-business-owners

McLean, R. (2013, October 15). *How Positive Cash Flow Properties Can Make You Financially Free (Ep6)*. On Property. https://onproperty.com.au/positive-cash-flow-properties-can-make-financially-free/

Merrill, T. (2015, March 6). *Key Principles of Real Estate Investing*. FortuneBuilders. https://www.fortunebuilders.com/the-key-principles-of-real-estate-investing/

Merrill, T. (2020a, October 9). *Passive Income Real Estate Investing*. FortuneBuilders. https://www.fortunebuilders.com/passive-income-real-estate/

Merrill, T. (2020b, November 13). *The Pros and Cons Of Real Estate Wholesaling*. FortuneBuilders. https://www.fortunebuilders.com/the-pros-and-cons-of-real-estate-wholesaling/

Miller, K. (2016, December 27). *10 Qualities of a Dream Tenant*. Rentec Direct. https://www.rentecdirect.com/blog/10-qualities-of-a-dream-tenant/

Miller, K. (2020, July 20). *The Lease Signing Process for Landlords and Tenants*. Rentec Direct. https://www.rentecdirect.com/blog/lease-signing-process/

Mo, F. (2018, January 1). *The Importance of Real Estate Investment Analysis Before Buying a Rental Property*. Investment Property Tips | Mashvisor Real Estate Blog. https://www.mashvisor.com/blog/importance-of-real-estate-investment-analysis/

Nadra, A. (2019, June 5). *8 Benefits of Owning a Rental Property*. Investment Property Tips | Mashvisor Real Estate Blog. https://www.mashvisor.com/blog/8-benefits-owning-a-rental-property/

Okoruwa, B. R. (2021a, February 19). *5 Questions to Ask Yourself If You're Considering DIY Property Maintenance*. Copyright (c)2004-2021 BiggerPockets, LLC. https://www.biggerpockets.com/blog/2015-06-19-pros-cons-single-family-home-investing

Okoruwa, B. R. (2021b, February 19). *5 Questions to Ask Yourself If You're Considering DIY Property Maintenance*. Copyright (c)2004-2021 BiggerPockets, LLC. https://www.biggerpockets.com/blog/property-management-vs-self-management

Owen, E. (2020, June 26). *How Will Unemployment Affect the Housing Market?* The Urban Developer. https://theurbandeveloper.com/articles/what-does-the-latest-employment-data-mean-for-the-housing-market

Owning a Long Distance Rental Property. (2021). Copyright (c)2004-2021 BiggerPockets, LLC. https://www.biggerpockets.com/forums/52/topics/212186-owning-a-long-distance-rental-property

Passive Income. (2021). Investopedia. https://www.investopedia.com/terms/p/passiveincome.asp

Peake, H. (2019, August 6). *A Landlord's Guide to Handling Difficult People*. Rentec Direct. https://www.rentecdirect.com/blog/a-landlords-guide-to-handling-difficult-people/

Plessis, E. (2017, April 10). *Can I Afford to Buy Rental Property?* Copyright (c)2004-2021 BiggerPockets, LLC. https://www.biggerpockets.com/member-blogs/5417/50015-can-i-afford-to-buy-rental-property

Postorino, S. (2020, July 29). *Self-managing My Property*. Landlords Choice. https://www.landlordschoice.com.au/self-managing-my-property/

ProsperiGuide - Beware: Risk Is Everywhere. (2021). Prosper Guide. https://ovintiv.prosperiguide.com/investing/grow-your-money/risk-and-return/000342?survey=true

R. (2021, January 28). *Pros and Cons of Investing in Multi-Family Properties*. Trion Properties. https://trion-properties.com/education/articles/pros-and-cons-of-investing-in-multi-family-properties/

Real Estate Investment Analysis. (2019, January 29). Maverickinvestorgroup.Com. https://www.maverickinvestorgroup.com/resources/real-estate-investment-analysis

Rental Properties: Pros and Cons. (2021). Investopedia. https://www.investopedia.com/articles/investing/051515/pros-cons-owning-rental-property.asp

Rental Property Inspection. (2020, November 30). Signature Home Inspection. https://www.signaturemore.com/rental-property-inspection/

Rozenberg, B. S. (2021, January 6). *Why Some People Will Never Succeed (& Others Always Will)*. Copyright (c)2004-2021 BiggerPockets, LLC. https://www.biggerpockets.com/blog/2015-04-25-success-principles-rental-property-owners

Rumora, B. E. (2021a, February 23). *8 Simple Steps to Close Real Estate Deals Like a Rockstar*. Copyright (c)2004-2021 BiggerPockets, LLC. https://www.biggerpockets.com/blog/2015-01-14-real-estate-business-not-hobby

Rumora, B. E. (2021b, February 23). *8 Simple Steps to Close Real Estate Deals Like a Rockstar*. Copyright (c)2004-2021 BiggerPockets, LLC. https://www.biggerpockets.com/blog/team-members-property-management

Santarelli, M. (2020a, June 5). *How to Self-Manage Your Properties*. Passive Real Estate Investing. https://www.passiverealestateinvesting.com/how-to-self-manage-your-properties/

Santarelli, M. (2020b, September 19). *Risks In Rental Property Investing - Norada Real Estate*. Norada Real Estate Investments. https://www.noradarealestate.com/blog/risks-in-rental-property-investing/

Student rental accommodations: The pros and the cons for landlords. (2021). Hawksby. https://www.hawksbys.net/news/2955/Student-rental-accommodation-the-pros-and-the-cons-for-landlords

T. (2019c, June 27). *How to make an offer on a house*. Trulia Guides. https://www.trulia.com/guides/how-to-make-an-offer-on-a-house/

Tak, C. (2019, October 17). *The Rental Application Process: What to Expect When Applying for an Apartment*. Apartment Living Tips - Apartment Tips from ApartmentGuide.Com. https://www.apartmentguide.com/blog/rental-application-process/

The Educated Landlord. (2021). *7 Ways To Increase Rental Property Cash Flow*. https://theeducatedlandlord.com/increase-rental-property-cash-flow/

Thinking About Buying a Foreclosure? Consider the Pros and Cons First. (2021). The Balance. https://www.thebalance.com/the-drawbacks-to-buying-foreclosures-1798184

Turner, K. (2018, February 6). *The definition of property investment*. Your Investment Property Mag. https://www.yourinvestmentpropertymag.com.au/news/the-definition-of-property-investment-246343.aspx

What do I need to know to self-manage my rental property? (2021). Ray White. https://nz.raywhite.com/blog/advice-and-tips/what-do-i-need-to-know-to-self-manage-my-rental-property/

What Is an Investment Property? (2021). Investopedia. https://www.investopedia.com/terms/i/investment-property.asp

What to Form an Exit Strategy. (2021). Investopedia. https://www.investopedia.com/terms/e/exitstrategy.asp

What to Include in a Rental Agreement [For Landlords] | SmartMove. (2021). My Smart Move. https://www.mysmartmove.com/SmartMove/blog/common-terms-include-in-rental-agreement.page

What's an MLS? (2021). NAR Realtor. https://www.nar.realtor/nar-doj-settlement/multiple-listing-service-mls-what-is-it

White, S. M. (2019, February 15). *What Happens if a Tenant Breaks the Lease Early and Moves Out?* RentPrep. https://rentprep.com/leasing-questions/landlord-guide-what-happens-when-a-tenant-breaks-their-lease/

WHY DO RENTAL PROPERTY OWNERS FAIL? (2021). Rental Property Investing Rivera Maya. https://rentalpropertyinvestingrivieramaya.com/why-do-rental-property-owners-fail.html

Why Does Property Location Matter in Real Estate Investing? (2020a, December 16). Vista Residences. https://www.vistaresidences.com.ph/blog/why-does-property-location-matter-in-real-estate-investing

Why Does Property Location Matter in Real Estate Investing? (2020b, December 16). Vista Residences. https://www.vistaresidences.com.ph/blog/why-does-property-location-matter-in-real-estate-investing

Wittwer, J. (2021). *Rental Property Cash Flow.* Vertex42.Com. https://www.vertex42.com/ExcelTemplates/rental-cash-flow-analysis.html

Woodruff, J. (2019, March 4). *The Advantages and Disadvantages of Debt and Equity Financing.* Small Business - Chron.Com. https://smallbusiness.chron.com/advantages-disadvantages-debt-equity-financing-55504.html